Third Edition

Secrets Of The Hidden Realms

Mystical Keys to the Unseen Worlds

Almine

An Extraordinary Revelation
of the Deep Mysteries

Published by Spiritual Journeys LLC

Third Edition: September 2011
Second Edition: June 2009
First Edition: October 2006

By Almine
Spiritual Journeys LLC
P.O. Box 300
Newport, Oregon 97365
www.spiritualjourneys.com

Cover Illustration–Charles Frizzell

Text Design and Illustrations–Stacey Freibert

Manufactured in the United States of America

ISBN: 978-1-936926-38-1 Softcover
ISBN: 978-1-936926-39-8 Adobe Reader

Disclaimer

Please note that *Secrets of the Hidden Realms; Mystical Keys to the Unseen Worlds* is a documentary and reflects the personal experiences of Almine. This book is not to be interpreted as an independent guide to self-healing. Almine is not a doctor and does not practice medicine, and any information provided in this book should not be in lieu of consultation with your physician or other health care provider. Any reference to the word "Healing" refers to the individual healing experience that a client may have had. Any reference to Almine as a "Healer" is not to be interpreted that she is a certified medical professional, or that she practices medicine in any way. The word "healer" only appears as a descriptive term used for Almine, as she acts as a guide for each client as they work through their own individual healing experience. Almine, Spiritual Journeys, or anyone associated with this book assumes no responsibility for the results of the use of any technique described in this book.

Table of Contents

Part IV – The Magical Realms

PART V – The Spirit Realms

PART VI – The Angelic Realms

PART VII – The Realms of the God-Kingdoms

Acknowledgements

The love and understanding of my children is a tremendous joy and support to me.

Thank you, beloved ones.

With love,
Almine

Preface

As a Toltec Nagual, Almine is dedicated to a life of impeccability and of setting others free from illusion. Whereas other wayshowers gather more and more students, she assists in creating more and more masters, freely sharing her vast knowledge. She has achieved the ultimate goal of the Nagual, namely, to conquer death.

The deep compassion this Immortal Master has for all life can be felt in her presence. Her writing and speaking are done from complete silence of the mind, accessed directly from Source. Because of this, she is a conduit for endless information, limited only by our willingness and ability to receive.

Foreword

Throughout the centuries, mystics and the alternate realities they live in have been shrouded in mystery. Their skills in working with the unseen have been held as closely guarded secrets deeply buried in the occult.

These mystics have had as their life goal the accumulation of techniques which would set them apart as bridges between worlds and often to establish them as sources of power among the populace. Sharing any of their secrets certainly did not serve either purpose.

It is to mankind's great benefit that Almine, acclaimed by scientists and leaders from all walks of life as the leading mystic of our time, differs from this philosophy. The philosophical difference lies in her unwavering focus on having perception as her goal, rather than power.

Because power is the consequence of having perception, she shares techniques that are perception-based. Many have wondered at her willingness to share information which previously would have been available only in mystery schools. But she holds firmly to her position that if the perception is there to practice the technique, it is also there to safeguard its use.

This book is a great gift to mankind and a timely herald for an age when a great many are pursuing their spiritual gifts. Looking through this great mystic's eyes is like seeing the dark side of the moon for the first time.

The life-altering experience of reading this profoundly mystical work will loosen reason's tyrannical grasp so that life can be seen for what it is: filled with endless possibilities.

The Rt. Hon. The Earl of Shannon
Former Deputy Speaker of the House of Lords,
Palace of Westminster, London

PART ONE

The Realms of the Goddess

Understanding the Divine Feminine

The use of the words 'Infinite' or 'Divine' has been a comfortable way to lull ourselves into thinking we comprehend the incomprehensible; to placate reason into believing it can grasp infinity. Words, by their very nature, deceive. We tend to think because we have labeled something, we can understand it.

Even the tiniest sparrow, a combination of a specific matrix and frequency, cannot be comprehended with the mind. The essence of this little life form has to be felt with the heart. It is unique in the way it will fulfill its destiny, which is, like that of all life forms, to turn the unknown into the known through experience.

In speaking of the Infinite, some are referring to the principle of indwelling life that animates and sustains form, called by many indigenous peoples the Spirit that moves through all things. But this cannot be the Infinite, for it originates within Creation.

But is the Infinite that which created Creation, referred to by most as 'God'? In almost all cultures this is regarded as masculine, and it is. Its polarity in relationship to Creation[1] is a positive polarity. For millennia this has been all that even the most profound mystery schools and the most enlightened teachers have been aware of as their highest deity. Some even knew that a male

1 Fully described in The Seven Directions, *Journey to the Heart of God*

3

god personified that from which Creation sprang - they called him The Creator. In higher realms he is called the Alumuanu King. But still, we would not yet have reached the Source of all life, the Infinite Being that created all things.

The Relationship Between the Divine Masculine and Feminine

The relationship between Creator and Creation can be depicted as a vertical figure eight, with the top representing God, or the Creator, and the bottom Creation. *(See Fig. 1, The Relationship Between the Divine Masculine and Feminine)* But where did God come from? From the Divine Feminine.

The many traditions like the I-Ching, the Mayan Tzokin, the Hebrew Tree of Life, depict only the vertical axis (known to mystics as the masculine principle). As a result the supremacy of the masculine has been indoctrinated into the masses.

The most holy secret of all was that the God principle sprang from a horizontal, divine feminine principle, the Mother of All. The most powerful being in all existence is in fact not a God, but a Goddess.

Why The Mother Reigns Supreme

In existence the feminine, non-cognitive aspects of mind access the unknown. The masculine accesses the known. The unknown is nine times greater than the known. In other words, if one pays attention to feelings (non-cognitive ways of accessing information), one can know nine times more than by simply relying on reason.

The one goal of all life is growth, whether it is an acorn becoming an oak tree or a cosmos. So too does the vast Being in

The Relationship Between the Divine Masculine and Feminine

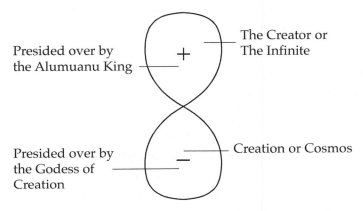

Presided over by
the Alumuanu King

The Creator or
The Infinite

Presided over by
the Godess of
Creation

Creation or Cosmos

The verticle axis is the masculine way of accessing reality.

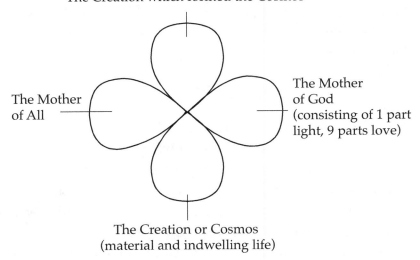

The Creation which formed the Cosmos

The Mother
of All

The Mother
of God
(consisting of 1 part
light, 9 parts love)

The Creation or Cosmos
(material and indwelling life)

The horizontal approach to life is feminine in relation to the vertical.

(Figure 1)

5

which we dwell seek to become more of what it is. Like all life within it, it seeks to grow.

But what is growth? Growth is turning the unknown into the known. Not only does it take a lot more energy and power to penetrate that which hasn't yielded its insights before, namely the unknown, but there are nine times more of it.

Because the unknown is the domain of the feminine, life has therefore invested far more power in the Goddess. Power, energy and illumination yield one another[2] in never-ending succession. She is therefore also exponentially more illuminated.

During patriarchal rule, large cycles of cosmic descension took place. During cycles of ascension there is matriarchal rule, supported by patriarchal orders. In February 2005, a 14 trillion year descension cycle gave way to a cycle of cosmic ascension. The long night has finally yielded to the dawn. The reign of the Goddess has arrived.

Symbols vs. Sigils

For us to familiarize ourselves with the power of the goddess symbols, we must first understand what symbols entail. We will also need to know the meanings of sigils in order to properly understand and utilize the sigils given later in this book.

A symbol **represents** something, whereas a sigil **describes** something. When someone sees a BMW or a Mercedes symbol, it represents upper middle-class vehicles of quality and distinction. On the other hand, the symbol for a Rolls Royce or Bentley represents elite vehicles that speak of a privileged lifestyle of dignity and wealth.

So much is deduced just from one symbol. That of a Rolls Royce evokes images of walled estates, chauffeurs, enough and

2 See The Anatomy of Change, *Journey to the Heart of God.*

accustomed money as opposed to the symbol of a Ferrari which speaks of more flamboyant taste.

Whereas symbols are common in our everyday world, the use of sigils is virtually forgotten. Even in mystery schools, their hidden knowledge eludes most mystics. But throughout the cosmos all beings of expanded awareness utilize sigils and only a few left-brain oriented races use symbols and those primarily in alphabets. The reason is this:

If we use the world 'LOVE', we have combined four symbols (letters representing certain sounds) to make one symbol (the word that represents a feeling). But love is one of the building blocks of the cosmos, like space or energy[3]. It can also represent many different nuances within the emotion of love (the desire to include) and many other dis-functionalities and degrees of need we mistakenly call 'love'.

As we can see, the symbol or word can be very misleading since what it represents to one may not be what it represents to another. The sigil for love describes the quality or frequency of what is meant. It maps out the exact frequency of the emotion.

The sigil for someone's name would do likewise. As the person or being rises in frequency, the sigil would change to reflect that. In the case of angels or lords of light, even their names would change. That is why the angel names or the goddess names have changed as the cosmos and earth have ascended to a much higher frequency[4]. In these higher realms the languages are different and reflect the higher frequencies.

It is for this reason we are including a glossary of lords and angels for the reader who may wish to call upon them. Lords are, except in very **rare** cases, male beings who govern left-brain, light-oriented tasks. For instance, if you need assistance with cash

3 Discussed in *Journey to the Heart of God*, p. 56, The True Nature of the Seven Directions
4 See higher goddess names in the topic Living the Goddess Traditions

flow or debt, a lord would be the better source of help. Angels would be called to restore harmony to a relationship or comfort to the dying.

When a person has accomplished a major task within the cosmos pertaining to that which they undertook with the Infinite to do, they also receive a 'meaning' with its accompanying sigil. When called to do a task that is for the highest good, a being will come if you have its name and meaning and absolutely **must** come if, in addition, you have the sigil for the name and meaning.

Having someone's sigil is like establishing a phone connection by having that person's phone number. Sigils not only describe what they represent, but are a means to communicate with what they represent. *(See Fig. 2, Wheel of Sigils and Symbols)*

Activating the DNA Through the Goddess Traditions

The human DNA is the roadmap to the sound or frequency patterns of the cosmos. It is a map of such detailed frequency that it can be used to create language and the previously discussed ancient form of writing that precedes letters—sigils. Many mystery schools and enlightened cultures patterned themselves in one way or another after the DNA template because of the power it has in representing the macrocosm.

When viewed in cross section by someone able to see frequency, the DNA strand would resemble the rose. *(See Fig. 3, DNA Frequency Chambers and Fig. 4, Thirteen Goddess Archetypes)* In looking at the rose pattern, we are looking at the frequency patterns that occur throughout the cosmos. The governmental structure of Mu patterned itself after this, and a map of the 4th dimensional city in the Himalayas and Shambala would look the same. It is also found in the Christian cathedral rose

Wheel of Sigils and Symbols
Used in Opening Cosmic Gates between Realms

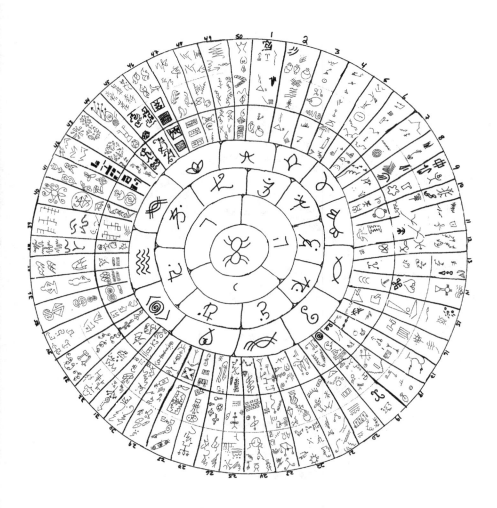

Ezekiel 1:16, "The appearance of the wheels and their work...
was as it were wheels in the middle of a wheel"

(Figure 2)

DNA Frequency Chambers

(Figure 3)

13 Goddess Archetypes

 1. PANA-TURA Goddess of germination. She is the essence of life-giving energy that births into form. She midwifes potentialities into materialization.

 2. AMA-TERRA-SU Goddess of history. On earth she is the keeper of the history stored in the rocks, sand, and soil. She keeps the record of the loop of time, which is our biggest history.

 3. KA-LI-MA Goddess of equity and destroyer of illusion. She brings balance by creating potentialities that can compensate for distortions that create karma.

 4. ORI-KA-LA Goddess of prophecy with the farseeing eye. She is the oracle and holder of the key to changing the future.

 5. AU-BA-RI Goddess of sound or frequency. She utilizes the rage of Lucifer to break up stagnant portions of Creation. She is the cosmic sound healer who works with the potential manifestation the spoken word creates.

 6. HAY-HU-KA Goddess of reversal energy. She works with indwelling life's purpose to evolve awareness, through manipulating the outer currents. She is the teacher who tricks others into learning.

 7. ISHANA-MA Goddess of beauty, grace and elegance. She facilitates the peaceful interaction among her children for harmonious co-habitation. She is a mediator and promotes joyful cooperation. She is the goddess of self love.

 8. APARA-TURA Goddess of cycles. She is the operator who opens doors for cycles that are opening and closes doors for cycles that are closing. She celebrates the beginning and end of cycles.

 9. HAY-LEEM-A Goddess of resources. She is the weigher of the consequences of today's actions on all life, including nature and future generations.

 10. UR-U-AMA Goddess of creativity and inspiration. She knows true art inspires altered perception and that life should be lived creatively.

 11. AMARAKU Goddess of new beginnings and forging new ways. When the old is gone, she invents a new approach. She is the innovator.

 12. ALU-MI-NA Goddess who guards the unknowable. She guards the source of all spiritual knowledge from being accessed by those with impure motives. She is the gatekeeper who determines who may cross.

 13. ARA-KA-NA Goddess of the power to transcend all boundaries. She is the guardian of the portal or passageway between Creator and Creation. She represents the gateway hidden within the core of human DNA that enables us to become the I AM that I AM.

(Figure 4)

windows. The rose pattern represents the orders of ancient female (goddess) mystery schools that once existed on earth. Sadly, most were prematurely exterminated, taking the secrets of the DNA activation through frequency with them until now.

The power held in the pattern of the frequency template that exists throughout Creation can be used in establishing government, in drawing the sigil of your name, or in developing a map of evolution. For instance, throughout many lifetimes, initiates would move from one through thirteen of the mystery schools in order to master the thirteen facets of the divine feminine and the accompanying attitudes that would activate the frequency chambers of the DNA.

During the thirteen lunar cycles of each year (from new moon to new moon), we can live the principles embodied by each of the goddess orders, focusing particularly on the specific one of that moon cycle. We end the year by exploring Ara-ka-na, practicing on allowing the aggression and negativity of others to move through us as we become a portal.

The power of a sigil for one's name lies in the energy behind the spoken word. *(See Fig. 5, Using the Frequency Template to Create Sigils)* If we take the name Michael for instance, it maps out the individual's contract with the Infinite; their destiny and the frequency that is their unique perspective within the universe. An advanced being knows that the frequency of the name contains its essence, or meaning. He will know that 'Mi' is consciousness, 'Ka' is energy and 'El' is matter, revealing that the entity so named has undertaken to step consciousness through energy down to matter. El also means 'lord', and Mi-ka-el's name also says he is lord of consciousness and energy.

The petals in the rose pattern of DNA are various sound chambers of frequency activated by attitude. Someone who follows the right-

Using the Frequency Template to Create Sigils

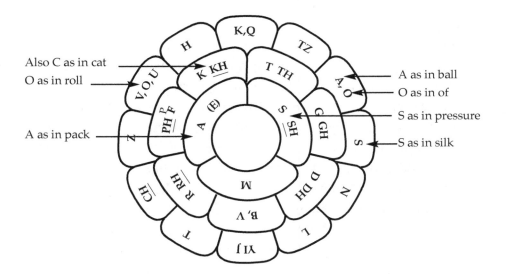

Also C as in cat
O as in roll
A as in pack

A as in ball
O as in of
S as in pressure
S as in silk

The sigil on the template spells out Michael (Mi-ka-el)

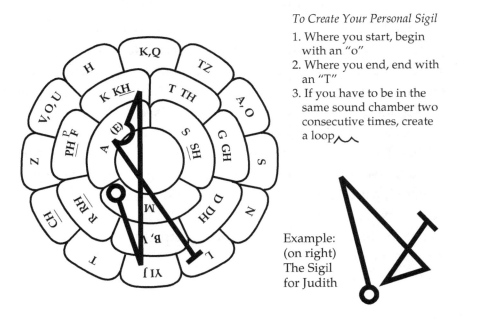

To Create Your Personal Sigil

1. Where you start, begin with an "o"
2. Where you end, end with an "T"
3. If you have to be in the same sound chamber two consecutive times, create a loop

Example:
(on right)
The Sigil
for Judith

(Figure 5)

brain method of ascension would use praise, love, and gratitude, activating the three middle petals or sound chambers. These three main attitudes activate the seven supporting attitudes (and vice versa): grace, reverence, self-reliance, calmness and poise, the embracing of failure as a learning tool, the ability to work with time and live in the moment, and generosity. These attitudes bring the middle row of seven sound chambers on line. Incorporating the thirteen divine feminine attitudes activates the twelve outer petals and the doorway within the center of the DNA opens[5].

The sound or frequency chambers activate the corresponding DNA strands, bringing them on line. Thus attitude can be used to activate the strands, 10 of which are formed from sub-atomic particles. In a left-brained person the strands are activated through insights gained and that, in turn, activates the sound chambers or corresponding petals of the rose.

In the same way that our names emphasize our unique mission or destiny in the cosmos, our DNA chambers are emphasized in a specific pattern as well. This provides us with a unique perspective that in turn gives us each a special way of looking at the world (one could say it gives our world a special flavor). *(See Fig. 6, The Supporting Attitudes and DNA)*

This is done because material life is like the eyes and hands (the physical body) of the Infinite. Diversity at this level of density is essential, especially diversity of perception. It is here where all new knowledge is gained. Because it is at this level of density where the known meets the unknown, this diversity maximizes learning opportunities.

---

5 For more detailed information, readers are referred to the book *A Life of Miracles* and to audio recordings *Flowers of the Heart* and *Journey to the Heart of God*, IV

The Supporting Attitudes and DNA

The activation of human DNA through the ascension and supporting attitudes

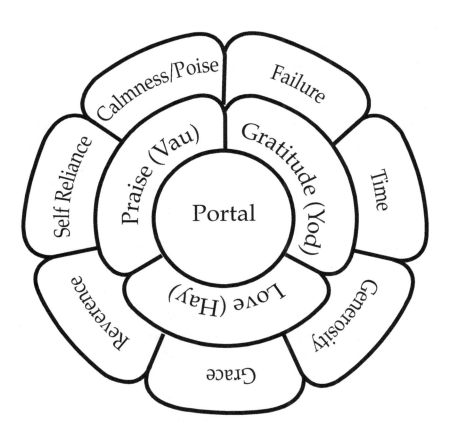

The three primary ascension attitudes and supporting attitudes that activate chambers within the DNA after we integrate the goddess archetypes into our lives. This results in the activation of the inner circle which is a portal to higher consciousness through our DNA.

(Figure 6)

The Goddess Archetypes and Their Relationships with the Gods

The fields of the human brain resemble a dodecahedronal field around each of its hemispheres. A dodecahedron looks like a soccer ball with twelve pentagons connected at each of their five sides, creating a faceted sphere. The left brain has a dodecahedron with twelve pentagons, but the right brain has a dodecahedron with twelve pentagons and an additional pentagon in the middle.

These facets represent aspects of the divine masculine and the divine feminine; the god archetypes and the goddess archetypes. *(See Fig. 7, Twelve God Orders)* Part of our evolution of awareness is to incorporate these aspects into our lives and merge the left brain's field with the right brain's field.

An example of how a left brain aspect (represented by a pentagon) merges with a right brain one, would be as follows:

If someone were to have mastered the ability to manifest money whenever needed, he wouldn't concern himself with expenditures or having to save or to buy insurance. Whenever there is a bill, he somehow finds the money to pay for it. One day, however, he notices he is suddenly starting to run into debt; the funds aren't manifesting as they used to.

He has already learned how to create a flow of supply (the goddess aspect). It has become time to master the god, or left brain facet of supply, which is the ability to harness and plan, budget and regulate by projecting what income will be necessary to meet demands. This new set of skills, in conjunction with the right-brain skills, will enable him to master harnessing the flow of supply throughout all areas of his life.

12 God Orders

 1. LA-U-MI-EL Lord of all consciousness. The symbol is the hieroglyph for reciprocity, also used to indicate wisdom in harvesting. This lord works with the law of compensation in nature to bring about the balanced evolution of species.

 2. AKASHA-EL Lord of the Akashic records and keeper of history. He is also the keeper of the spoken word and language. He determines the insights of history by being the holder of the big picture. The symbol means permanent record.

 3. KARAMA Lord of karma. He determines where karma can best be learned and experienced. The symbol stands for the opening of all 12 chakras, which only occurs when a being has removed the seals of unresolved karma by learning the lessons past experience teaches.

 4. URI-EL Lord of intelligence. He is the interpreter of insights gained and redesigns the evolution of awareness accordingly. He turns information through intelligence into the known.

 5. KI-AS-MUS Lord of time and space. He works within the allotted amount of time to evolve awareness within a certain space (in Creation, time and space have established limits).

 6. MI-RA-EL Lord of symbols of hidden knowledge (includes DNA coding). He determines what must be hidden and what must be revealed within DNA coding or through symbols. He also works with pivotal energy.

 7. OM-KA-EL Lord who holds the vision. He creates the template that fulfills the purpose of a certain part of creation. The symbol stands for focus and will, or focused intent.

 8. KA-PA-EL Lord of the cycles. He works with the cycles of change all life goes through: transformation, transmutation, and transfiguration. The spiral is either positive, resulting in a higher form of the lifeform, or negative, resulting in death.

 9. LEEM-U-EL Lord of the flow of awareness. He oversees the interaction of the different forms of awareness during the large creational cycles.

 10. ILLUMINATI Lord of illumination. He creates the grid lines along which creation will be formed. He is the architect and engineer for wielding sacred geometry.

 11. KU-MA-RA Lord of hierarchy and government. He brings stability through structure to growth. He represents the perfect balance between the neutral, feminine and masculine elements.

 12. KA-LI-SA Lord of energy distribution. He determines the amount of energy a lifeform can hold.

(Figure 7)

When these two specific aspects are fully integrated into his life, the two pentagon facets of the fields around the brain halves meld into one, like a sacred marriage of the divine masculine and feminine. When all twelve pairs have 'married' as aspects of our lives, the sacred fire (kundalini) rises through the pranic tube and the chakras burst open. It is then that the thirteenth facet within opens and ascension becomes possible.

What is applicable to man is also applicable to the planet and, ultimately, the Infinite and its Creation as well. Since 1998, the fields around the planet have been merging their facets and in 2005, the opening of her seven chakras took place.

This process precedes entry into God-consciousness (the expanded state of awareness in which one no longer identifies with the ego) and involves thirteen goddess facets *(See Fig. 3)* plus twelve god facets *(See Fig. 7)* and seven neutral elements (chakras), equaling thirty-two total components. Representing these aspects, thirty-two gods, goddesses and neutral archangels oversee Creation.

Because of the vast importance the earth and man are playing within the big scheme, aspects of these thirty-two creator gods have come to earth and created bodies for themselves that resemble man. They created very large caverns within the crust of the earth, including the Halls of Amenti,

"...that they might dwell eternally there, living with life to eternity's end. Thirty and two were there of the children, Sons of Light, who had come among men seeking to free from the bondage of darkness those who were bound by the force from beyond." (The Emerald Tablets of Thoth, Tablet II).

They represent and oversee thirty-two aspects of life on earth and also thirty-two geographical areas; twenty (thirteen goddesses and seven neutral chakras) are on the surface of the earth, and twelve god aspects represented by geographical areas are within the earth. *(See Fig. 8, The Twenty Sacred Symbols)*

Also upon thrones of light in Amenti, but not in the form of man, are seven Lords of Light that dwelled on earth in a previous cycle of life. Only seven are mentioned in the Emerald Tablets but an additional two were called to service as we entered the 4th dimension in March 2005. Together with the great master, the Dweller also known as Horlet, they direct the destiny of humankind. *(See Fig. 9, The Seven Lords of Light)*

The god and goddess archetypes, represented by pentagons, touching five others at the pentagon's five sides, each interact with the functions of five others. For example, one of the sides of the pentagon representing the god, Lord Ki-as-mus, would be touching that of Lord Karama since they work together to balance the way the cosmos unfolds. Lord Ki-as-mus designs the time and space in which this outbreath of God/Goddess will unfold. Lord Karama decides when and where during this Creational cycle, the unresolved portions of life need to be experienced in order to solve them.

The gods work with measure (the matrix), and the timing in which Creation will unfold. The goddesses, on the other hand, work with how it unfolds (movement) and fill in the creative details, overseeing the quality of the journey.

Living the Goddess Traditions

Our failure to comprehend the necessity for individuals to balance the archetypes within has created distortions in the way they express in everyday life. Some examples are:

• In many cultures where spiritual practices and traditions are

The Twenty Sacred Symbols

The icosahedronal field around the earth and the placement
of the 20 sacred symbols: the 13 goddess symbols and the 7
symbols of the Lords of Light. The 12 god symbols are within
the earth in a dodecahedronal pattern.

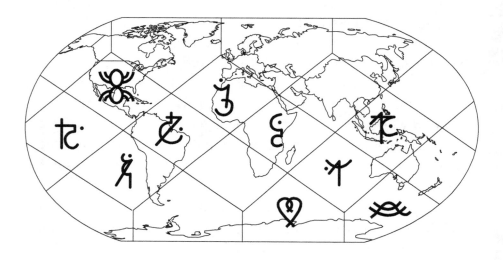

(Figure 8)

The Seven Lords of Light

LORD 3   Untanas
Lord of the Halls of the Dead. He is the director of negativity that is allowed to enter the earth's plane.

LORD 4   Quertas
Lord of Life. He is the giver of lifeforce who frees the souls of humankind.

LORD 5   Chietal
Lord of the power of intent. He is the giver of the frequency that forms life.

LORD 6   Goyana
Lord of hidden mysteries. He is the guardian of powers bestowed upon men, protecting the path of light from those unworthy.

LORD 7   Huertal
Lord of space and time. He works with the purpose of life and the process by which the purpose unfolds.

LORD 8   Semveta
Lord of karma and cycles for humankind. He weighs the hearts of man.

LORD 9   Ardal
Lord of white light. He turns chaos into order.

(Figure 9)

prevalent, men have autonomy over these areas of life. Examples include the Jewish, Tibetan and indigenous cultures. Because women are barred from fully participating in the spiritual practices of these cultures over centuries, they have attracted suppression from races of a more masculine nature.

• The movement of women into the job market, corporate world and factories—the domain of the male—has often come at a cost. They have had to hide their goddess tendencies in order to compete and 'fit in'. In other words, women have had to forfeit their essence, becoming more like men to be acceptable in these environments. Because our cultures have not understood the power of the feminine, it isn't taken seriously.

• In most cultures, men find it 'embarrassing' to be in any way engaged in the goddess aspects of life, especially in front of other men who might suspect them of homosexuality. They therefore live barren and stark lives and because the overbalancing of maleness causes separateness, they live disconnectedly from the web of life. This causes great damage to the environment, great disregard for the coming generations and disrespect for the sacred traditions of others.

• In medieval Europe, the sacred rites were performed by women and acknowledged to be the domain of the goddess. After the Inquisition exterminated between 9-10 million women (10% are estimated to have been children), these rites were performed only by men and turned into a ridiculous parody of their original holy nature. The Inquisition had successfully suppressed the expression of the divine feminine.

When men are taught the goddess traditions, they often have responses like the following: "Well, you place great emphasis on this information, so it must be important, but how is it relevant to me? ...Oh, by the way, can the class have a dinner for you at the end of our week to celebrate what we've learned?"

I then point out to his amazement that he has just demonstrated two goddess aspects, those of Alu-mi-na (Goddess of celebration) and of Hay-hu-ka (Goddess who tricks into learning).

The dynamic balance that incorporating these archetypes into our daily lives brings, prepares us for God-consciousness where we no longer identify with the ego. Studying a goddess aspect for every one of the thirteen moon cycles of the year, and a god archetype for every month is a very helpful approach.

Higher Aspects of the Goddess Archetypes

The goddess archetypes express throughout the lower densities of the cosmos. But, they also have higher aspects that form the divine feminine of the higher frequencies as well as the highest levels of cosmic existence. The languages used in these other realms are entirely different and the goddess names change accordingly. Since June 2005, our goddess archetypes merged with their higher selves twice as we opened to two higher cosmoses.

PANA-TURA

In the original mother tongue of the earth, 'Pana' means earth element or matter and 'tura' means door. Pana-tura holds the door to material life and from this the legend of Pandora's box was derived. She manifests that which the frequency emitted in material life calls forth.

In the mid-heavens or realms, this archetype is known as: **Lesplanaursamakrufbiparshlavushparirbu.**

In the highest realms she is: **Auveanuma.**

23

Application in daily life.

• For at least one hour a week, explore and list your own desires. Take ten minutes a day to contemplate the list and visualize what each desire would mean to you if it were fulfilled. Pana-tura creates realities by first creating the frequency that draws them in. If we deny our own desires to the point that we no longer even know what they are, this archetypal energy cannot assist us in creating a path that makes our heart sing.

• Immediately after waking and before sleeping, when the mind is at its most receptive, spend a few minutes envisioning your dreams and desires already fulfilled. Every day should add more detail to the pictures in your mind. The old sages called it 'fanning the dream with warmth'. It is as though we are blowing a tiny flame into a raging fire.

• Once a month create plans to put a foundation under your dreams. Analyze what it would take to accomplish one of the desires on your list. Design a strategy to achieve the realization of your dream.

• Watch yourself hour by hour to eliminate fears that control your life and create the frequency that actualizes them. When confronted with a decision, ask whether our choice is born of our highest vision or our fears.

Jack London, author of *The Call of the Wild*, lived during a time when it was virtually impossible to move from one socio-economic class to another. He was the son of Welsh immigrants, a dock worker and barely literate. But he became one of the highest paid authors of all time (taking inflation into account) through strategy and a dogged focus on his dream. In the very early morning hours before his grueling day of manual labor, he would practice his writing. After work, he would take grammar and creative writing classes at the local library, persevering until the successful publication of his first book.

The strategy we design must organize into projects the requirements for fulfilling our desire. The projects are then divided into tasks and the tasks assigned time slots within our days when we work on them.

Meditation

Take time to breathe deeply. Sit or lie with the spine straight, legs uncrossed and muscles relaxed. With each exhalation, breathe out all tension through the base of the spine and the bottoms of the feet. If an area is tense, envision a little mouth in the skin over the area and blow the tension out.

When the body feels heavy and relaxed, start the meditation. With every inhalation, envision all the wonderful things life has to offer being pulled into your life; loving relationships offering mutual support; abundance in every area of your life; a perfectly healthy body; time for fun and laughter and self.

With every exhalation, release all things within your life that limit you; all disfunctionalities in your relationships; fears of failure; ruts and soul-deadening work; all lack of self-worth or lack of any kind. Continue until none of these remain.

Suggestion

Follow this with a warm bath in which you dissolve a cup of Epsom salts or coarse salt. This will draw out the toxins held in place by negativity.

AMA-TERRA-SU

'Ama' (mother) 'terra' (earth) 'su' (awareness) is the keeper of the earth's history. Her symbol resembles a tongue, for the feminine method of history-keeping is the oral tradition. The symbol also stands for the largest history humankind has, the loop of cosmic descension and ascension, also known as the in-breath and out-breath of God/Goddess.

Aspect of the mid-heavens; **Kreunimiravael.**

Aspect of the highest heavens; **Aushbleshveda.**

Application in Daily Life

• Research the lives of your parents and grandparents. Their life experiences have shaped yours by the way they raised you, either inspiring you to emulate their characteristics or instilling in you the conviction that you would live differently. Understand what made them the way they were and take time to look at their specific prison bars of social conditioning. Document any acts or choices that were heroic, especially as seen against the background of the times they lived in.

• Research your family lineages, their national origins and any events that inspired them to seek out a new land or territory. Find a family member's achievements or overcomings that would inspire courage in your own life. The Mormon Church has documented the lineages of a great many families all over the world and gladly and freely shares that information. Contact them for details.

• Create your own historical journal. Document your insights and experiences. Use photos and meaningful letters. Putting our experiences down on paper has the very beneficial effect of bringing order to our mind and more firmly imprints the lessons gained from experience. Help your children do the same.

Meditation

Calm the mind and relax the body by the methods previously described.

Envision a chamber made of pinkish purple light. Inside, an angel of magnificent white light awaits and beckons you through an open door. As you enter, he shows you a table and a chair where you should sit. A pen and documents are on the table. As you see them more closely, you recognize they are pedigrees or family trees divided into two lineages; one through your father's lines and one through your mother's lines. Take time to observe them in detail. Some names have photos next to them. The angel now hands you two scrolls, one for each of the two lines. He hands you a pen and asks you to fill in the blanks. Each document reads:

"As light-bearer for this family lineage, I (NAME) hereby declare all contracts previously entered into by any of these family members that necessitated suffering as a requirement for growth, to be null and void. I declare on behalf of this family that growth shall henceforth come through effortless insight, support and grace. I decree that triumph shall replace failure and compassion and mercy shall eliminate disfunctionality and unkindness."

(Signed) _____

(Date) _____

Give the scrolls to the angel who will immediately take them to Ama-terra-su to place within your family's past. If we change the past, we change the present and that changes the future. As the angel leaves, envision golden light flooding the lineages of men and women who are your ancestors, filling them with hope and health.

KA-LI-MA

There is an on-going balancing to create equity beneath the surface of life. This constant adding and subtracting to bring about justice is the domain of the goddess Ka-li-ma (ka=energy, li=to illuminate, ma=mother); the mother of illuminating energy.

Aspect of the mid-heavens; **Lanatrubiunim.**

Aspect of the highest heavens; **Treanumaurudaada**.

27

Application in Daily Life

• Make a list of all perceived injustices you have suffered in your life. Take time to understand the motivation behind the injustice inflicted by another; the blindness that prevented him or her from seeing that to injure another is to injure oneself, since we are each a consciousness as vast as the cosmos superimposed over all that is. See how in not realizing the oneness of all life, the other person has warped the web of life through his actions, creating karma. Really internalize the truth that the person has but injured himself.

If you now wish to mercifully help him off the repetitive treadmill of karma, you can learn his lessons for him by gaining the insights of the events so that he may now progress into higher perception.

Make a list of all compensations and gifts the hardships and their overcomings have brought you. Imagine how barren life would be without them until true gratitude fills your heart.

• Examine all areas of your life to see whether or not you treat others inequitably. Does your treatment favor one over another because he or she is more beautiful or wealthy or famous than another?

Meditation

Put yourself into a relaxed state. Place your attention on the heart center. See it rotate open in a clockwise manner, continuing to do so until first the moon, then the sun, then the solar system appear. Continue to open beyond the speed of light until the entire galaxy appears as but a speck of light in the spiraling arms of the vast central sun. Continue to open until the vast central sun is in the middle of your heart and you meet the slight resistance of the membrane that contains the cosmos. Remain here for a long time, observing from your identity as a being as vast as the cosmos, the ages pass and the solar systems come and go. Then, contract until you are just slightly larger than the earth. Again watch the ages come and go, civilizations rising and falling until you find your current lifetime. Scan your lifetime, and then home in on a perceived injustice. Just observe it from this expanded perspective without any judgment. Keep observing without any thought until the scene dissipates like mist before the morning sun and the 'injustice' dissolves as the illusion it is.

ORI-KA-LA

'Ori' (lights the way or lamp), 'ka' (energy), 'la'(all), means she who lights the way for the energy of all. She is the oracle and the visionary. She guides and holds the key to the future. The word 'key' comes from ka-la (more obvious in French).

Aspect of the mid-heavens; **Kellusinblivaset.**

Aspect of the highest heavens; **Bliiminaruaad.**

Application in Daily Life

- Ori-ka-la holds the key of the future for all because in seeing a possible future, that future can be re-written. Focus on a single portion of your life for a week, working on it every day in the following way:

  For instance, imagine in great detail how your work will play out in the next year. Then play out the year after, and so on until you can see how the next five years will transpire. Then go through it all again, visualizing it as you would like it to be.

- Learn the language of dream symbols given in this book and familiarize yourself with it by reading it through before you go to sleep. Sleep next to a pen and paper and write down your dreams the minute you wake up. Interpret them by using your list of symbols. Be sure to focus on any question you have about your life immediately before falling asleep. Mugwort in a small pillow helps in remembering dreams.

• When confronted with a choice between two possibilities, utilize the following meditation to help you choose:

Meditation

Determine an area within your life where you would like to make some changes. After placing yourself in a relaxed and meditative state, envision two doors in front of you. Spend time envisioning the doors. Behind the door on the left lies a possible future choice and behind the door on the right lies another possibility. Step through the first door and observe the future. Stay in deep meditation, scanning the next five years. Step out of the door and close it. Note any feelings that arise as a result of what you saw. Now do the same for the other door. The images and the associated feelings should clearly point out the preferred path to follow.

AU-BA-RI

'Au' means to listen, 'ba' is body—or sometimes baby, 'ri' is to shine or be luminous. Au-ba-ri means she who through listening creates a luminous body. It is the origin of the name Audrey and the root for the word embryo. Her symbol represents a left ear which is governed by the right brain and implies listening with the heart.

Aspect of the mid-heavens; **Priurtaemkrasunmavetel**.

Aspect of the highest heavens; **Meshmenenada.**

Application in Daily Life

• Create an oral tradition for your family. Television has become a substitute for the conversation necessary to bond a family. Schedule an hour once a week that is a priority for everyone in the family and that is not to be pre-empted by conflicting interests.

Have family members take turns in picking a favorite meal and preparing the questions to discuss. The object is to learn about the life of each family member. If grandparents participate, they can tell about ancestors. Other questions could include:

–What did you learn about the people around you during the past week?

–What was your greatest achievement?

–What was your greatest challenge or most embarrassing moment?

–What would you change if you had unlimited resources at your disposal?

–What is your secret dream?

Questions need to be brought to the level of the youngest family member so that everyone can participate in a non-critical environment where they can be truly heard.

Create 're-entry' time for each family member. Take 10 minutes each day when they come home to ask questions about how the day went at work, school or the babysitter's. Truly listen with your heart. A loved one may suppress unpleasant experiences you may need to know about, breaking down vital communication.

Listen to your heart. Do not allow a busy life to hurry you into situations and decisions that aren't life-enhancing. Always ask yourself, "How does this make me feel?" Do not be afraid to tell others you need to think about a given matter, whether for a few minutes, overnight or a week.

Teach children the validity of their emotions. Acknowledge their emotions and create a safe place and way for them to be expressed. Re-direct anger at the situation rather than a person. Teach them the healing power of tears and pain for it is the precursor to change. Help them to be guided by fear as it either leads them away from harm, or teaches them about acquiring courage.

Meditation

Every creation has a signature frequency and accesses a unique portion of Creation. As such, each creation can become a doorway into infinity if we can hear the song it sings with its life. Sit in front of your potted plant, cat or a flower (and later, more distant objects like the moon or a star so we may begin to hear the music of the spheres) and go into meditation. When in an altered state, become one with the object in front of you. You can imagine walking into its body or shape. Stay in a place of no thought as you feel its frequency and experience the miracle of another life. This exercise will provide practice for true listening, which can only take place in the absence of the internal dialog of one's mind and in complete silence as we enter into another's perception.

HAY-HU-KA

Hay-hu-ka is the goddess of the reversal energy of indwelling life and her influence is under the surface of material life. She tricks into learning and is often called the trickster or Loki, or the coyote teacher.

She uses laughter as a teaching tool and is also known as the sacred clown. She uses the ridiculous and unexpected to break up stagnant energy and to keep us from becoming pompous and taking ourselves too seriously.

Aspect of the mid-heavens; **Barsunnamahirutparva.**

Aspect of the highest heavens;

Trumaniedvadablaumenaeshbluvaatrnermate.

Application in Daily Life

• Ruts close down the lifeforce needed for evolution of awareness and create stagnation. This goddess aspect breaks up stagnation by identifying these stuck areas and bringing in new energy. Make the distinction between personal rituals (consciously done to add meaning to certain moments) and ruts (mindlessly performed habits) and deliberately eliminate the latter. Rituals enhance life. They can be as varied as the daily soak in a scented bath to relieve the stress of driving home in traffic; listening to beautiful music through headphones while riding on the bus; connecting with the earth during lunch break. Ruts result from lack of creativity, such as eating the same food in front of the television instead of meals creatively prepared and served. They can also be the product of mindless, shallow living and inertia; throwing on serviceable clothing that blends with the masses rather than taking the time to adorn the body and dress in a way that reflects our uniqueness and personality. Bring deliberate changes to the areas of your life that are in a rut by introducing the new and exciting, that which enhances our pleasure in living.

- Regularly identify areas in relationships that have become predictable. When stereotypes form in the roles people play in relationships, labels form. "Sue is always so hardworking—she'll get the job done." Labels trap awareness and keep us from being fluid. Growth slows down as we become caught in the web of others' expectations.

Meditation

In a meditative state, picture one of the obstacles in your life in as much detail as you can; for instance, a rageful boss yelling at you over a small error. See the scene disintegrate before your eyes like a seltzer, in a glass of water. The same process can be applied to a memory that has a hold on you or a bad habit or mindset. You can also imagine erasing it with an eraser. Replace it with a detailed scenario of how you would like the situation to be. This is best done right before falling asleep or right after waking up. An accompanying affirmation of, "I am filled with new energy moment by moment" is a good way to close this meditation.

ISHANA-MA

'Ish' means come, 'ana' means from heaven and 'ma' means mother. Ishana-ma is the mother who comes from heaven. As the name implies, she is concerned with creating a family life that is like heaven on earth. She is the Aphrodite archetype.

Aspect of the mid-heavens; **Klueshmispataranuvir.**

Aspect of the highest heavens; **Silmaanavubaratre.**

Application in Daily Life

- This goddess enhances the lives of others with small gestures of graciousness and kindness such as a rose for a wife or the desk of a colleague, a favorite cigar for a boss or an uncle, a love note or movie tickets in a teenagers lunch box, a note or a truffle on a pillow, genuine praise and compliments freely given, surprise visits, thank-you notes and phone calls.

- This archetype has respect for the self and it reflects in the environment through things like a favorite chair with a handy blanket or quilt, well-organized cupboards creating order and harmony, comfortable bedding for cold winter nights, beautiful china and crystal for special occasions, pleasing music, inspiring books, photos of loved ones, a handy stash of stationery.

- Throw out clutter. If you haven't read that old magazine by now, you aren't going to. Get rid of clothes that pinch or fit poorly. You are worth more. Throw away makeup or aftershave you didn't like—it won't improve with time.

- If you are in a romantic and sexual relationship, never take your partner for granted. Instead, truly see him or her as the miracle of a life unique in its expression of the divine. Feel his or her sexuality and potency. Don't let life crowd out the magic. Get a babysitter and re-connect by going on a date. Go to bed at least one night a week prepared to make love.

Meditation

Place yourself in a meditative state. Envision yourself rising up out of the body and ascending through layers of light. As you rise into higher and higher frequencies or dimensions, more and more angels accompany you and the light increases. Finally, amidst joyous angel choruses, you ascend before the throne of God (if you are a man) or the Goddess (if you are a woman). You kneel before such magnificent glory because you can see that the radiance of this divine being fills all the cosmos. The God or Goddess rises and places a hand on your head, sending waves of bliss through every cell. Then you are given the command, "Arise!" and you feel complete awe as the divine being walks into you and you hear the words, "But my child, I am you." The angels now accompany you as you descend, merged with your godhood, to re-enter your body. Lie or sit a while in stillness, feeling the increased frequency in your cells. Then ask yourself, "In what way will I now live in order to honor the divinity dwelling within me?"

APARA-TURA

'Apara' means operator and 'tura' means door. The word aperture comes from her name. The name Dorothea that has survived in some of our languages means the door goddess. Apara-tura is the operator of the 'doors' that open and close the cycles of life.

Aspect of the mid-heavens; **Lizibriraunamir.**

Aspect of the highest heavens; **Kuluvabisandra.**

Application in Daily Life

• In the journey of life, many cycles of existence play themselves out. Deep, meaningful living requires that we acknowledge their beginnings and their ends. The simplest of these are the passages of night and day. If the dawn came but once a year, people would be lined up on mountain tops to see such beauty. Yet, day by day most take it for granted. Let us honor the miracle of a new day by taking time to sit in stillness for even 10 minutes to see the dawn and set our intention for its accomplishment. Let us pause to watch it close as stars appear. It has been observed among the baboons and other primates in Africa that the entire tribe's activity ceases for a few moments at the close of day. Even the activity of the rowdy young subsides as though reverently offering an invocation to the passing of the day. It is the time to evaluate the lessons of that day and gain the wisdom they offer.

- In honoring the cycles of life, input (receptivity or beingness) should alternate with output (activity or doingness). Cycles of passion, the desire to know, should alternate with cycles of joy—the desire to live. Let us do what it takes to clear the calendar and make the time to live in this healthy balance, ensuring that neither rest and leisure nor work and activity are neglected within our lives.

Meditation

Facing the south, sit by a fire (in a ring of stones if you want to indicate to the universe that a sacred ceremony is taking place), having a pile of previously gathered sticks. Start from your earliest memories, work through each painful memory by asking the questions below to gain their insights and properly close the cycles of your past. When you have completed each incident, symbolize its closure by burning a stick.

1. **What is the lesson?** Look for the lesson that our higher self wishes us to embrace. For example, the lesson may be that we need to speak our truth. It could manifest as laryngitis, or someone may appear to mirror to us that we frequently suppress

36

our voice. He or she may violate our boundaries to get our attention. We need to protect ourselves by voicing our truth that this behavior is unacceptable. Accepting the unacceptable isn't saintly, it is dysfunctional.

2. **What is the contract?** Everyone who interacts with us has made an agreement prior to this incarnation to assist with our growth and for us to assist in theirs. They may have agreed to push us over the edge, and we may do likewise for them. Ask, "What is the contract we are playing out?" It is with great love that many agreed while in the spirit world to be our catalysts. When we are in perfect equilibrium, there is no growth so it is a signal to the universe to knock us off balance so the lessons may continue. Thus we pull relationships into our lives that test us in every way imaginable.

3. **What is the role?** Am I playing the victim? Am I playing the teacher or the student? What role am I playing within this contract? Also look at the role the other person is playing. For example, we may have a tyrant in our life. It may be our spouse, mother, or boss. Once you establish that, see what you are enacting in relation to that person's role. Remember, we may change our role at any time because we create our reality.

4. **What is the mirror?** We pull relationships into our life that mirror one of the following things: an aspect of who we are, what we have given away, what we still place judgment on, or what we haven't developed yet. For example, if our innocence is gone, we may find ourselves intensely attracted to a young person. If we have given our integrity away, we might fall in love with a missionary who, in our eyes, represents integrity. Another thing that can be mirrored is that which we judge. If we have resentments against people who lie, then we are judging them and therefore attract liars.

5. What is the gift? Every person we encounter has come to give us a gift and receive one as well. This applies even with the most casual acquaintance. Ask, "What gift am I supposed to give this person?" It may be something as simple as offering him the gift of unconditional love; or we may recognize something beautiful in him that nobody else has seen. We may genuinely listen to someone and for the first time in years, he feels heard and understood.

(Note—The last four questions deal with our attitudes surrounding the answers to the first five questions)

6. Can I allow? This is the point of discerning what has to be allowed, what has to be changed, and finding the courage to act. Imagine yourself as the water in a river. If a rock is in front of you, should you oppose it or flow around the rock? We have masterfully created every situation in our life, even the rock. Is this a test of flexibility and surrender? Or is this a battle for us to fight? A battle is only worth fighting if the stakes are worth having. If you have already learnt the lesson, no need to re-fight this battle.

7. Can I accept? We cannot accept the painful things that happen to us unless we begin to see the perfection underlying the web of appearances. A common belief is that we were placed on the wheel of reincarnation, suffering lifetime after lifetime, until we have lived enough lives to become perfect. We have been created perfectly with the ability to be a creator. Thoughts combined with emotions create our environment. The heart is like a microphone, the stronger the emotions, the stronger the universe's response to manifest our desires. But the universe doesn't discriminate; it will manifest whatever we think— positive or negative. It is important that we accept that we have co-created the situation, which removes any feelings of having things done 'to' us.

8. Can I release? To release is to let go of the energy surrounding the person or event. If we don't release, we keep it alive by feeding it energy through thoughts (sometimes subconsciously). Even if someone has violated us in some way, working through these steps to gain the larger insights behind the appearances, changes the focus to an eternal perspective, revealing the underlying perfection.

9. Can I be grateful? If we have gone through the previous eight steps and can feel true gratitude for the insights gained, it raises consciousness. Gratitude is a powerful attitude that can assist us to transfigure into a higher state of being. It changes stumbling blocks into stepping stones.

HAY-LEEM-A

'Hay' means goddess, 'leem' means water and flow, 'a' means of. From this goddess the name Halima, common in the Middle East, is derived. Hay-leem-a has stewardship over the supply and demand of resources. As the goddess of flow, she sees that today's actions do not deprive future generations of the supply needed to fulfill their destiny.

Higher aspect: **Vichelibispirtama.**

Highest aspect: **Ratrunamachbelvedavaridi.**

Application in Daily Life

• This archetype guards the resources of life. When we take more than we need, we deplete not only ourselves but also our environment. Identify areas of life where you waste, and eliminate them.

• Always leave yourself a cushion—it is only when we have prepared for the worst that we can have the luxury of expecting the best. We don't want to be taken by surprise, because surprise drains energy and loss of energy lowers consciousness.

– Establish and build with discipline a savings account.

    – Have enough food supplies on hand for two weeks.

    – Have enough savings to live on for a few months in case of a job loss.

    – Don't completely fatigue yourself—destiny may knock on your door and you may need energy to respond.

• Guard your personal energy like gold dust. It is your passport to higher states of consciousness. Watch for others who drain your energy through neediness, control or manipulation and agendas. Interact sparingly with them, if at all. Take short breaks during the day to touch the earth, or a tree, to replenish your energy. Above all, have as your daily guide the mantra "I cease to oppose life" and live it with diligence.

Meditation

Place yourself in a deep meditative state while lying with your head to the North. Envision the river of life flowing in through your head and out through your feet. See it as continuing indefinitely. Connect the life-force center behind the belly button (a grapefruit sized ball of white light) with an umbilical cord to the earth's life-force center, a bluish white ball of light in the Halls of Amenti, the sacred ancient temple located inside the earth's crust. With every in-breath, envision yourself drawing white light in through the cord and with the outbreath blowing it through every cell. Continue until you are completely energized.

UR-U-ANA

Her name means Light of the Heavens. She is also the mother of creativity, artistry and new thought. Her symbol is a weaving, as she brings artistry to the weaving of life. She is the muse that inspires and the dream weaver that turns dreams into manifestation.

Aspect in the middle heavens:

Klubartarumkusmarvatalusbimatesh.

Aspect in the highest heavens: **Salavachbuvulama.**

Application in Daily Life

• Use the technique of brain-storming in problem solving. It engenders fluidity of thinking by causing slight movements of the assemblage point. This is a ball of light about the size of a tennis ball, located on the outer edge of the 7 bodies of man *(See illustration of the Bodies of Man in Identity Consciousness in Part VII, Realms of the God-Kingdoms)*. Its placement and position determines how we view life and, in extreme cases, the reality we assemble. This helps us think out of the box so we can cultivate creativity in problem solving.

• Make time for some form of creativity or art. Study art so that your appreciation of it is enhanced. Good art brings new energy into our lives by changing our perspective and adding grace and elegance to our daily lives.

    – Read a poem every few days.

    – Visit an art exhibit or museum.

    – Browse through your local art gallery.

    – Go to an opera, play or ballet.

    – Become familiar with the world's great composers.

    – Vary your music selections.

    – Bring art into your living environment. Dress artistically and serve food in an aesthetically pleasing manner. Honor your children's artwork.

Meditation

In a meditative state and to music that inspires you, envision yourself dancing among the stars. Let colored lightning flash forth from your feet, coagulating into rings of stars. Spread a veil of stars around you as you create a cosmos.

Suggestion

Regularly seeing yourself dancing evokes the same physiological response as exercise. Weight loss and toned muscles could occur.

AMARA-KU

'Ama' is mother, 'Ra' means father and 'Ku' is the kundalini or sacred fire energy (also called the serpent energy). Her name stands for the birth of the new. The ku is birthed by the mother and father coming into balance. She is the innovator finding new paths.

Aspect in the middle heavens: **Verchspirirakritmarva.**

Aspect in the highest heavens: **Kiusalmanivabre.**

Application in Daily Life

- Amara-ku inspires innovation in our lives. At least twice a year, set aside a day to go over all areas of your life, streamlining and bringing innovation to each area. The goal is to become more effective, organized and to expend less energy.
    - Make sure you have emergency tools, supplies and a first aid kit in your car.
    - Keep a spare set of clothing at work, school or in the car in case of spills, accidents, etc.
    - Keep spare toiletries and snacks in a carry-on bag during flights for use during layovers.
    - Keep a hand-held recorder in the car in case you have a rare insight while driving.
- Organize cupboards in a way that separates items into categories to streamline access. Have a container of spare tools and utensils like can openers, scissors, corkscrews, etc. Have emergency candles, matches and fire extinguishers where they can be easily found in the dark. Use clear containers for children's toys so they can see the contents at a glance.

• Flat trunks under beds can store out-of-season clothes so closets have more room. Clothing should be checked for loose buttons, tears and dirt before storing. If you don't have time for repairs, find a cleaner who provides that service. Put buttons that come off inside an envelope and pin it to the garment.

Meditation

In meditation, see yourself as having all power and resources on earth at your disposal. Look at areas of suffering on earth and find innovative ways to alleviate them. For instance, envision how many light-filled children are suffering in a school system that does not allow them to express. Imagine how government money can be re-directed into creating a school environment where there are enough teachers and a curriculum that focuses on the gifts of every individual. In doing this, you lay these thoughts into the grid[6] of the earth, helping to bring these innovations about, further empowering yourself and practicing your innovation skills.

ALU-MI-NA

'Alu' means of everyone, 'mi' is consciousness and 'na' is wisdom. This word is also the root for illuminated. Alu-mi-na holds the wisdom of the consciousness of everyone. One has to be illuminated to pass the gate to the unknowable and the source of all knowledge that she guards. *(See Fig. 10, The Sacred Symbols that Pull Higher Light-Bodies or Soul Pieces into Body)*

Aspect in the higher heavens: **Lisugraviniskahurep.**

Aspect in the highest heavens: **Belmundisilvater.**

Application in Daily Life

• Create your own celebration days in addition to the normal

---

6 Grids are lines of light along which information flows to tell each species how to live and be. Whoever can affect a grid can, in short, effect trillions and trillions of beings.

The Sacred Symbols that Pull Higher Light–Bodies or Soul Pieces Into Body

The Symbols of Alu-mi-na

  As in the sarcophagus above

  So in the sarcophagus below

  The sacred fire is born

(Figure 10)

44

festive holidays. The day of a special spiritual initiation or peak experience could be celebrated with a feast, music and dancing and what the North American Indians call a 'give away'—a time of giving sacred objects to friends who come to celebrate. Examples include a container of ashes from many ceremonial fires that can be strewn on their own property; stones from holy sites; crystals that have been prayed over, etc.

- Give importance to accomplishments and milestones in the lives of loved ones and yourself with special dinners, parties or presents. Respect the occasion by dressing up and asking guests to do the same. Candles, flowers or balloons for children add a festive air.

- Alu-mi-na celebrates the high points of life, but we can celebrate whenever we wish with the slimmest of excuses: to cheer up a friend, introduce a prospective romantic partner to someone or show off a new dinner service. There are days such as All Saints Day, Twelfth Night, May Day, equinoxes and solstices, Chinese or Mayan New Years as occasions for celebration.

Meditation

Along the journey of life we sometimes have higher aspects of ourselves that have been placed along the way for us to assimilate. The entry of such a higher aspect into one's body provides an instant initiation and boost in consciousness. Higher pieces we may be entitled to receive can be called forth with symbols in (*Fig. 10*) and with the following words after going into deep meditation.

Either draw the symbols in (*Fig. 10*) directly on the body 3 times, write it 3 times on a piece of paper and place it on your chest or sign it 3 times in the air above your chest while saying:

"As in the sarcophagus above, so in the sarcophagus below, the sacred fire is born,"

Gold, frankincense and myrrh help bring higher frequencies into the physical and should be in proximity to the body. If there is a feeling of imbalance, do the ritual 3 more times. The soul piece may be half in and half out. Chakra clearings beforehand help prevent this.

ARA-KA-NA

Her name means 'Of Light, Energy and Wisdom'. Her symbol is a stylized spider in the form of a figure eight. The figure eight represents the point of convergence (the zero point) between Creator and Creation, as illustrated earlier in (*Fig. 1*). Like the spider sitting in the middle of her web, Ara-ka-na is at the center of all levels of Creation—zero point. All the frequency bands of Creator and Creation meet at this portal, the place of no frequency.

Aspect in the middle heavens: **Planatuuchbrispiheks.**

Aspect in the highest heavens: **Peleandermaraset.**

Application in Daily Life

• During the thirteen lunar cycles of each year (from new moon to new moon) we can live the principles embodied by each of the goddess orders, focusing particularly on the specific one of that moon cycle. We end the year by exploring Ara-ka-na, practicing on allowing the aggression and negativity of others to move through us as we become a portal.

As we have seen, the human DNA is the roadmap to the cosmos. The petals in the rose pattern of DNA are various sound chambers of frequency activated by attitude. Praise, love, and gratitude activate the three middle petals or sound chambers. These three main attitudes activate the seven supporting attitudes (and vice versa): grace, reverence, self-reliance, calmness and poise, the embracing of failure as a learning tool, the ability to work with time and live in the moment, and generosity. These attitudes bring the middle row of seven sound chambers on line. Incorporating the thirteen divine feminine attitudes activates the twelve outer petals, and the doorway within the center of the DNA opens. To activate this portal of Ara-ka-na, we should closely study and incorporate these attitudes into our daily life:

The Seven Supporting Attitudes

- **Time:** Our lives hinge on the moment. One key event or insight can alter the course of a life forever, pivoting destiny into an entirely different direction. With it the outcome of events in the cosmos could pivot also. If, for just this moment, we can see ourselves as being the center of the cosmos; as having the ability to influence with the quality of our thoughts the very fabric of existence, what would we contribute? If we can see ourselves as this central point of influence affecting all of existence, for even one second, then we can do so for the next and the next. Then suddenly without even realizing, at some point we'll discover that we have transfigured ourselves into a being of great light through the power of our thoughts; a being that has power over death and a love so great that through grace it melts the illusion of others.

- **Failing Successfully:** A day without failure is a day without growth. Our battle in life is not against outside circumstances. After all, one strengthens that which one opposes. The true battle of a light promoter is against illusion. Every encounter with opposition is a chance to pierce the illusion and find the hidden perception. In that case, how can we really ever fail?

  The most common mistake made when confronted with a

challenge is to measure it against past experience. This leads us to believe we have it identified and labeled. There are four steps to help us avoid strengthening old belief systems and failing to grasp the insights.

1. *We don't back away from a challenge if it is ours to tackle.* We remind ourselves of the covenant we made with the Infinite to find understanding through our experiences. Therefore, we embrace a challenge if it is ours.

2. *We know that there is far more to this challenge than just its initial appearance.* We take time to see behind the appearances, because we are ever mindful that what we have undertaken to solve is uniquely ours. It can not be compared to anything anyone else has ever experienced.

3. *We remind ourselves that we are really working on our destiny.* Our destiny is to solve that portion of the mystery of the Infinite's being for which we took sole responsibility. When we do this, failure versus success becomes meaningless. The only failure in the true meaning of the word, is failure to learn.

4. *We realize that we created this challenge.* We did so by carefully manifesting outside circumstances to learn our next insight. The solution has to benefit the growth of all.

- **The Attitude of Grace:** The attitude of living with grace is a composite of various factors that blend into one admirable quality, inspiring to observe and imperative to cultivate, for higher consciousness awaits the one who does.

  Impeccable timing is the side effect of a life of grace. There is a moment to act and a moment to cease. There is a moment to advance and another to retreat, often indicated by signs in our environment.

  The other key component of grace is fluidity. The fluid being does not bring the last moment into the present. The past becomes a ball and chain if we drag it into the future.

- **The Majesty of Poise:** The calm poise detected in masters of power is the culmination of a lifetime of discipline and the unconditional surrender to the unfolding of life. It is the crowning glory of a life well lived; a life in which the larger vision was the determining factor rather than a focus on the vicissitudes of every day life.

- **Self–Reliance:** Great gains in self–reliance have been made during the last 25 to 30 years, in large part as the result of an escalating de-structuring of family life. Both men and women have been plunged into single parent units where they have had to play many roles and often find the only nurturing afforded them will have to be self-nurturing. In addition, no one can advise us on a course of action, since every individual's challenges are unique. Suddenly one day we realize that our being is our sustenance. Such a realization is the very foundation of self-reliance.

- **Reverence:** Reverence stems from the ability to glimpse the divine within form. If there are parts of Creation we exclude from our reverence, let us look a little deeper and there too we can find abundant reasons for seeing the perfection of indwelling life. It is often easier to feel reverence for nature or the genius reflected in the works of man's hands, than for our fellow man. Reverence leaves the mark of refinement upon the one who makes it a way of life. The answer to pollution, poverty and homelessness is not more technology; it is reverence for the purposes of indwelling life in order to co-operate with it.

- **Generosity:** If there is one thing that characterizes nature perhaps more than anything else, it is abundance. Generosity is the allowing of this natural abundance to use us as a vehicle. It is therefore simply life giving to itself. The minute we close ourselves to the flow of life, we not only close ourselves to giving, but also to receiving, and stagnation and atrophy occur.

When all outer petals have activated their frequencies by our living their corresponding attitudes, the center portal of Ara-ka-na opens within our DNA. This great event signals that we have moved to the next level in the evolution of consciousness.

Meditation

• The portal into eternity lies in the moment. Higher levels of consciousness demand that we live in the moment, that place of power called eternal time. When peak spiritual experiences catapult us into God-consciousness, linear time can pull us back out. The solution is to have at least three 20-minute periods a day of going into eternal time until this becomes a way of life.

The goal is to enter into full awareness of the moment. Resist the temptation of entering into meditation or falling asleep—an entirely different placement of the assemblage point. Start by deepening your breaths and clearing thoughts from the mind. When thoughts do arise, don't engage them. Just observe them rising and falling like waves upon the ocean. Blow stress out of tense areas as previously described.

Gradually, as stress leaves the body, the stomach or chest will still feel tense without going into meditation. This stress is linear time. Imagine it as talons or claws, gripping your body, and deliberately undo each talon through visualization, breathing any residue of tension out until it is released.

The change in the assemblage point, as you now simply sit and observe your environment as a child would, is felt as bliss trickling through the cells, or the crown of the head opening. Avoid clocks, noise, public places, phones, TV and even music. Use a timer to end the session if you have to get back to work.

Living and internalizing the goddess archetypes revives, rejuvenates and revitalizes our lives. Sex appeal for both sexes is enhanced, life force is increased and higher states of consciousness become possible. The goddess archetypes bless our lives with grace, elegance, harmony and peace. The gift we can receive by acknowledging the divine feminine is at hand, not only in the cosmos but in every personal life.

The Deeper Mysteries

1. Pana-Tura's Realms Of Manifestation

Within our cosmos the feminine principle of frequency is the primary factor in manifesting circumstances or objects in physicality. Very few beings in the etheric realms can assist with this; they are after all, on the other side of the veil, the non-physical side.

It is a lot easier for human beings to materialize than for even the mighty angels or guardian spirits to create material objects. We are on the physical side and if we create the correct frequency, materialization must follow.

This doesn't mean that assistance from the angelic realms doesn't come and shouldn't be requested. It does mean, however, that we have to do part of it. The dynamics work as follows:

> • If we ask the angels to help us lose excess weight, fervent prayer to an appropriate angel *(See Glossary for individual names)* will definitely pull them in. They will work diligently to form your etheric body into what you have visualized as your desired weight. When they have completed transforming you in the etheric, you will look exactly that way to them. Then, congratulating each other on a job well done, they'll leave.

But you, on the other hand, will think your prayer hasn't been answered. The scale still reads the same and your pants still don't fit. For seers who perceive energy directly, you may look thin, since the angels have altered your etheric body.

Will the physical body follow and lose weight as well? Not necessarily, if you continue to see yourself as fat and broadcast the frequency of despair about your weight. Because we are more able than they to determine the manifestation of the physical, we could keep the illusion of our weight in place indefinitely.

But why is the weight now an illusion? Because the 'real' or etheric part has been removed; just the illusion remains. If we could see ourselves losing weight every day, gladly anticipating how nice we will look in our swimsuit, the illusion will give way to the reality the angels created.

If we wanted to do the same thing the angels have done, we would have to envision ourselves leaving our bodies (placing ourselves on the non-physical side of the veil to influence our non-physical aspects) and see ourselves shrink to the desired size, fanning the vision with joy. We then do the same on the physical plane by consciously envisioning what we want.

To materialize from the ether, life goes through the following steps: *(See Fig. 11, How Matter is Formed)*

- The etheric or Indwelling life is separated from Material life by a 'membrane', called the veil in many scriptures. Material life has a positive polarity in relation to the etheric or Indwelling life.
- The blueprint is held within Indwelling life. The blueprint is the product of the interaction of the masculine (the matrix) with the feminine (the frequency). Imagine two circles overlapping to form a vesica pisces—the mother circle and the father circle forming the blueprint.

How Matter is Formed

STEP 1

Within the etheric realms or Indwelling Life the blueprint is formed

Membrane dividing blueprint from manifested life

(a) The blueprint starts to push against the membrane

(b) The blueprint is now in manifested life

STEP 2

A corresponding frequency within manifested life calls the blueprint forth. (With frequency, like attracts like.)

Pocket of frequency created by devas

The blueprint begins to fill the space of like frequency

STEP 3

The blueprint is negatively charged (having come from the etheric or Indwelling Life) and attracts atoms (positively charged— within matter, opposites attract.)

(a) Atoms rush into the designated space and arrange themselves according to the matrix and frequency
(b) The form is

materialized

(Figure 11)

- The blueprint can also be called a pocket of potentiality of matter waiting to become. As yet the pocket of potentiality has not birthed through the membrane to take form.
- In order to understand the next sequence of steps, it is important to know that opposites attract if we are referring to energy and matter (atoms), but with frequency and light, the same poles attract.
- The deva responsible for working with a particular creation decides that it is time for the image to be created. First, he defines the space in which the object will form by creating its frequency (each creation has a signature frequency) only in that space. The frequency aspect of the blueprint within Indwelling life on the other side of the veil is attracted by the similar frequency played by the deva, and the blueprint is pulled through the membrane.
- Indwelling life on the other side of the veil is negative in polarity, as opposed to material life. The pocket of potentiality, having come from Indwelling life, is therefore negatively charged. As we've pointed out, it's the opposite polarity to material life. With atoms and energy, opposites attract and so they rush into the pocket of potentiality to form themselves according to the blueprint.
- The same principles are used by us to manifest our life's circumstances through thought and feeling. This goddess aspect births all potentials into form as we call forth our reality by emitting certain frequencies.

2. Ama-Terra-Su, Keeper of Her Story

Within the physical, etheric, emotional and mental bodies of man is stored past karma and history. If the information consists of unyielded insights, it shows up as a distortion or constriction. This

The Seven Bodies of Man

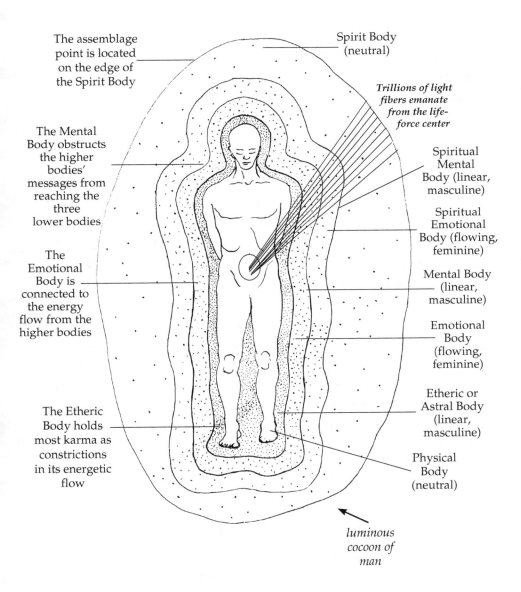

The assemblage point is located on the edge of the Spirit Body

Spirit Body (neutral)

Trillions of light fibers emanate from the life-force center

The Mental Body obstructs the higher bodies' messages from reaching the three lower bodies

Spiritual Mental Body (linear, masculine)

Spiritual Emotional Body (flowing, feminine)

The Emotional Body is connected to the energy flow from the higher bodies

Mental Body (linear, masculine)

Emotional Body (flowing, feminine)

Etheric or Astral Body (linear, masculine)

The Etheric Body holds most karma as constrictions in its energetic flow

Physical Body (neutral)

luminous cocoon of man

The bodies are superimposed over each other. The trillions of light fibers from the lifeforce center penetrate all other bodies forming the luminous cocoon.

(Figure 12)

is karma. If the information stored is the result of insights gained, it manifests as light. In the case of the mental and etheric bodies the light forms lines, or meridians. (*See Fig. 12, The Seven Bodies of Man)*

In the physical body as well as along the meridians of the etheric body, any blockages caused by suppressed memories, incorrect attitude or unyielded insights from past experience cause constrictions in the flow of energy. The result is that eventually physical disease manifests in these areas.

As vital as the proper flow of energy is to a human body, so too is it vital to the vibrant health of our planet. Forgotten memories and unyielded past insights likewise form constrictions in the flow of energy through the earth's meridians.

The numerous humans within the inner earth[7] have (until the merging of the inner and outer grids in March 2006) formed the etheric body of the earth and we, the humans on the surface of the earth, the physical body. If unacknowledged history exists among us, the earth has blockages in its energy flow. The time is imminent when the inner earth's people bring their written history to the surface.

The tradition of sharing the stories of our lives from generation to generation is encouraged by Ama-terra-su. It engenders a sense of belonging to a larger history than just our individual lives and puts our roles into the perspective of the whole.

Multi-generationally, it helps bring life to the earth. Many secret stone libraries around the earth have kept the histories of civilizations long gone.

But history hasn't stopped—we're still creating it—let us therefore keep a record of our own. Unraveling the insights of

---

7 Millions of humans live inside the hollow earth. See Part III, The Forgotten Realms.

memories of our own lives with a journal helps our own energy flow, restoring physical health and emotional well-being.

3. Ka-Li-Ma's Law of Compensation

Although we understand that inherent within challenges great gifts of insight await, relationships can still push our buttons.

Planet Earth has great diversity in the levels of consciousness among its inhabitants. Great masters are birthed in the midst of illusion. Wayshowers and light-promoters often choose to be born into dysfunctional homes. This seeming discrepancy in awareness has caused great pain to the more enlightened.

But, the goddess Ka-li-ma decrees that for every obstacle there must be a blessing. The obvious blessing is the insight hardship provides such as the strength, patience and self-reliance that are cultivated when light-beings recognize that their source of strength is within, rather than from their fellow man.

Yet, the feeling of disappointment that key people in our lives, such as parents, don't have more awareness seems to persistently linger. The expectations that adults we encountered during childhood should have 'known better' or seen more clearly, can leave light-promoters with much pain.

The earth has a pivotal role in the ascension of material life within the cosmos into higher realms. For this role to be properly fulfilled, the most dynamic growth needs to take place here. Within the cosmos the following principle applies: Movement or growth is the most rapid and pronounced where the poles are furthest apart. Thus, the difference between the enlightened and the unenlightened on earth is quite vast.

Where relationship is concerned, the greater the diversity in perception, the greater the discomfort. For the enlightened, seeing or experiencing others acting in an unconscious way that damages other life-forms is painful. For the unenlightened, being in the presence of purity and light flushes up their suppressed pain and, if resisted, results in chaos. Customarily they have attacked the source of their discomfort rather than change.

This situation resulted in a cosmic descension as the light-bearer's pain dimmed their light. The cosmos, like the earth, is currently in ascension. It is now a time of perception; a time for light-promoters to reap the compensation of Ka-li-ma for the previous hardships.

Growth comes from turning the unknown into the known. The unknown is experienced by the mystic as a grey, moving energy lying outside the boundaries of the known cosmos. It is faceless and nameless.

The ageless dance between the enlightened and the unenlightened consists of those without perception acting out the unknown and the enlightened making sense of it. Through their experience, they give the unknown a face and a name. The enlightened then pierces the illusion with their ability to see behind the appearances in order to turn the unknown into something they can understand. Both roles are vital for transmuting chaos to a higher order for the growth of the cosmos.

In summary, someone has to volunteer to play the role of the fool and someone has to play the role of the sage. Within the folly of our fellowman lies the gift of growth and the compensation of our enhanced perception.

4. Ori-Ka-La Invites Us to Enter the Seven Gates of Dreaming

To master the third of our lives we spend sleeping and dreaming, we must acquire certain skills and accomplishments (called gates) during our dreamtime. Ori-ka-la reigns over the dream states.

Gate 1. The first goal is to be able to have full recall of our night's multiple dreams. Like all accomplishments, the goal is achieved through several steps. We prepare for this gate by keeping a pad and pencil by our bed. Initially we write down our dreams in the morning when we wake up.

We interpret them according to the dream symbols found in this book. This encourages the non-cognitive portion of mind to speak to us through dreams all the more. The next step is to set the alarm for 4:00 a.m. and once again to record the dreams carefully. Eventually, we automatically wake up at that time. If at first we only remember a small part of the dream, we use that piece like the end of a string that we follow into the labyrinth of our dream memories. As we use the dream symbols as guides, our lives become more streamlined, requiring less energy. The more energy we have, the better our recall. Try going to bed earlier to see if remembering your dreams improves. Eventually we pass through this gate when we can easily recall the night's dreams.

Gate 2. To go through this gate, we have to be able to choose the dream we wish to have. This is done by watching ourselves fall asleep. Some describe it as rolling out of the body or falling out of the body backwards. As we do this more and more, the experience deepens and we feel as though we're walking out of one room into another. As we continue to practice, we can choose which room we walk into. If we don't like the scene we see, we can walk out of that 'room', or dream, into another. This will take practice.

Gate 3. The goal of this gate is to become a lucid dreamer—to know we're just having a dream even as we experience it. The first step is to ask yourself many times a day: Am I asleep or awake? If you think you're awake, how can you be certain? Perhaps this too is some sort of dream. As we thoroughly practice this, we will start to ask the same thing during the dream state. Then, as we answer affirmatively, we can start to enjoy the dream for what it is.

Gate 4. This gate requires that we consciously choose to do some action within our dream. Every night as we fall asleep, let us have one goal in mind; to remember to look at our feet in the dream. Are we barefoot? Wearing slippers or shoes? This gate may take some time, but it is a most important gate separating those who just happen to be gifted dreamers from those who are serious about mastering the mystical skill of becoming dreamwalkers, fully able to use their dream body.

When this skill is mastered, the next step requires the dreamer to be able to lift a foot. Even if he can just lift it a few inches, he has mastered a significant skill. Practice, even if it takes months for it to become easy to do. The success of the next gate depends on it.

When this skill becomes second nature, the next goal is to actually move an object such as a cup or a pencil even a few inches while staying aware that it's a dream. This usually makes the dream dissolve. So to prepare for it, we keep staring at our feet as we've been practicing, but start giving quick looks about the room (or whatever location you're in).

For example, as the dream begins, you're aware you are dreaming and staring at your feet. You give a quick look at the clock on the table, and then look back at your feet. Then a quick look out of the window or at a painting and then back again at the feet.

As the looks away from your feet become longer and longer, you can eventually stare at other objects in the dream. With a great deal of practice you can eventually move them a few inches from their original location.

Gate 5. As we continue to 'roll' out of the body into a dream, we now simply roll out of the body but not into a dream. The goal for this very advanced mystical technique is for your dreambody to be able to stand next to your bed and watch yourself sleep. As you fall asleep, roll out of the body but stay near the bed; don't enter a dreamscape. It may take a few months of practicing every night.

Again, conserve energy; don't expect to have success after eating a large meal just before bedtime.

Gate 6. The next goal is to be able to move your dreambody at will. But start out small. As you stand there observing yourself sleep, just take a tiny step **towards** your sleeping body. At first you may get sucked back into the body, but sooner or later you can be successful at moving about your bedroom.

Gate 7. As the gates become increasingly challenging, it may take longer and longer to master them. Don't be discouraged. Even if it takes a year, the results are well worth having. You are becoming a dreamwalker, a rare accomplishment for even a serious mystic. During preparations for this gate, practice moving with your dreambody until you become very good at it. Look at the dog or other family members as they sleep.

The next huge goal the aboriginals of Australia master so well is the ability to move physical objects while in the dreambody. The success of this endeavor depends very much on how comfortably you can move about in your dreambody. If eventually it is as real as being awake, try pushing a small object. Keep working at it until finally you can pick up something. If you can accomplish this, you have become a dreamwalker and graduated from the seventh gate of dreaming. You have become a master of the third of your life you spend asleep.

5. Au-Ba-Ri's Gift—Listening from the Heart

Thoughts arise as resistance to life. As we cease to oppose life, our minds become more and more silent—the only way to hear with the heart.

Pain is the desire for change. Thus, as pain arises signaling that change is needed in some area of our lives, we either have to make that change or resist. Most choose the latter option because humans have the tendency to want their lives to change, while strenuously resisting any thought of changing themselves.

The way our mind suppresses, rather than deals with, the pain is to direct our awareness away from the heart to the head. There it engages our awareness with an internal dialog—keeping us from feeling the pain. This also makes true listening impossible unless we regularly learn the lessons pain wants to teach us. We have to take time to make the necessary changes, either in our lives, attitudes or perception to be able to eventually silence the mind.

To truly hear, we have to enter into another's worldview. The word 'love', for example, could mean a hundred different things to many people. We therefore have to see through their eyes what their words meant to convey.

To do this, we firstly empty our minds—listening is a lot like meditation except the assemblage point is not as far left. If one of your own thoughts interrupts, ask the person speaking to repeat himself. Stay completely focused, entering their mind completely, feeling each word with your heart. Practice this technique until the image they are trying to convey flits across the screen of your mind and you can feel what they mean. True listening is now taking place.

6. Hay-Hu-Ka's Power of Reversal

The direction in which our life is moving is determined by our perception and our perception is kept in place by the position of the assemblage point. To be able to change perception in order to progress, it has to have mobility. We have to cultivate fluidity and flexibility in our lives.

Life does not travel in a straight line and a great deal of fluidity is needed in order to change direction at a moment's notice. Hay-hu-ka's god counterpart, Mi-ra-el, orchestrates the key moments that provide for those dramatic changes that require us to be able to spin on a dime to catch the opportunities looming before us.

Hay-hu-ka helps reverse the flow of awareness in the direction of greater life-force and growth as needed. One of the aces up her sleeve is the element of surprise. After all, she is known as the trickster. Through surprise she loosens the grip of reason, even if only momentarily, so new concepts can enter the awareness.

The principles underlying this method are not dissimilar to those employed by surrealistic art. It amuses, astonishes and shocks our reason until mind relinquishes its tyranny of control and the art (in the goddess's case, life) can be experienced with the heart. The heart can recognize the real and the true even where mind cannot conceive it.

The more aware we become and the more responsive to her intent to trick us into learning, the more she plays with us. Her nature is to be light-hearted and fun-loving; to lighten the way with laughter. As we become a willing playmate, she will teach and cajole by means of the ridiculous until our life becomes a comedy of errors. But the greatest gift of all she bestows on those she enlightens, is the elimination of the number one impediment to growth—self-importance.

In not taking ourselves too seriously, we travel lightly, discarding identity along the way. Since we have seen ourselves as sacred clowns too many times, we discard belief systems, knowing we known nothing for certain and that today's truth is but tomorrow's folly.

Then suddenly, without even realizing, we find we have become a being fluid and wise; one who has surrendered to the dance of life even if we alone can hear the music.

7. Ishana-ma's Gift of Communication Within the Family

Throughout existence, all beings can be divided into the four directions, forming the family of Creation. Those who primarily function in the South are the nurturers; those who function in the North, the warriors; those who function in the West are the child races and those functioning in the East are the elders or sages.

The same family exists as sub-personalities within the microcosm that is man, i.e., the inner nurturer, inner child, etc., in exactly the same way races form the sub-personalities of the cosmos. *(See Fig. 13, Relationship of Sub-Personalities)*

Ideally, the strategy for this inner family is created by the warrior after careful analyses and input from the sage provides as much information as possible. All personality pieces must cooperate for this plan to be effective and for our life's strategy (formed from our highest wisdom) to succeed.

Perception yields emotion and emotion yields perception. The warrior and sage function primarily from perception. The nurturer and inner child use emotions and non-cognitive information for guidance. In many cases, we fail in our purposes because the emotions of the child override the higher wisdom of the sage. When the inner child is in terror, it can confuse and obscure the

Relationship of Sub-Personalities

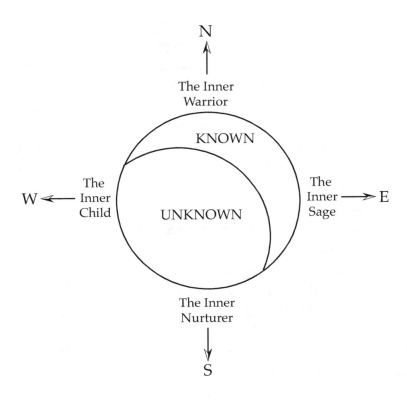

- **The Inner Warriors**
  (deals with the known)
  Within the cosmos: The dragons
  Their role is to protect

- **The Inner Sages**
  (deals with the known)
  Ascended masters of all races
  Their role, to see beyond appearances

- **The Inner Children**
  (get information from unknown)
  The elves and fairies
  Their role, to express their feelings

- **The Inner Nurturers**
  (get information from unknown)
  Those races that have human form
  Their role to receive symbols

(Figure 13)

perception of the warrior and sage; thus, decisions can be made based on need or fear rather than insight.

The emotion of fear can be a valid indicator of danger or simply an indicator that we are encountering the unknown or have unresolved childhood issues. It is the duty of the inner sage to determine which. Simply overriding it could expose us to danger, sensed by the inner child, but undetected by the inner sage and the inner warrior. For this reason, the communication that Ishana-ma fosters among family members is essential.

Communication requires respect. If the inner child's ability to sense the unknown is not respected as valid, he or she will not feel safe enough to voice it, resulting eventually in the loss of soul force. Without acknowledgement that nine-tenths of what can be known can only be accessed by the inner child and nurturer, the sage and warrior could dismiss the emotional response as invalid.

But even if the inner sage determines that the child's emotional reaction is simply the result of unprocessed childhood trauma and that it must be ignored or repressed, it could still interfere in our decisions. Firstly, just repressing it will strengthen unwanted emotion. Secondly, because emotion determines perception, unclear emotion could cloud judgment.

We therefore have the following dilemma: we cannot let the fearful child dictate our course of action, nor can we repress the emotion. Once again the goddess advocates communication among her children. The inner child is not logical, therefore reasoning with him or her will not work. The inner nurturer must now step in to soothe the child by parenting it in the way one would calm the fears of a five-year-old. The child needs to know that it cannot run the decision making process; that its fears were considered but that the nurturer will comfort and hold the child's hand.

Ishana-ma wants the smooth interaction of all her children to take place. But peace in the world does indeed begin with peace within—the peaceful and respectful communication among the members of our inner family.

8. Apara-Tura and the Death Song

As we have seen, with frequency and light the same poles attract (with matter and energy opposites attract). It is this principle that Apara-tura uses in opening and closing doors of opportunity and experience, as well as bringing to a close the mortal life of an individual and ushering it into the spirit realms. In fact, the tunnel often seen at death, with the light at the further end of it, was known in ancient cultures as Apara-tura's door.

The Gates of Transfiguration

Between one level of existence and another—like life or death, or one phase of growth and the next—there is an unseen doorway that keeps the unworthy from progressing through it. It is a membrane separating the frequency of one level from that of another.

In the always-changing cycles of life, transformation, which sheds all that no longer serves, yields to transmutation, which turns challenge into perception. Transmutation in turn becomes transfiguration, because any being can hold only so much light before it must transfigure to the next phase of its evolution. To do that, one must pass through Apara-tura's gates.

If the frequency rises to meet that which lies on the other side of the membrane, the attraction between the two opens the door. For example, at the end of the phase of transmutation when increased light and frequency result from turning challenge to perception, the door opens and a new cycle begins.

The Gates of Death

What happens, however, if we refuse to learn our lessons and progress through the cycles of change to immortality and beyond? Forced change comes. Life will not be stopped in its evolution and movement forward. The one constant in the cosmos is change. The change is then forced onto the individual in the following way:

• The soul's frequency is untainted by human experience. It matches its higher self on the other side of the membrane separating physicality from the etheric. At birth, the two aspects are fully compatible when the soul embodies. If the physical body resists life, it gets worn down as a result of life experiences, and the body's frequency becomes lower than that of the soul.

• Opposite frequencies repel, so the body with its lower frequencies gradually repels the soul. Soul-force is lost and moves through the membrane to rejoin its higher self on the other side. Eventually, the higher self has such an abundance of the frequency that the weaker, but similar frequency left in the body is pulled through the portal of death.

In some cases even in younger people, if enough soul-force has left because of trauma, heartache or because the soul yearns for the spirit realms, the body will attract disease, accidents or violence. This doesn't apply to babies or very young children who contract to enter physical life for a very brief period in order to initiate specific events or results. If a small child or someone who loves life suddenly has a heart attack or fatal accident, that event would be occurring at the point where that person originally chose to end this particular lifetime.

A very little known truth is that often the soul leaves the body hours before physical death occurs, even though this may not be discernible to others. In many brutal murders and other highly traumatic events, the soul leaves prematurely so it does not experience that trauma as the body goes through the motions.

There are many reasons why children contract to die early. Sometimes a soul must incarnate as part of its next step, but does so reluctantly and stays only long enough to fulfill its obligation. Many spirits will do anything to avoid incarnation.

Or a child may come in briefly at a high or special frequency as a gift that alters all humanity by its brief presence. The child could also agree to die early as part of a contract to give growth to the other family members through the 'tragedy'.

When asked why children were permitted to die of hunger, one of the goddesses answered, "For the other children." She confirmed that the continuing deaths of large numbers of children raise the consciousness of others. When many members of a soul group leave, the energy released enhances those who remain. She went on to say, "They don't suffer and they don't know they are dying of hunger unless you tell them."

How does Apara-tura entice spirits through the door of death? She does it by singing the death song. On the other side of the membrane, she sings the 'Song of the Soul' by temporarily greatly increasing the frequency of the higher self until it is so strong that it becomes irresistible to the soul.

The perfection governing all life also governs the passages of life and death. Within the perfect timing of life's cycles, the goddess Apara-tura plays a major part.

9. Hay-Leema's Principles of Ample Supply.

Hay-Leema advocates wisdom in managing resources to provide for the needs of tomorrow, without hoarding in a way that cuts off the supply. The subtleties underlying the principles of creating flow and harnessing resources can fill our lives with abundance when understood. It is definitely worthwhile taking a careful look at these laws of supply.

1. Desire, the driving force behind flow:

The foundation of all emotion is desire. There are 8 basic emotions:

Joy/Passion—When joy (negative pole) is not alternating with its positive pole, it can become self-centeredness. When passion (positive pole) is not balanced with joy, it can become aggression. For joy and passion to be in balance, both poles (which yield each other alternately) must express in equal measure.

Anger/Protectiveness—Anger is the desire to attack or break up. When not balanced by the desire to protect (negative pole), it can become rage. When in balance, it attacks that which is stuck or suppresses light. Protectiveness identifies what is worth fighting for. Once again these opposite poles yield each other.

Fear/Love—Fear shrinks from certain aspects of life, which could serve as a warning that we have encountered something we are not yet prepared to handle. Love is the desire to include.

Pain/Contentment—Positively expressed, pain is the divine discontent that leads us to seek a better way, a higher road, a way out, or a way forward. The opposite pole of pain is contentment – the desire to retain or keep. It is the feeling of having arrived at the right place or having found the right thing; of living a perfect moment.

Desire is vitally important for growth since it creates the movement and direction of our lives; without it, stagnation results. Yet many religions have shunned emotion as unenlightened. It is essential that we take time to create the flow of our lives by getting to know our own desires and to joyously anticipate and envision their fulfillment.

2. Obsession halts the flow of supply

When desire no longer is just a preference, but has instead become a need, we have entered the realm of obsession. Suddenly the movement of our lives towards the fulfillment of the goal stops. The harder we push, the further across the horizon it recedes. Desire wants something in the future but appreciates and enjoys today. Obsession finds it cannot be happy today because it doesn't have the object or circumstances it wants. Yet perception changes year by year and what would have pleased us today may not tomorrow. If therefore we continually need what we don't have, we not only cut off our supply but condemn ourselves to a life of unhappiness.

3. Gratitude increases our present supply

We empower what we focus on. If we focus on lack, our lack increases. If we focus our gratitude on what we have, that increases, too. It is a simple but very powerful tool and even in the depths of despair, finding one thing to be grateful for can change the direction of our lives.

4. When saving becomes hoarding

A large part of what makes saving hoarding has to do with attitude. Do we hoard based on fear and doubt in our ability to create as much supply again? Saving, on the other hand, looks at what areas of our life need to be prepared for the unforeseeable, makes the preparations and then focuses with gratitude on the present.

5. When we take more than we need—greed

Nothing depletes our environment quicker than greed. Greed takes more than it needs, is self-centered and self-serving and therefore exclusive versus inclusive. Because we are part of the whole, we cannot deplete the environment without depleting ourselves. The universal laws are quite clear: Whenever we benefit at the cost of the whole, we must pay the debt. The more we take beyond our needs, the larger the debt. We are permitted to enjoy abundantly as long as we also give abundantly. In this way we continue to receive an ample supply.

10. Ur-U-Ama's Song of Inspiration

To hear the song of creativity Ur-u-ama sings (the song of the muse), we have to delve into the wildish places of the psyche.

Those places exist beyond the confines of mind in the lush and unexplored valleys of our imagination. Her song whispers to us upon the night wind and entices us to throw off the shackles of propriety and with vigorous creativity paint with vibrant colors upon the canvas of our lives.

We follow her song, unconcerned about the opinions of others whose lives stand starkly revealed as lusterless by comparison. For having once danced within the hallowed temple of artistry and beauty to the enticing tones of the muse, we are enchanted forever. Our lives have become a living work of art.

11. Amaraku and Living a Life of Vision

Growth is achieved by turning the unknown into the known. Once it is known, however, it must be implemented, no matter how revolutionary or how starkly it contrasts with previously held views.

Amaraku oversees the incorporating of new vision into daily life. The clinging to old ideas and belief systems is much like a pond that isn't fed by a stream of new, clean water. Its water quality must eventually deteriorate until it can no longer sustain life. It is because of this principle that civilizations rise and decline.

The ideal, however, is that as a fresh stream cleans a stagnant pond, new ideas should invigorate a society. But traditionally, change has often been heavily resisted and slow in taking form. The establishment has seen it as a way it might lose control over its citizens and, more frequently than not, has suppressed new information. New thinkers have been ostracized, opposed, discredited and, in some cases, killed.

Amaraku has sent 'system busters' into mostly the grass roots levels of society from whence change filtered into the masses. Gandhi, Mozart, Martin Luther King and Christ came from humble beginnings and rose into the public eye to realize their visions.

Sometimes the grass roots movement had no particular leader, but raged like a wild fire nevertheless, freeing perception from the confines of old belief systems. An example is the gentle cultural revolution fueled by music and art that took place during the 1960's with the 'free love' movement.

At other times, prominent rulers like Marcus Aurelius, Julius Caesar and Akhenaten came into power for their often heavily opposed and abbreviated reigns to imprint changes into society.

Changed perception precipitating changed living begins with the individual. In our lives, growth can either be the result of forced change, which comes through pain, or the way of Amaraku: Learning from our daily experiences and implementing those perceptions courageously into our lives. As we watch where our buttons are pushed, or where observations about others stand out in our minds, we will find the areas where insights are waiting to be gained. Life becomes an interactive dance between us and our higher selves, becoming lives of grace.

12. Alu-Mi-Na's Message: No Point of Arrival

We are embarked on a journey of exploration that never ends. To rest upon one's laurels at any point of the journey and feel we've arrived, is to retard growth. Our ongoing adventure resembles a multi-tiered maze. We can't see the end or the goal and sometimes when we feel as though we may not be making much headway, Alu-mi-na opens a door to the portal of Ara-ka-na. Once there, we suddenly find we have to do it all over again, but at a much higher level.

The journey can be discouraging if we have not learnt to do the dance of movement and measure taught by the god and goddess archetypes. By now we must have heeded the message of the goddesses to value the quality of the journey rather than desiring the outcome.

It is for this reason Alu-mi-na encourages us to celebrate our achievements, creating high points along the way. By being grateful for achievements and spiritual victories, we increase them. In addition, the moments of celebration add markers to the map of existence that otherwise seems to stretch into eternity.

When our lives become vibrant by our lighting candles of celebration along the way, it illuminates the lives of everyone else we touch as well. It shows love and respect for others when they are included in thoughtfully prepared celebrations. They feel included in our lives and learn by our example the deep satisfaction of living the archetypal feminine.

When our hearts finally rejoice at the wholeness and vitality we feel from merging all previous archetypes and incorporating them into our lives, Alu-mi-na knows we have the key to unlock the door to higher levels. We are then permitted to pass into the realms of transfiguration presided over by Ara-ka-na.

13. Ara-Ka-Na and the Opening of Portals

Change proceeds like the seasons that follow one another in a never-ending procession: over and over again in the cycles of transformation, followed by transmutation, followed by transfiguration.

When enough of these stages of change have been lived, we finally find ourselves at a gate of initiation, a place where large leaps of consciousness are made. At times, these are large enough to advance us into a whole other line of evolution such as the God-Kingdom.

Ara-ka-na, the keeper of gates and portals between realms, is the only goddess that doesn't have a god paired with her to complement her function. She requires from those who would pass through her gates that their masculine and feminine aspects be capable of perfect balance. In other words, they have to have a certain level of mastery in expressing emotion and to have achieved the accompanying perception.

Perfect balance is stagnation, however, and a master utilizes the deliberate imbalancing of perception and emotion to bring about growth. It occurs in this way:

Perception yields emotion and emotion yields perception. Each stage of initiation and growth alternates with the next in that strong emotion is felt and perception has to catch up or, expanded perception is experienced and the corresponding emotions must be generated.

When mastery is not complete, many who enter expanded perception shun emotion as being undesirable. The result is that they stop short of Ara-ka-na's gate and are unable to proceed on the journey of progression. At a time when awareness is so vast that emotions seem non-existent, the master must, through raising the kundalini, or sacred fire energy (which can be done through sexuality or intense and passionate creativity or praise), once again generate them.

In this way, Ara-ka-na will feel satisfied that the mastery of the masculine and feminine components within justifies her opening the gates to higher states of awareness.

The Lords and Their Symbols

"Meditate on the symbols I give thee, keys are they, though hidden of men." Emerald Tablets, Tablet III

1. **Untanas**— The Keeper of the Halls of the Dead. He quenches life and the right to incarnate when light or the life-force is greatly diminished through resistance to life. In this way he plays his part in the evolution of awareness. The soul or life-force of man appears as floating flames of various degrees of brightness in the Halls of the Dead. When the light grows to a great luminosity, he sets that individual free from the bondage of death. He is called Lord Three. (Lords One and Two are Lords of Darkness)

2. **Quertas**— The one who gives life to form. As Untanas quenches life by 'swallowing' the flame with his darkness, so Quertas kindles the flame of indwelling life, called the inner fire, to bring life to form. He is the one that will gauge when humanity's light has grown bright enough to be set free from mortality. He is Lord Four.

3. **Chietal**—Holds the key to the power of intent. He is the great lord of manifestation who guards and guides the abilities of humankind to manipulate reality. Humans are endowed with abilities to manifest reality that astonish higher races. This entire holographic environment of denser material life is held

in place by our minds. We daily manifest our environment but because our thoughts have tended to be chaotic, we have manifested a large degree of chaos, not realizing how powerful we are. This is monitored in a way that allows the race to fulfill its destiny and not prematurely self-destruct. Chietal is Lord Five.

4. **Goyana**—Is responsible for the initiations and the unveiling of the mysteries along a path of enlightenment. The sacred powers and keys must be guarded from the eyes of the profane, yet accessed by those who have relinquished their personal desires upon the altar of enlightenment. Many keys to knowledge are hidden in language and symbols. He is Lord Six.

5. **Huertal**—Master of space and time, he regulates the earth's various timelines and the speed at which time passes. For example, we have come to a close of many cycles and in preparation many karmic requirements had to be met. Over the past years, time has felt as though it has sped up—two years feel like ten. But, time actually slowed down in order to fit everything in before the cosmic ascension started in February 2005. In other words, time had been compressed (as in the moments before an accident when it seems like an eternity) so we can fit more into it. Every two years may have had ten years of change and hardships and growth packed into them. Huertal opens up the ability to travel through time and space to those who have mastered themselves. He is Lord Seven.

6. **Semveta**—He is the weigher of human hearts and works with timing. The great service density brings, is that rapid growth is possible because of it and it acts as a timing mechanism. Density can either be used by the aware lightseeker to speed up progress by transmuting hardship to wisdom, or it will slow the progress of others who choose to stay on the treadmill of

karma longer by failing to learn their lessons. Timing is vitally important in any evolution or else the growth will lack strength. An example is the struggle of the chicken emerging from an egg—if we pull the chicken out sooner than it would have emerged on its own, it lacks the strength to survive. Semveta is Lord Eight.

7. **Ardal**—is Lord Nine, holder of white light and the keeper of keys. The master orchestrating chaos and order, he works with humanity's destiny. He balances the unfolding of the purpose of the Infinite through individuals as well as the race into which they incarnate. He keeps chaos at bay.

"Few *there were among the children of man who looked upon that mighty face and lived, for not as the sons of men, are the Children of Light when they are not incarnate in a physical body.*" *Emerald Tablets, Tablet I*

The Dweller—is the one who is in charge of the loop of time in which humankind finds itself. He is instrumental in guiding the role of humanity as a blueprint for the cosmos; the microcosms that are the way-showers of tomorrow. He ensures that we stay on track in our pivotal role within the big picture.

The Symbols as Used in Teleportation

In working with the unseen realms, relationships are a key factor in cultivating various abilities. Although perception seekers are discouraged by the masters from paying so much attention to the fascinating beings of the hidden realms that they forget to work on themselves, interaction with them becomes a way of life during Ascended Mastery.

But there is one relationship that cannot lead us deeper into ego

The Wheel of Teleportation

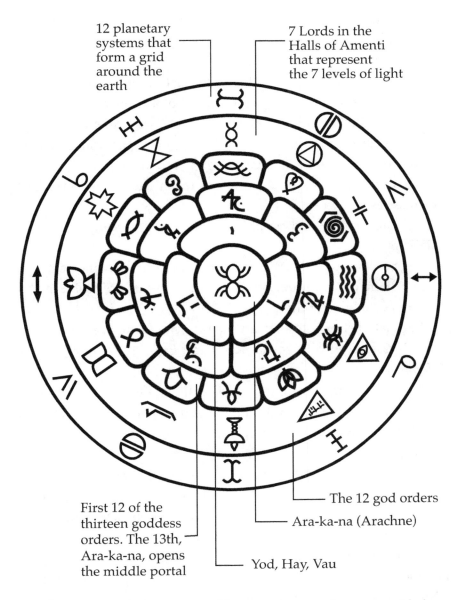

12 planetary systems that form a grid around the earth

7 Lords in the Halls of Amenti that represent the 7 levels of light

First 12 of the thirteen goddess orders. The 13th, Ara-ka-na, opens the middle portal

The 12 god orders

Ara-ka-na (Arachne)

Yod, Hay, Vau

The outer symbols represent 12 star-systems and were provided by the Wonderful Indigo Child, Grandmother Chandra.

(Figure 14)

and is the key to cultivating all other relationships. It is the one we have with the earth. The earth is a sentient, living being who knows when our intent is pure. The aid she will lend is therefore based on the purity of our hearts and proportionate to that which we can receive. This is the case in using this method of teleportation.

Be aware that the skill of teleportation will take time to develop. Driving a car for the first time or playing a new instrument seems overwhelming at first, but then becomes second nature.

How can I share such an advanced technique with the reader? The reasons are twofold:

If it's not for the highest purpose, none of the beings involved will help.

Anyone who loves Mother Earth and these holy beings enough to gain their cooperation, will have lost any desire to harm the interconnectedness of life.

The relationship with the earth is the vital element in operating the teleportation device depicted in *(Fig. 14, The Wheel of Teleportation).*

The next strong relationships you will need to cultivate will be the ones with the seven lords and the god and goddess archetypes. Each one needs to become a friend, able to be felt as a presence inside one.

The Yod, Hay and Vau principle is the matrix of existence. Everything changes as all life pulses between the positive, negative and neutral poles. The positive pole is action-oriented. In regards to fun, an example of the positive pole would be water-skiing; the negative would be watching a movie (input vs. output) and the neutral part of fun would be lying on the grass on a Spring afternoon, doing absolutely nothing.

The symbols around the outer ring are for the twelve star-systems that form a star-grid around the earth—something that was activated during February 2005 in an area near the pyramids, underground in a secret chamber.

This chamber is mentioned by Thoth in *The Emerald Tablets of Thoth*. Its location is mapped out by drawing a line from between the paws of the Sphinx to where the apex of the great pyramid would have been if the capstone were there. The line would then be drawn in the same direction down the other side, at the same degree, forming a triangle with the apex of the pyramid as the top.

To teleport an object such as a chair from one room in your house to a room in the house of a friend, follow these steps:

- Envision the wheel in *(Fig. 14)* around your body as you lie down, with the center circle large enough to fit around the chair. If you wish, you can practice with 19 of these wheels placed around you (19 being the number used by mystics for teleportation). The wheel around your body as you are lying down would be parallel to the floor.

- Think of the principles behind the Yod, Hay, Vau symbols in the three middle petals. Start to spin the ring of three petals **counter-clockwise.**

Next, name the 7 lords: Untanas, Quertas, Chietal, Goyana, Huertal, Semveta and Ardal. Really think of their functions and feel their meanings. Call on them to assist you with your purpose. Then spin their ring **clockwise** as fast as you can. Briefly see the three-petalled led one still spinning fast in the opposite direction (inner seeing).

- Then think of the goddess orders one by one. Call on their assistance as you feel the unique contribution of each to the cosmos. Then spin their ring as fast as you can **clockwise.** Briefly glance at the previous two rings to make sure they're spinning rapidly as well and in the correct directions (through inner vision).

- Go through the god orders, honoring them for the way they regulate and govern the cosmos. Spin their ring **counter-clockwise** as fast as you can. Briefly check that the other rings are still spinning very fast in the appropriate directions.
- Next, spin the ring with the star-system symbols[8] as fast as you can **counter-clockwise**. You will start to feel great heat in your body.
- Envision sending the wheel of spinning rings to encircle the chair in your room. Make sure the chair is centered. Now ask Ara-ka-na to open the central portal.
- Call on Mother Earth to create a tunnel between the present location of the chair and the place to which you want to send it and to 'dial' the correct coordinates.
- A swirling tunnel will begin to form around the chair. Even though there will be a lot of sensation in your body, don't break your concentration for a moment. You are anchoring the wheel around the chair with your mind.
- The different rings, spinning in their different directions, will now get different clicks, similar to those heard when dialing the combination to open a safe as the earth 'dials' the coordinates for the location you hold steady in your mind.
- See the swirling bluish tunnel form all the way to your friend's house. Hold that vision and without any action on your part, the chair will begin to move upwards and through to its destination.
- When the teleportation is complete, with your mind, close both ends down to a pinprick of light.

---

8 These symbols given by Grandmother Chandra, the wonderful Indigo child.

PART TWO

The Realms of Dreams

How Our Dreams Communicate To Us

The importance of understanding the language in which the non-cognitive portions of mind communicate to us through our dreams is almost always underestimated. Nine-tenths of the information we're exposed to each day is non-cognitive. The unknown eludes the cognitive mind and reveals itself instead through dreams, feelings, meditative states and symbols.

So much of what we think of as 'known' is in fact unknown; people, words, the future and its outcomes being some examples. Dreams containing information about these areas come up to be interpreted by our left brain, or cognitive mind. That information addresses areas of our lives pertinent to the evolution of our awareness. In this way it tells us our next step.

Dream language is symbolical in that one thing can represent another. For example, a concrete item may represent a symbolical concept. The exception to this is when a dream is in fact a visionary experience. In this case, one thing doesn't represent another but is exactly as it seems. The feeling or mood of such a dream is different. Objects seem lit from inside—even in a dark room one can clearly see them. This is because we are in fact experiencing the reality of the etheric or astral realms, rather than messages in symbols from the right brain. A visionary dream seems very vivid and its impressions linger much longer.

Following is a list of dream symbol interpretations that have come down through the ages from Toltec seers. These seers made in-depth studies of dream language techniques to utilize the power of dreaming and control the intrusion of other beings into an individual's dream state.

Use your common sense to extrapolate and understand the meaning of symbols not mentioned; look at the characteristic of the symbol. A broom might mean you need to clean up a portion of your life; a breadbasket would mean the ability to hold or receive bread daily spiritual sustenance, and so forth.

The Language of Dreams

Toltec Dream Symbols And Meanings

Activities

Birthing own or other's child	new awareness is about to happen
Boating	need or desire for emotional change
Buying	giving power away or exchanging power for approval of others
Can't move	stuck in a world view, or stagnation
Coughing	difficulty to accept
Dancing	self-expression in everyday life, living with grace
Drinking	accepting emotional support (or desire for)
Drowning	feeling suppressed or overpowered
Dying	release, success or being afraid of release

Exercising	preparing for or building energy and power
Falling	fear of failure
Flying	freedom, or need for freedom
Learning in school	humility is needed to learn something
Mending clothes	trying to mend our self-image
Mending roof	holding on to old limitations
Never-ending work	fear of being overwhelmed or not up to the task
Parachuting	abandoning a world view or life's direction by changing perception
Persecution by	fear of victimization authority
Reading	searching for answers within old world views
Running	desire for freedom or window of freedom
Running a race	being attached to outcome
Singing	finding your voice or life's calling
Skiing	our ability to love is too shallow; others can't give us the love we need
Sneezing	desire to express passionately
Stealing	feeling inadequate to provide for ourselves
Suffocating	loss or lack of personal power
Surfing	utilizing an opportunity
Swimming	desire to be loved and accepted
Talking	need to communicate
Teeth falling out	no need for aggression
Teeth being brushed	getting ready for a battle

Theft of money	power has been stolen
Tripping	fear of inadequacy; letting ourselves or others down
Travel	change or need for change
Washing hands	need to fix our relationships
Winning trophy	need to give self credit; gold for spiritual achievement, silver for worldly achievement
Working	desire or need to take action
Writing	communication
Yawning	need to pull in more energy

Activity—Sexual

Flirting	desire for vitality
Heterosexual sex	receiving and giving power
Homosexual (male) sex	desire to know one's own maleness; feeling inadequate as a male
Kissing	desire for or lack of energy/power
Lesbian sex	desire to know one's own femaleness; feeling inadequate about being a woman
Prostitution	compromising our standards, making choices from less than our higher perspective
Rape	sense of being a victim; or allowing others to plunder our life
Sex w/juvenile	need to connect with the inner child to receive vitality
Sexual perversion	low self-image

Anatomy

(See Figs. 15 &16, The Body Parts as Dream Symbols)

Ankles	flexibility in moving forward in daily life (left = feminine aspects or relationships of life like spirituality; right = masculine aspects or relationships of life)
Arms	the way others treat you or you treat others (males = right, females = left)
Back	upper—responsibility or ability to carry work load mid—expression, self-expression lower—support or lack of
Belly button	sustenance or life force
Blood	love
Bones	parental and hereditary information
Breath	expressing life force
Breasts	nurturing or need of
Chest (lungs)	self-expression when expelling breath, pent up grief
Colon	letting go of what no longer serves us
Duodenal/transverse	mothering or insufficient mothering colon (solar plexus area)
Ears	desire or ability to hear
Elbows	fluidity in how we treat others
Eyes	desire or ability to see
Feet	ability to move forward
Gall bladder	ability to process density
Genitals	self—self-perception of one's maleness or femaleness ; other—one's maleness/ femaleness as reflected by another or, if opposite sex, one's male or female aspects

The Body Parts as Dream Symbols

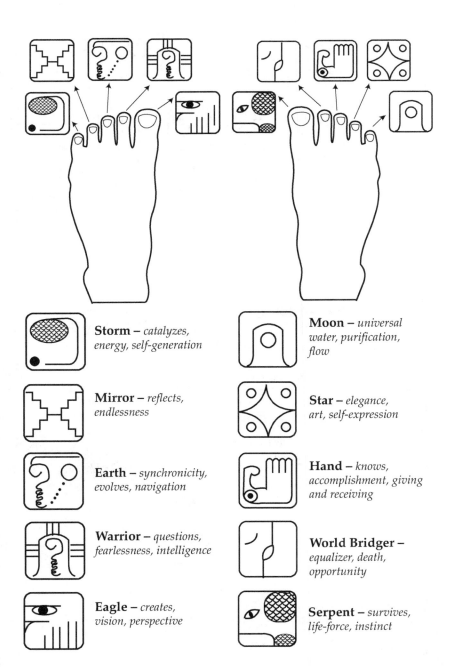

Storm – *catalyzes, energy, self-generation*

Mirror – *reflects, endlessness*

Earth – *synchronicity, evolves, navigation*

Warrior – *questions, fearlessness, intelligence*

Eagle – *creates, vision, perspective*

Moon – *universal water, purification, flow*

Star – *elegance, art, self-expression*

Hand – *knows, accomplishment, giving and receiving*

World Bridger – *equalizer, death, opportunity*

Serpent – *survives, life-force, instinct*

(Figure 15)

The Body Parts as Dream Symbols

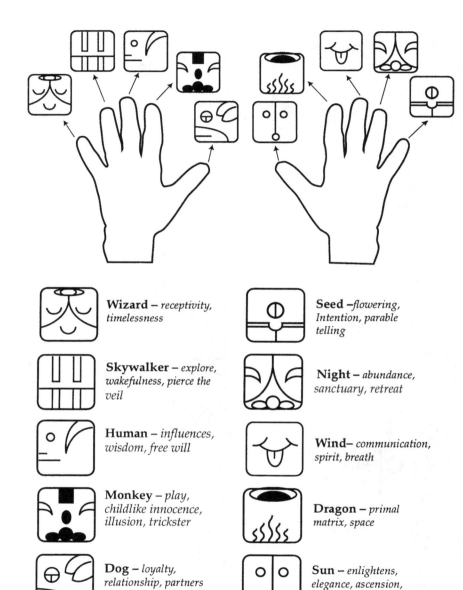

Wizard – *receptivity, timelessness*

Skywalker – *explore, wakefulness, pierce the veil*

Human – *influences, wisdom, free will*

Monkey – *play, childlike innocence, illusion, trickster*

Dog – *loyalty, relationship, partners of destiny*

Seed –*flowering, Intention, parable telling*

Night – *abundance, sanctuary, retreat*

Wind– *communication, spirit, breath*

Dragon – *primal matrix, space*

Sun – *enlightens, elegance, ascension, universal fire*

(Figure 16)

Hair	social self-image
Hands	relationships
Head	intuition, idealism, through
Heart	ability to give love
Hips	where the way we want to move through life and the way we move through life meet
Kidneys	fear
Knees	flexibility with relationships and our required roles (left = feminine, right = masculine)
Legs	progress thru life
Liver	anger
Mouth	ability to receive sustenance
Neck	ideals vs reality; the place where the way we want life to be and the way it seems to be, meet.
Nose	the right to happiness, to flourish; personal power
Ovaries/testicles	procreation or offspring
Shoulders	responsibility
Skin	interaction with others and outside circumstances
Stomach	acceptance of life's circumstances
Teeth	need for aggression
Thighs	sexuality
Throat	unspoken or spoken words
Wrists	fluidity in relationships

Animals

Armadillo	need for defense
Bat	ability or need to find the way through the unknown
Bear	time to go into or come out of seclusion or rest; also rebirth, ending of hardship
Beaver	need to control outcomes, lack of cooperation with one's higher self
Cat	black—black magic, white—white magic, all others—temporal affairs; everyday activities
Camel	ability to flourish during and be prepared for opposition or hard times; need to bolster emotional resources
Caribou/reindeer	instinct as guidance
Chameleon	fluidity and flexibility needed
Cow	nurturing of others
Crab	warriorship against illusion; spiritual warriorship
Crocodile/alligator	pitfall set up by another
Deer	tranquility and peace
Dog	loyalty in relationships and friendship
Dolphin	right brain awareness, non-cognitive information
Donkey	allowing others to drain our energy or use us; false humility
Elephant	expanded awareness
Fox	being tricked into learning the unexpected; expect the unexpected

Hippo	need to approach through feeling rather than mind
Frog	experiencing other realms, frequencies or realities
Horse	balance and freedom in material life
Hare/rabbit	need for awareness—quick change may be needed
Lion	creation; also destruction
Locust/grasshopper	destruction producing blessings
Monkey	need to play or playfulness
Octopus	control or confinement of or by another
Penguin	there is far more to something than meets the eye
Raccoon	brashness, impudence; also toughness
Rats/mice	secrets; white rat means wisdom
Snake	wisdom or need for it
Spider	shortcomings that feed on ourselves; self-destruction
Swan	mastery
Tiger	sovereignty; white tiger means initiation
Whale	superior wisdom or need for it
Wolf	stalking[9] one's own motives or a situation
Wolverine	need to be tough or toughness in the face of greater odds
Zebra	indecision

9 In Toltec terminology, stalking means to not think we know and to approach with great awareness.

Birds *(Refer to thoughts–observe any colors) (See section on Colors)*

Birds of prey	power
Any blackbird (except raven or crows)	treachery
Crow/raven	path of power
Dove	peace, tranquility
Eagle	power through perception
Hummingbird	energy
Owl	seeing or being led thru the dark
Sparrow	fun, joy, being carefree; if white, peace and contentment
Turkey	clinging to old patterns or obsolete habits
Vulture	de-structuring; the end of the old

Clothing *(self-image or image to others)*

Coat	need to shield self
Crown/hat	self importance
Handkerchief	time to get rid of our own or others' negative emotions
Shoes	understanding
Shrunken clothing	we're made to appear less in eyes of others
Socks	that which prevents us from understanding what is really going on behind appearances

Underwear	private life

Colors

Black	need for wholeness; the unknown
Brown—*observe the feeling around it*	dirty brown could mean pollution or unwholesome; clear brown could mean stability or groundedness
Red	need or desire to fight or be aggressive
White	peace/wholeness, purity, high-mindedness
Yellow	spirituality and faith
Green	healing and fertility
Blue	humility and understanding
Pinkish purple	unconditional love
Pink	lightness of being, well-being
Orange	need for shrewdness, cunning, mental strategy
Indigo	need for deeper vision
Violet	mysticism, unseen realms
Turquoise	need to stay centered and go within

Directions

East	direction of sobriety or need to analyze behind appearances
West	feeling or need to notice feelings; listening to guidance from inner child

North	place of power and warriorship; viewing the large picture objectively
South	need to meditate or watch dream symbols for guidance, self-nurturing
Right	left-brained, cognitive, masculine aspects of life
Left	intuitive, feminine, spiritual
Above	effortless knowing will be there
Below	instincts should be trusted

Gems/Jewels/Metals

Copper	healing; transmuting harmful energies
Diamond	mastery through overcoming
Emerald	open heart or healing of heart
Garnet	need to trust instincts
Gold	spiritual matters
Ruby	personal sovereignty, dignity, strength
Sapphire	need for courage and clarity
Silver	everyday matters
Tin	rational mind

Insects

Insects in general	aspects of shortcomings
Ant	labor or hard work, and cooperation needed

Bee	cooperation with destiny
Butterfly/moth	gift of power from the cosmos
Hornet/wasp	someone with anger in environment or directed at environment
Termite/louse/ Parasite	allowing others to use us and drain our energy or usurp our life

Locations

Cliff	trust to make a dramatic change
Desert	despair and hopelessness
Forest	shelter and place to rest
Jungle	unforeseen adventure
Mountain/hill	hope
Open area	need or desire for freedom
Public place	fear of exposure
Valley	place of security

Numbers

0	completion
1	interconnectedness of life, oneness
2	humility and understanding needed
3	trust the intuitive to help create
4	stability and balance or need for

5	freedom and change
6	having to choose the old or new; guidance within physical life
7	information, perception
8	opening or closing of a cycle; harmonious interaction
9	feminine side of spiritual gifts; intuition, non-cognitive information
10	inclusiveness, not thinking in separative way
11	transformation or need for; chance to go to the next level
12	strength and power, enlightenment
13	new birth or beginnings

Objects

Air	ability (or lack of) to see behind appearances, to understand what is really going on, mental activity
Angel	protection and guidance from the higher self
Ashes	remnants of the old

Ball	if it's your turn to throw it, action is required; if you're catching it you have just received a challenge
Basement	sub-conscious, hidden flaws
Basket	possibilities through cooperation
Books	looking for answers within the prison bars of social learning
Boxes	something hidden in a box means secrets kept; storage boxes = that which we have put behind us; boxes in general are limitations through social conditioning
Buildings	view of the world, perspective; public buildings—social conditioning
Candle/lamp	guidance through perception; guidance from unseen realms
Caves	subconscious programming
Ceiling	limitation
Chimney	outlet for anger
City/town/village	common world view or social conditioning
Clock (alarm)	time to wake up; indicates time for awareness to move or awaken; time for change; when we're late it means change or action is overdue
Cupboards/closets	the subconscious or storing of events that have not yielded their insights

Curtains	fear of exposure or that which obscures vision
Dam/lake	conditional or conditioned love
Door	possibilities
Earth/soil	groundedness, return to basics, stability
Eggs	fertility awaiting birth
Egg yolks	the luminous cocoon of man
Feces	money or desire for money
Fire	de-structuring or dramatic change
Fish	beware; treachery; all is not as it seems
Floor	perspective of life, world-view
Food	spiritual nurturing
Flower	beauty and grace; dead flower, lack thereof
Furniture	bed—need or desire to rest chair—comfort zone lamp—illumination or guidance screen—something obscuring vision table—decisive action needed
Garbage	that which isn't properly done or of use
Grass	walking a path with heart and joy
Greenery	fertility, good results in everyday practical matters
Hearing	ability to receive guidance

Key	solution or missing piece; missing puzzle piece indicates the same
Law	balance and integrity
Lighthouse/foghorn	guidance through cataclysmic change or through uncertain times
Lightning	dramatic shifts in awareness
Military	navy—emotional action needed airforce—mental action needed army—action needed in everyday life
Money	crystallized power
Moon	our dreaming body, intuitive self
Music	harmonious interaction
Musical instruments	percussion—harmony with destiny string—harmony within relationships wind—harmony with concepts/thoughts
Newspaper	common view of the world
Nudity	feeling exposed
Ocean	life in general
Optician/glasses	ability or need to see clearly
Path/road	direction
Photos	events or interactions that have not yet yielded their insights; events that need closure
Podiatrist	needing advice to understand the next step

Police	when acting protectively, boundaries need to be established; when acting oppressively, victimization or fear thereof
Rain	the process of life
Report card (grades)	time to account for ourselves; time to live what we know
Reward (money) (trophy)	a gift of power acknowledgement
Ring	power
River	unconditional love
Roof	self-imposed limitation
Sand/sea/beach	that which the process of live has taught us
Secret mission or Agent	destiny
Shooting star	time to be clear about our wishes
Sight	ability to see behind appearances
Smelling	ability to discern
Snow	frozen emotion
Smoke	indication of suppressed anger
Stairs	going up or down in levels of awareness
Storm	cataclysmic change
Tablecloth	tactful action needed
Target	goal is in sight or focus

Taste	nurturing, self-nurturing or spiritual nurturing
Tools	assets and talents
Walls	blockage of perception,being trapped by labels or belief systems
Washing machine	time to clean up our social image
Water	emotion
Weapons	need to protect yourself
Wheels	primary supporting relationships
Wind	thought
Window	vision, ideals
Zipper	unzipped = exclusiveness, separateness zipped = inclusiveness

Transportation

Air	changes in perception, ideas or ideals
Animal	change in aspect represented by animal; i.e., donkey = false humility
Car	the way we travel thru life, e.g., jobs, relationships
Going backwards	slipping back into old habits
Public (bus/train)	change in social conditioning
Road direction	change in general awareness,

PART THREE

The Forgotten Realms

Secrets of the Inner Earth

It seems unrealistic that the largest population on earth would be living in the hollow earth. How can such a large number of people be sustained? We, however, have very large oceans, deplete our environment due to unsound environmental practices and have vast regions of land and deserts that aren't arable. Not so with the inner earth.

The Hopis call it the Land of the Smoky Sun. The temperature is very hot and hovers around 102 degrees. Because many from the inner earth will soon make their way to the surface, some are making their blood thicker by staying for some periods of time in the snow located in mountain ranges on the outer surface. Mt. Shasta is one such location. There is usually no rain or snow in the inner earth but mind-controlled weather produces very high humidity four times a year to water the verdant plant life and maintain the water sources.

The last twenty years (on our calendar) have seen incredible changes to the landmasses and inhabitants of the inner earth. *(See Fig.17, Map of the Inner Earth Before 20 Years Ago, Fig. 18 The Map of the Inner Earth Since 20 Years Ago, Fig. 19, Geographical Names of the Inner Earth)* In fact, what occurred is perhaps one of the greatest miracles on earth. Twenty years ago, the climate

Maps of the Inner Earth Before 20 Years Ago

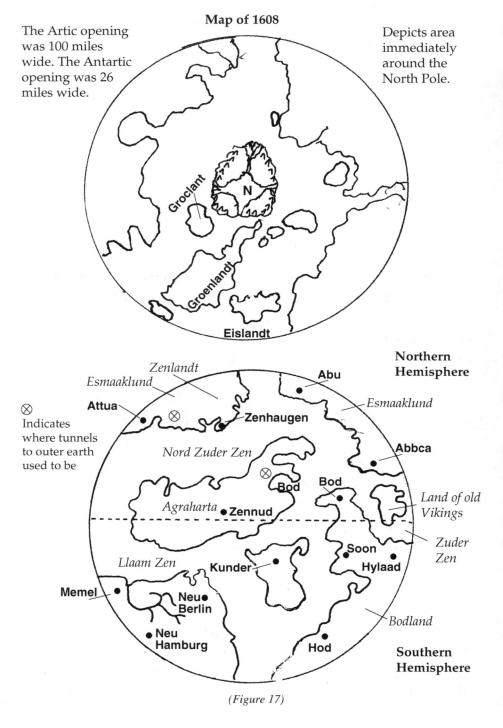

Map of 1608

The Artic opening was 100 miles wide. The Antartic opening was 26 miles wide.

Depicts area immediately around the North Pole.

Groclant

N

Groenlandt

Eislandt

Northern Hemisphere

Zenlandt

Esmaaklund

Attua

⊗ Indicates where tunnels to outer earth used to be

Abu

Esmaaklund

Zenhaugen

Nord Zuder Zen

Abbca

Bod

Bod

Agraharta ·Zennud

Land of old Vikings

Zuder Zen

Llaam Zen

Kunder

Soon

Hylaad

Memel

Neu· Berlin

Neu Hamburg

Bodland

Hod

Southern Hemisphere

(Figure 17)

Maps of the Inner Earth After 20 Years Ago

Southern Hemisphere View

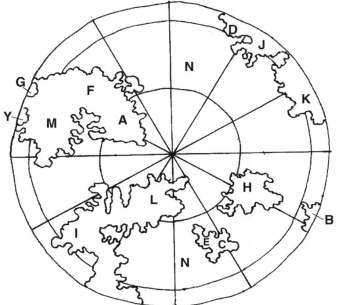

Northern Hemisphere View

(Figure 18)

Geographical Names of the Inner Earth

Southern Hemisphere View

A – Hervingenstadt

B – Pelengrud

C – Gelshpi

D – Sparendoch

E – Nor

F – Brepski

G – Ur

H – Hetva

I – Nenhursva

J – Peleursk

K – Vrilsk

L – Netvi

M – Skrubahirk

Northern Hemisphere View

N – Klarenmeer (Ocean)

O –Baringnud

P – Peleninsk

Q– Harsklutva

R – Trechvarutski

S – Trechbar

T – Hurenepski

U – Gruag

V – Balaur

W– Kranuch

X – Rurbahurch

Y – Elvi

Z – Pruchba

Vrilsk is the land of the giants

(Figure 19)

turned very severe. One of my friends within the inner earth calls it 'the time of the big freeze'. Everything froze and then the climate became warm again, melting all the ice and snow and causing such massive floods that the entire map of the land masses changed. According to my friends, the disruption in the weather was caused by incorrect thinking.

Amazingly enough, only 2% of the population was lost because of a great miracle. The Creator Goddess sent an aspect of herself as a vision that appeared to 55% of the population, sending them into God-consciousness, silencing their minds and greatly expanding their awareness. This group went into the stillness of mind just prior to the freezing conditions.

When their world became disrupted enough to disintegrate old thinking patterns and over half the population had already entered God-consciousness, programming their grid accordingly, another 43% entered this state of expanded awareness. This happened after the freeze, but before the thaw and flooding.

Because their minds were still, 98% of the inner earth's population could therefore feel in their hearts where they should go to wait out the coming cataclysms.

The people of the inner earth had a separate grid (an array of lines of light that tells a species how to act) from ours. They represented the etheric body of the earth, even though they are as physical as we are, and we represent the physical body. In March 2006, our grids merged into one and because they are more numerous than we are, it affected our consciousness very positively.

The only exceptions to the physicality of those in the inner earth are the giants who are one level up in frequency. This makes them invisible and intangible to us. During the freeze, 40 giants were lost, leaving a current number of 200.

All people within the inner earth live in eternal time versus linear time. This means they live with complete focus on the present moment. It is a very pastoral life without any day or night as we know it, under a sun that pulses every 24 hours.

They are very respectful of all life forms and highly respectful of nature. I asked my friend, the 30-foot giant Egsplauvitpata, how he got water for his bath and if he had to pay for it. He said he did not. It came from the ocean, passed through a filter to remove the salt and was heated by fire. He had a large garden and lived through bartering. Asked how they knew when to meet a friend for lunch since they couldn't tell time by day and night, nor had they used clocks for twenty years, the answer was that as a result of being in eternal time, they could feel in their hearts when it had to happen.

There are several population groups with the same variety of skin colors as we have on the outer earth, but with slightly different features:

- 1,800 Hebrews who found their way there a little after the Babylonian invasion of Judah. They are the descendants of those generally referred to as the 10 lost tribes. Height is 4'6" to 5'1". Some still speak Hebrew.
- 22,000 German descendants. 21 entered there through an opening at the headwaters of the Amazon during the 15th century. 14,000 Germans entered at the same place at the end of WWII. No SS soldiers or Nazi leaders were permitted in. They had obtained maps from some of the original Germans who had returned many centuries before. Some still speak German. Their height is the same as ours.
- Atlanteans and Lemurians comprise the rest and, being vastly in the majority, make Atlantean the most widely spoken language of earth. The Atlantean catastrophes occurred 1 million, 200,000

and 75,000 years ago respectively. The last one sank Atlantis—then known as Poseidonis— and occurred 11,586 years ago as of 2006. Many Atlanteans escaped these by going into the hollow earth;

- Lemurians entered there in large numbers 1,600,000 years ago. The Atlanteans and Lemurians range in height from 6' to 12'.
- The Giants range in height from 28' to 30' and can live to be a million years old. They came from Lemuria and later also from Atlantis. They are mentioned in the Old Testament in Genesis 6:4, Numbers 3:33, Deuteronomy 2:20, Joshua 12:4 and Samuel 21:22. The other races live to an average age of 86 years.

No currency is used in the inner earth but inhabitants use barter systems as in the case of Egsplauvitpata. Whatever their labor produces is freely shared among themselves.

Some of the major governments on the surface of the earth are aware of the populations in the inner earth. They have as yet not found their way in. According to my friends, the entrances are shielded from observation even by satellite technologies. If they choose, the people from the inner earth are able to see the outer earth. *(See Fig. 20, The Atlantean Alphabet, Fig. 21, Atlantean Numbers)*

NOTE:

Many of the future spouses and partners for the major lightworkers on the planet will, within the next few years, be emerging from the inner earth. They will be bringing with them an evolved Atlantean culture. Their advent will enrich our lives, raise planetary consciousness and bring some humility to the arrogance of the minds of men who thought they knew the cultures of earth. It is therefore important for us to begin to study their culture.

The Atlantean Alphabet

1. KA

2. PH

3. QU

4. S

5. D

6. M

7. G

8. I

9. E

10. L

11. PHL

12. C

13. N

14. R

15. X

16. Z

17. Y

18. ST

19. TH

20. CHL

21. OOO

22. TL

23. B

24. J

25. ZU

26. V

27. CH

28. NG

29. WH

30. MA

(Figure 20)

114

The Atlantean Alphabet Continued

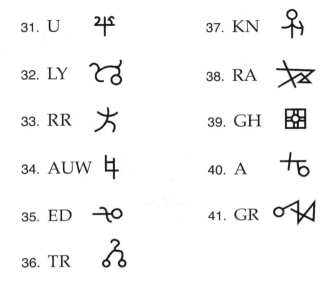

31. U

32. LY

33. RR

34. AUW

35. ED

36. TR

37. KN

38. RA

39. GH

40. A

41. GR

Additional letters used to accommodate
other languages' sounds.

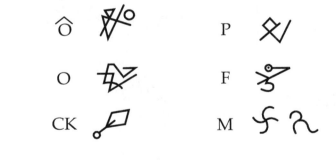

ô

O

CK

P

F

M

is for m as in name   is for m as in mean

Atlantean is written from right to left.
When there is more than one figure per letter,
it means that there is more than one sound.

Atlantean Numbers

1.

8.

15.

2.

9.

16.

3.

10.

17.

4.

11.

18.

5.

12.

19.

6.

13.

20.

7.

14.

In 2005 Atlantis sank 11,587 years ago. It is written like this:

11,587 =

(Figure 21)

The Most Accurate Calendar on Earth

To understand the Atlantean calendar, we must understand the meaning and great significance of a day out of time. Since we cannot see the vastness of the etheric realms, nine-tenths of existence is unknown.

Before the last sinking of Atlantis dropped the consciousness of man, much more of the unseen realms were as real as the seen. The etheric realms are where materialization begins and it is the etheric that moves through all things, giving life to matter. If something in the etheric changes, it will also change in manifested life unless we prevent it by clinging to our illusion-based belief systems.

A day out of time is a day that exists in the etheric, but not in the physical (though it seems it does to those who cannot see the difference). It is therefore a day that presents the golden opportunity to change aspects of manifested life by changing them in the etheric.

On the Atlantean calendar there are five days out of time; September 23, December 21, January 21 March 23 and June 21. To illustrate this, imagine 365 soldiers standing in a line. If 5 take a step back, there would still be a lineup but those soldiers, like those 5 days, would be on a different plane. *(See Fig. 22, Atlantean Calendar and Fig. 23, Key to the Atlantean Calendar)*

Current Use

As we have noted, the largest population group lives in the inner earth. This Atlantean calendar is the one they use, making it the most widely used calendar on earth. It is able to indicate time to within five minutes.

But, how can a world that cannot see an earthly rotation with its passages of day and night know when a 24-hour day has passed? Because the inner 'smoky' sun pulses every 24 hours. Complete

Atlantean Calendar

July 26th
(1st day of the new year)

June 21st

September 23rd

March 23rd

January 21st

December 21st

The year's numerals are written in here from right to left.

The days of the 13th month have no color but were indicated by holes or indentions.
This signifies that the month functions as a portal to a new spiral of consciousness.
The Atlantean year count began after the major catastrophe of 75,000 years ago

(Figure 22)

Key To The Atlantean Calendar

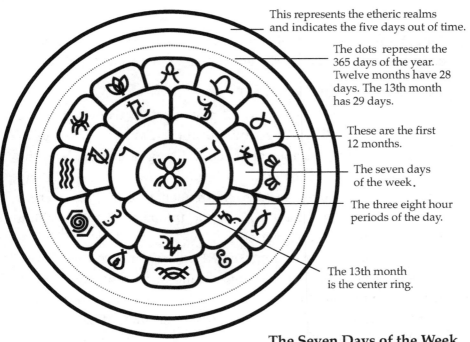

This represents the etheric realms and indicates the five days out of time.

The dots represent the 365 days of the year. Twelve months have 28 days. The 13th month has 29 days.

These are the first 12 months.

The seven days of the week.

The three eight hour periods of the day.

The 13th month is the center ring.

The Three Eight Hour Periods

Yod = midnight to 8 a.m.

Hay = 8 a.m. to 4 p.m.

Vau = 4 p.m. to midnight

Understanding the Spider

The eight legs represent the hours within each eight hour segment starting from the upper right hand and proceeding in a clockwise manner.

The Seven Days of the Week

Untanas – Monday

Quertas – Tuesday

Chietal – Wednesday

Goyana – Thursday

Huertal – Friday

Semveta – Saturday

Ardal – Sunday

(Figure 23)

darkness is unknown in this inner realm, but a 12-hour period of dimming and another of brightening mark the days and nights.

Features Of The Calendar

The Atlantean calendar has 12 months of 28 days each and a thirteenth one with 29 days. Five of these days are days out of time. As a more conscious civilization living in eternal time, the Atlanteans mapped out frequency segments for use in their daily lives. There is a big change in the frequency of the day every 8 hours, marking a dramatic shift in the frequency 3 times within any given day or 24-hour period.

The 8-hour segments represented polarity in that one 8 hour segment is positive and therefore a time to be proactive; one is negative and a time to be receptive and one is neutral in that it is positive and negative. The calendar is so accurate it can indicate exactly during which segment of the day, or the frequency band of the day, an event occurred.

Within each of the three 8 hour segments or frequency bands, 8 one-hour segments form mini bands with more subtle frequency changes. Structuring life to cooperate with the frequency of every given hour was a way of life to the ancient Atlantean civilizations, as it is to the people of the inner earth. Like the changes they noted in birdsong as these frequency bands transitioned from one to the other, their music was composed to balance and enhance each hour of the day.

The smaller one-hour frequency time periods were also mapped out on the calendar and by indicating during which part of the one-hour mini band an event happened, the calendar could place it to within 5 minutes.

The thirteen months are arranged in a circle of twelve with the thirteenth in the center. There are many hidden truths behind a thirteen-month calendar: The number 13 stands for the goddess or feminine principle that gives birth. Time is, in actual fact, the movement of awareness and the movement aspect of the cosmos is feminine. Hence time is feminine.

Time is the birthplace of potentiality into actuality. Thirteen always has the potential to birth something new. In conception, at least 12 sperm must pummel the ovum so that the 13th can enter. In being born into God-consciousness, the twelve archetypal god and goddess facets of the surface mind blend, so the 13th goddess can open the doorway within mind to birth the expanded state of awareness called God-consciousness.[10]

The 13th month is positioned within for another reason. It is the month that marks the end of a year—a time for evaluation and introspection. In this way the past year's lessons are incorporated into formulating the desired changes that must be put into effect during the new year.

The months were named for the goddess archetypes.[11]

Number of the Month	Goddess Archetype
1st	Pana-tura
2nd	Ama-terra-su
3rd	Ka-li-ma
4th	Ori-ka-la
5th	Au-ba-ri
6th	Hay-hu-ka
7th	Ishana-ma
8th	Apara-tura
9th	Hay-leem-a
10th	Ur-u-ama
11th	Amaraku
12th	Alu-mi-na
13th	Ara-ka-na

10 See *Journey to the Heart of God*
11 For the qualities of the months, see the qualities of the goddesses in Part I of this book.

The days were indicated by a ring of dots; the first day of each of the 13 months around the ring marked by a different color dot (color is tone or frequency made visible.) Each of the first 12 months has a tone and color. The 13th month is represented by a 'hole' or portal, indicating that it is a passage to new consciousness.

The days out of time are marked with a separate ring indicating not only that they exist as a separate reality, but also their exact placement in relation to the regular days.

The year is written on a separate part of the calendar in Atlantean. Atlantean is written from right to left and so the numbers read from right to left.

How to Indicate Time

To indicate a specific date (the way we would circle a date on our calendar), a line is drawn from one of the days, or dots, on the outer or second outer ring, depending whether it is a day out of time or a regular day. *(See Fig. 23)* For example, if it's the 7th day of a specific month, one would count the colored dot, indicating that month, as one and then count six more dots in a clockwise direction. That's where the line begins. The line then moves through one of the corresponding goddess symbols to show at a glance the goddess archetype governing that month.

If it's the 12th month of Amaraku, it is a time of testing our worthiness and a time to celebrate our achievements. It is a time of bringing closure to our unfinished projects and to prepare for the 13th month of introspection and rebirth—the month of Ara-ka-na that lies ahead.

The line next goes to the day of the week we want to indicate. The seven days of the week were named after the seven lords of light who dwell in the Halls of Amenti. *(See Fig. 8, The Seven Lords of Light)*

Monday	Untanas
Tuesday	Quertas
Wednesday	Chietal
Thursday	Goyana
Friday	Huertal
Saturday	Semveta
Sunday	Ardal

The line next indicated in which 8 hour segment the event occurred. But we find the 8 hour segments progressing counter-clockwise. The section of Yod is the 8 hour period from midnight to 8 am. The section of Hay is from 8 am to 4 pm. The section of Vau is from 4 pm to midnight. The counter-clockwise progression represents the structure (or masculine pole) of time, the windows through which time flows.

There are deeper, esoteric meanings about the core of the calendar progressing backwards, or counter-clockwise. One reminds us that time can flow backwards and that certain portions of history were actually lived backwards. Humans appeared on this page of creation, in this loop of time, at a given time. Other cultures actually lived backwards in time, extending history backwards.

In the God-kingdom there is a constant feeling of déjà vu in that the next minute is remembered as the past. To decide what to choose, one looks back at the past to see what has already been chosen. It's as though the time of the gods is backwards. This therefore represented the time of the gods.

We then draw a line to one of the spider symbol's (Ara-ka-na's symbol) eight legs. This indicates which hour segment we are talking about. The right hand upper leg (*see illustration*) marks the first hour and, proceeding in a clockwise manner, the subsequent legs mark the other 7 hours.

Each leg of the spider, however, has 3 segments to indicate in which 20-minute segment an event happened. Each segment can be divided into quarters, to place the event within 5 minutes. The cross-over point of the spider's body (drawn as a figure eight), is the eternal now. The line always ends there, reminding us that time is illusory in nature and the eternal now, the moment, is all that exists.

Understanding Time

We need a lot of humility as we approach this very complex subject of time. We know a mere fraction of how time flows. It is the movement of awareness and as such can travel in any direction—and yet we have assumed we understand it.

Scientists have puzzled about where Sumeria, a complex and advanced civilization, could have originated since it didn't seem to have evolved from previous known civilizations. The actual truth about it, as explained by one of the goddesses, is that it is the result of a 'backwards' evolution of time that occurred as follows:

- Life doesn't occur in trillions and trillions of years of one uninterrupted story. Instead, a series of stories or short plays on the stage of life are designed to explore through life's experiences the unknown portions of beingness. These are called 'pages'. When we emerge on a new page with a whole new stage set, play and sometimes characters, we have no history on that page.
- To make life seem as though it has existed for a long time on that page, some of the characters or civilizations live backwards on an accelerated timeline. For example, if we emerged onto this page for what to us seems like 200 years ago, we have traveled 'forward' 200 years, but other civilizations could have traveled

backwards 3,000 years during the same time period, giving us an apparent history. Otherwise, everything would just be blank prior to 200 years.

• When Thoth was asked when he built the pyramid, he said "200 years ago, but I traveled back into the distant past to do it."

In the advanced stages of Ascended Mastery, mastery of time travel becomes a way of life. The master learns to loop back to correct errors or give himself insights. By changing the past, today becomes changed as well.

The master also learns to utilize the time traveling tunnels located in various places on earth, such as the Great Pyramid, Ireland, Bali, Nepal and others. These tunnels enable one to travel between the pages of existence, whereas with his own abilities, he could only travel through time on the particular page of existence he occupies.

My first experience of time traveling while in the body came when I was sent to take information to a future inter-stellar dynasty that would have formed (this future has since changed). My body left in segments, like rings stacked together that fell over one at a time. Upon arriving at my destination, my body re-assembled the same way. When I returned, my body again came together in a series of rings or segments. Although I had spent days in the future, only 45 minutes had passed on the clock. My body felt refreshed and filled with energy.

The Loop of Time

The Atlantean calendar was circular. Circles indicate the feminine. Time, as the movement of awareness, represents the feminine aspect of awareness.

The calendar is also circular because it reminded the ancients of a deeply mystical and obscure secret I re-discovered quite by accident: that humanity's past lies in the future and we have been on a backwards loop of time.

Hints of this esoteric principal began to show up while working with students to uncover their destinies. Painstakingly going through past life regressions, we identified repetitive themes that manifested during the cycles of their lives.[12] The goal was to see the specific theme they had undertaken to solve on behalf of the Infinite and to see how those that contracted to 'injure' them in a particular life have corresponding themes.

As we worked over years to uncover the students' destinies (a life-changing event that puts challenges into perspective), the past lives looped into the future. Exploring this in detail, we learned that a template had been designed to explore the concept of unity within diversity among races. A dynasty across this area of the cosmos formed, but ended disastrously as it was infiltrated by hostile races and by internal corruption within itself. At least one planet was blown out of the sky. Many of the souls who were lost had no place left where they could incarnate.

Soon after (remember, this happened in the future) as recounted by some of the star-brothers, emissaries from Mother were sent to 32 different planetary systems, representing the 32 root races of the cosmos.

They were to send their best geneticists back to what is now about 12 millions years ago. These geneticists were to go to a planet that had formed when a larger planet, formerly located on the other side of Mars, had two-thirds of its surface destroyed. The remaining piece had spun out, forming what is now Earth. The old planet had been called Tiamat, which means "Eternal Mother" and its fragmentary remains became the asteroid ring.

12 More information on this process may be heard on the CD Painless Past Life Regression

These geneticists had to form a being that incorporated the best each race had to offer, knowing only that the result would benefit all at some point in the future. The Andromedans gave 'man' their mental bodies, the Orions gave the reptilian brain and pineal gland, the Pleideans gave artistic ability and so forth.

But another unique anomaly had occurred. From the great trauma caused by the shattering of the planet, the souls themselves had fractured into what is called the four sub-personalities. In this way, although every race represents one of the four directions, man has all within. Truly made to be the microcosm of the macrocosm, man would now have within the ability to solve the communication problems that occurred between the races.

Throughout various short incarnations (not the case on other planets), man would solve the problems of the future dynasty's downfall so that when we caught up with it, its conclusion would be changed. Humankind would in actuality be solving the karma for all races through the experiences of their lives.

This would help all 32 root races of the cosmos be able to maximize their abilities to resolve all, or at least a significant part, of their karma before the cosmic ascension began in February 2005. From that point on, with each successive cosmic ascending shift, more and more races that had not eliminated enough karma would disappear back into the sea of consciousness. No longer would they be individuated beings.

Because many races could time-travel, they were able to foresee that humanity would lead the ascension and one day pull them into oblivion. Every attempt was made to obstruct, mind control and even abduct major players in this epic drama of ascension.

The repressive races of Orion abducted 300 of the Indigo Children's aspects and 50 brilliant Chinese children.

Ships hovered over God-conscious masters, gathering the neutrinos emitted by those in such elevated states (the reason why people heal in their presence by grace). The neutrinos were then used to beam their effects back through radionics to the ships' home planets to eliminate karma.

Aliens tampered with governments and introduced repressive technologies to prevent the people of earth from rising in consciousness. But none of this managed to save them.

After spending 2004 studying the issues of the future through the lives of my students, enough information was gathered to take 'back' to the future, to 16 generations before the disastrous ending of this dynasty from which we originated.

Using a technique described in the *Emerald Tablets of Thoth*, I was able for the first time to travel with my body, which left in rings from the feet up as previously described. Disheveled and in my jeans, I arrived in a locked chamber with no windows, containing only a small throne on a raised platform. Seated on the throne was a very regal queen. She had dark skin, very finely defined features, dark eyes and black hair streaked with a little grey. She had no wrinkles and very prominent cheekbones. Her robes of teal and bottle green changed colors when she moved. She wore a tall headdress. The throne was made of a pewter-like substance with no seams; jade-like overlays created a beautiful design.

In addition to the queen, there were two men dressed in white robes and appearing to be of a different race. They were fair and had white hair. To the right of the queen stood another woman, seemingly of high rank. My feeling was that she was like a lady-in-waiting to the queen.

My arrival had startled them and the queen reached for a cord hanging from the ceiling of the room (possibly to summon help).

By gesture, I conveyed this was not necessary and kept smiling. Then she spoke and I recognized one of the star languages I knew.

I remained in that place for six of their days and nights, giving in as much detail as I could, the information I had unraveled about why the dynasty would fail. I had found solutions for the problems with the students by studying their lives. I relayed these insights in detail during those days as their guest.

In May of 2005 while working on preparing angel sigils for an assignment given to me by the Mother Goddess, I felt something shift throughout my body. The beings in my house confirmed that the loop of time had disappeared. We had gained all the insights needed for the principle of unity within diversity to be instilled within the cosmos. The future was no longer written for us and we could live it any way we chose.

When Time Wrinkled

As the cosmos ascended from one frequency to the next, Mother was giving instructions as to the preparation of ceremonies that had to be done by proxy in physicality. They were called the opening of gates, and as preparations for what was the ninth gate were under way, thousands of symbols were being inscribed for a wheel approximately 8' in diameter.

The spirits suddenly starting saying, "No" to every symbol. Asked why, they said: "You've already used all those symbols at the ninth gate!" "But this is the ninth gate we're preparing for! Remember, we did the eighth gate last time?" Despite walking them through each successive gate we'd passed, they insisted we had already done the ninth, tenth and eleventh gates.

There were pages of symbols I had not yet reviewed with them, but they continued to insist all had been used at either the tenth or eleventh gate. Asked what the current date was, they gave one that was months ahead of us. I was very concerned. The symbols stood for groups of beings and races and if the spirits were wrong, those beings and races could be wiped out when we ascended. Ezekiel 1:9 "And when the living creatures went, the wheels went by them: and when the living creatures were lifted up from the earth, the wheels were lifted up."

Continuing to work on gate nine, I began to feel ill. The spirits said that if I did not do the right gate soon, all humanity would feel ill since we were living in the wrong time. Students were faxing and e-mailing with reports of feeling strange, ill or experiencing dread, as did I.

That night I dreamt the earth was telling me she was scared. The next day the spirits explained, "She's afraid you're going to pull her backwards." Still unsure, it was becoming increasingly difficult for me to think. There was an unusual volume of jet aircraft and helicopters flying above our little town.

I asked the dragon named Beautiful One, that guarded the house, about the air traffic, she just kept saying, "Too busy."

Finally, she answered, "They're aware of the wrinkle in time and they're hoping to pressure you into making the wrong decision and pulling us backwards. They can't see you because of the shield,"

"But how do they know where I am?" "They have an alien working for them and have been tracking all the UFO's into this area."

That was really a great relief and blessing, because now I knew exactly what to do. I immediately started preparing for the 13th gate. Ironically, it was this gate that dissolved the 'they' who had sent the jets and made so many plans to control humankind, back into the sea of consciousness.

Atlantean—The Most Widely Spoken Language On Earth

As previously mentioned, the possibility that the most densely populated area of humanity might not be on the surface of the earth, but inside the hollow earth, might seem preposterous to some. But the changes happening on earth during its ascension are coming rapidly and occurring dramatically. Soon, there will be ample evidence of the millions of people living within the hollow earth.

Of these, 200 are giants; 38 of those are babies born during the week of June 13, 2005. Giants like to give birth during the same week and only reproduce every 300 years. (Since the earth's ascension started in February 2005, this is changing).

The inner world is governed by two male rulers of very high consciousness: Sol and Som[13]. Sixty-two percent of the inhabitants speak Atlantean, making it (as we pointed out) the most widely spoken language on earth. Atlantean is a derivative of Lemurian and Nibiruan, the language of the Annunaki who settled here from the planet Nibiru 467,000 years before the crucifixion of Christ[14].

The Lemurians and Annunaki who settled Atlantis came from two very divergent historical backgrounds. *(See page 136)*

Mu Re–Visited

About 10 million years ago, 12 races that would eventually form a star-grid with the earth and play a major role in the ascension of the cosmos, were contacted by the emissaries of the Creator Goddess. They were told that it would benefit their race if they sent their geneticists to earth to develop the human race.

---

13 Sol's son, called Hervingenstadt, is currently on a walking journey to the surface. He will emerge through Mt. Shasta in California.
14 *The Lost Book of Enki*, by Zecharia Sitchin

About 6 million years ago, the seven root races of Lemuria, the motherland, were formed. Some were giants, some were not. Those that migrated to Atlantis were the Ramouhal, the 5th root race.

But 1,000,000 years ago, a major cataclysm hit the planet; a giant comet tilted the earth's axis. The Lemurians had advance notice and found safety by going into the hollow earth. *(See Fig. 24, The Alphabet of Mu, and Fig. 25, The Lemurian Numbers)*

A Visit to the Motherland

One night in the summer of 2005 while lying awake in my bedroom, a mist appeared next to my bed. It soon became more defined and compact, and then it started swirling in a clockwise rotation. I felt myself swept up and after several minutes within a pulsating silvery tunnel, found myself standing in sunlight.

I was in a small courtyard surrounded by stone buildings. I stood in complete bewilderment, barefoot and in my nightgown. I had the uncomfortable feeling of 'programming' in my mind breaking down, as if it were fragmenting into pieces like mosaic tiles. I was struggling not to lose my composure, but I was not the only one.

A man, about 5' 11'' tall stood staring in complete disbelief. When I saw him, he hid his shock and smiled. He had dark wavy hair cut short, very white skin and soft, almost black eyes. He was slender and wore a green suit with pants made from an unfamiliar fabric. The closest I've seen is what is called 'boucle', with lots of thread loops on its surface.

He spoke and beckoned me into one of the buildings where he pointed for me to sit on a bench. The first language I had received in my gift of tongues had been Lemurian. From his speech, I knew I had somehow been sucked through a time tunnel into Lemuria.

The Alphabet of Mu in Order

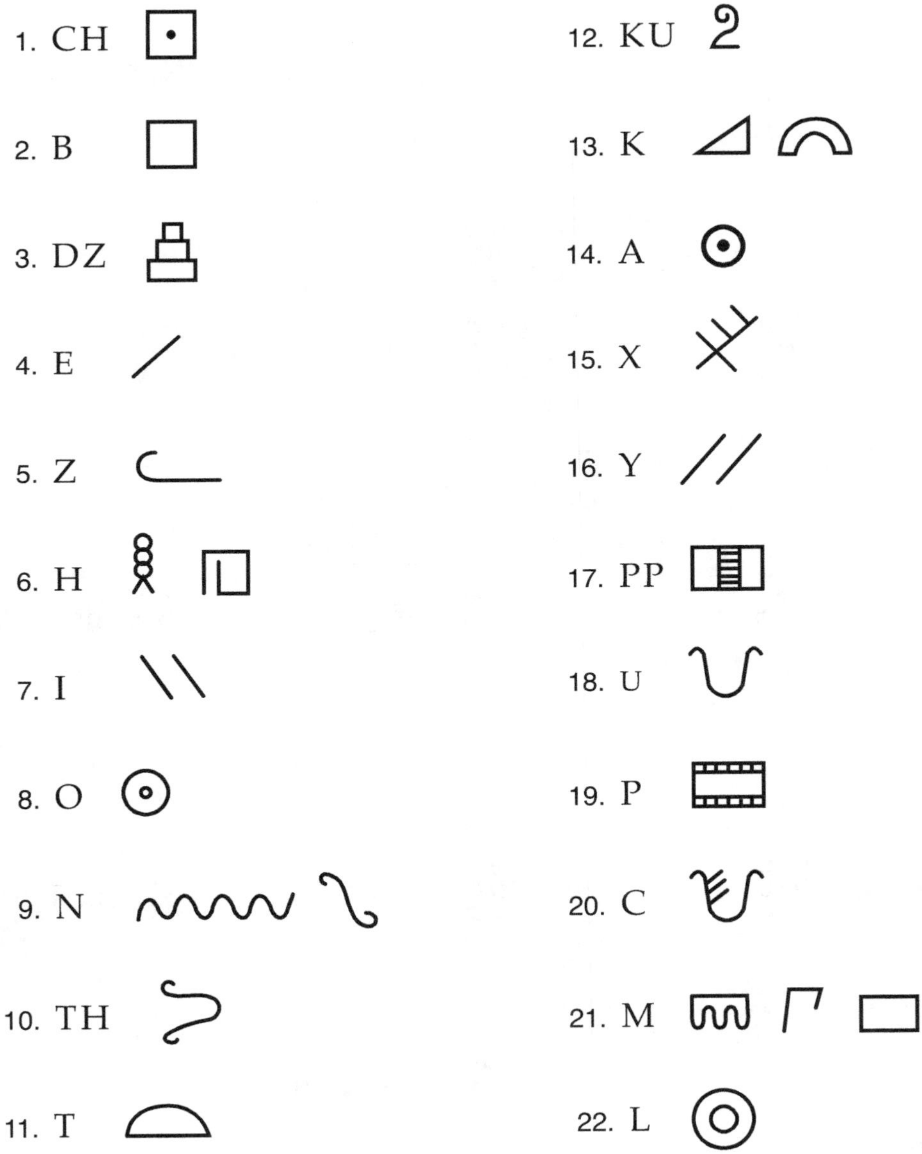

1. CH [·]

2. B □

3. DZ ⊟

4. E /

5. Z ⊂

6. H ⚇ �𝌆

7. I \\\\

8. O ⊙

9. N ∿∿∿ ∿

10. TH ∿

11. T ◠

12. KU 2

13. K ◺ ⌒

14. A ⊙

15. X ⤬

16. Y //

17. PP ▥

18. U ∪

19. P ▤

20. C ℧

21. M ⋒ Γ ▭

22. L ◎

(Figure 24)

Lemurian Numbers

1.  Hu   5. HO   9. BOLAN

2. CA   6. UAC   10. LAHUN

3. OX   7. UUC   11. BULUK

4. CAN   8. UAXAX   12. LAHAK

13.  OXLAHUN

(Figure 25)

134

Perhaps it had opened by mistake from my work with time that had been done in my bedroom.

The man went to speak to someone in the adjoining room. I heard their excited voices while I looked at my surroundings. It appeared to be a laboratory of some sort. Suddenly two heads appeared around the corner, looking inquisitively at me. The new man was slightly fairer, but with dark eyes. They smiled when I saw them. I hadn't said a word and didn't let on I could understand some of what they were saying. Although I still don't understand the meaning of their terms, the following conversation could be overheard as they retreated around the corner:

"I think she's an ambassador." "No, I think you're wrong, she's at least an eagle."

The two heads peeked around the corner again, but suddenly and without warning, the room appeared to be spinning and immediately I was pulled back through the tunnel and into my bedroom.

A week later, strange music could be heard in my room as though from a festival. It used a whole tone scale, much like Middle Eastern music. It continued for about 8 hours.

Two weeks later I awoke to a loud 'POP' noise in my room and found a woman standing next to my bed. She looked as surprised as I must have seemed. She had long dark hair in a style vaguely similar to that of ancient Greek statues of women. Her skin was very light in the dimly lit room and her eyes were dark. She was very pretty and wore a long, dark purple dress drawn in at the waist.

For a few minutes she and I stared at each other and then she was gone. Somehow, the tunnel into this ancient civilization has now closed, but I will always remember the gentle-looking inhabitants of Lemuria I was privileged to meet during the brief opening of a window through time.

The Sunken Lumerian Temple

Off the coast of Maui is a sacred site that guards the base of the earth's pranic tube. This sacred site is where the earth's feminine, love-based, magnetic energy is at its strongest. Shielded from all but the pure in heart, a Lemurian temple lies beneath the waves— remnant of a civilization that lived the divine principles in every day life.

This sacred temple can be entered in meditation through its sixteen gates, if the truth-seeker can speak the names of the gates. He or she must also know the meaning of the sacred principles they represent and meditate on the deeper meanings behind the words. Once inside the Holy of Holies beyond the gates, the wheel on a white polished stone slab can be seen. In 2005 this wheel was turned to signal and initiate the rising of portions of Lemuria.

Gate 1—The Gate of the Light Family It honors those who work to promote light, the earth's star grid family, the value of relationship and in remembrance that this is the gate that began the journey of the family of Creation.

Gate 2—The Gate of the Wayshower—Earth She has with patience and compassion worked out the issues of many; now she becomes the bestower of grace.

Gate 3—The Green Gate of the Elemental Kingdom This gate is dedicated to the bringers of joy and beauty and the bounty of nature throughout the cosmos.

Gate 4—The Gate of Sacred Government To the journey home to the light, led by the sacred Matriarchy, supported by sacred paternal orders, that all species may prosper.

Gate 5—The Gate of the Angels Filled with light and love, they support the plan of Creation and the evolution of all life.

Gate 6—The Gate of the Radiant Lords of Light Steadfast in purpose, radiant of countenance, they are the pillars that uphold the structure of the cosmos.

Gate 7—The Gate of the Gods and Goddesses of Creation Forming life anew every eternal moment, the luminous ones guide and guard all life.

Gate 8—The Gate of the Ascended Masters To the few who, having overcome all, leave the many behind to become the wayshowers for others.

Gate 9—The Gate of Thoth The one who stands for dedication to service to all life and setting all beings free from illusion.

Gate 10—The Gate of the Lightbabies of the Cosmos Vehicles of communication are they, bringing messages between realms, filling mind with light.

Gate 11—The Gate of the Elements of the Seven Directions To the sacred building blocks of All that is and the Ancient Ones who represent Original Awareness, Light, Love, Time, Space, Energy and Matter.

Gate 12—The Gate of the Living God—The Alumuanu King In honor of he who represents the Infinite, Father of Creation that he inseminated through light.

Gate 13—The Gate of the Eternal Mother Having birthed all that is, she enfolds her children with compassion, yearning for their blossoming into the fullness of their being.

Gate 14—The Gate of the Beautiful One In remembrance that an individual's courage, impeccability and honor can be that which determines the outcome for the many.

Gate 15—The Gate of the Dragon Realms The living examples of dedication to duty and respect for order, they represent highmindedness, brilliance and elegance.

Space 16—The Space of Hope That the family of all creatures great and small may thrive and live in respect and love for one another's unique gifts, embodying the principle of Unity Within Diversity.

The Annunaki Arrive on Earth

When the first Annunaki arrived here from Niburu 667,000 years ago, they circled the earth but found no one. Only 15 years after they had made their first settlement did some of the Lemurians (some of them giants) emerge from the inner earth and re-populate the motherland of Lemuria.

After another major cataclysm took place 200,000 years ago, Atlantis was once again settled by the Lemurians. It was not until after the second last global cataclysm 75,000 years ago that Thoth, whose father Enki had come to earth from the planet Niburu, took over the kingship of Atlantis. This was the golden age of Atlantis. The Halls of Amenti that house the lifeforce center of the earth and the seven (there are now nine) lords of light as well as the great lord known as the Dweller[15] stood upon the Atlantean island of Undal. Thoth's father, Enki, was the liaison between the lords and the kings of the earth.

During this time, knowledge and wisdom flourished. Beautiful cities arose by the power of Ytolan, which is a way of creating instantly with thought (see the next section). In our calendar year of 2005, the key was again turned under the guidance of Enki for the rising of Atlantis to rapidly occur. *(See Fig. 26, Landmasses After Cataclysm of 800,000 Years Ago, Fig. 27, Landmasses After 200,000 Years Ago until 75,000 Years Ago, Fig. 28, Landmasses After 75,000 Years Ago until 9,564 Years B.C.)*

15 See the chapter on the Lords of Light for additional information on The Dweller.

Landmasses After the Cataclysm of 800,000 Years Ago

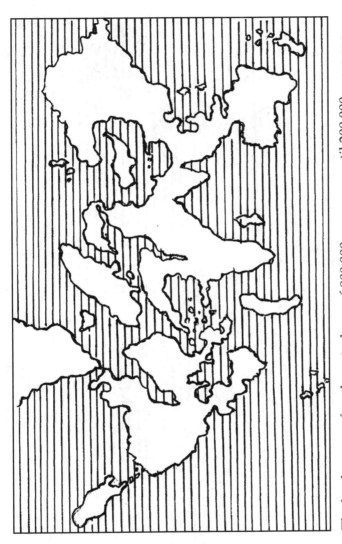

The landmasses after the cataclysm of 800,000 years ago until 200,000 years ago. Atlantis consists of islands.

(Figure 26)

Landmasses After 200,000 Years Ago Until 75,000 Years Ago

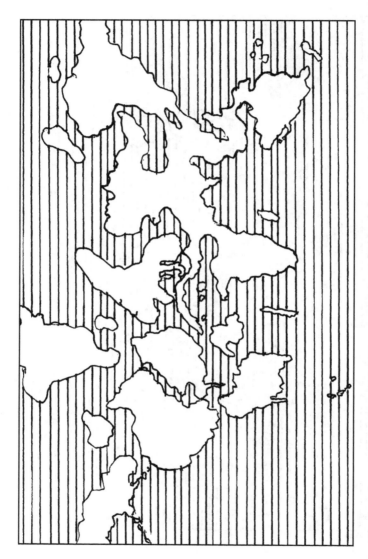

The landmasseses after 200,000 years ago till the cataclysm of 75,000 years ago. Atlantis consists of two islands, Ruta and Itaya.

(Figure 27)

Landmasses After 75,000 years Ago Until 9,564 Years B.C.

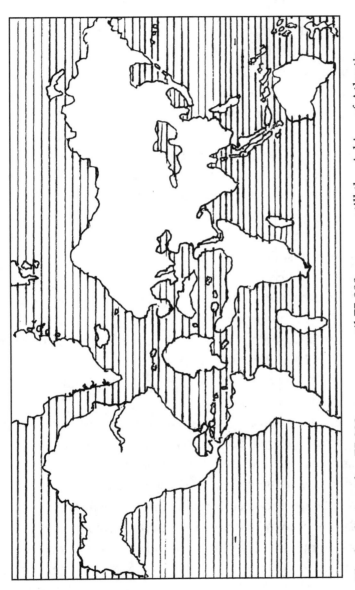

The landmass after 75,000 years ago until 75,000 years ago till the sinking of Atlantis (Poseidonis) 9,564 years before Christ's crucifixion.

(Figure 28)

The Power Of Ytolan

During the last week of February 2005, I was called by the Dweller to the Halls of Amenti. He led me to a chamber off the channel that runs through the earth and equates to the pranic tube in humans. In humans, it is the size of one's middle finger touching one's thumb tip to tip and it runs from the crown to the base of the spine. In the earth it runs from a location near the Great Pyramid to a point off the coast of Maui.

The Dweller showed me the key to the power of Ytolan. a sacred object that allows thoughts to materialize. It would be used in the near future by the soon-to-be Sacred Government to create beautiful and elegant living and supplies for all without depleting the environment, just the way Atlantis was built.

In the fifth of the Emerald Tables, Thoth states:

"Out of the ether called he (the Dweller) its substance, molded and formed, by the power of Ytolan, into the forms he built with his mind. Mile upon mile it covered the island, space upon space it grew in its might ... Swiftly the temple grew into being, molded and shaped by the word of the Dweller, called from the formless into a form."

The power of Ytolan not only creates, it also removes. Thoth came to see me in March 2005 for two hours of discussion about my work and I asked him about the garbage dumps of the earth. He was unconcerned about most, because he said that the power of Ytolan would be used to clean them up instantaneously.

His only concern was the old portions of the mountains of plastic bags dumped daily into the ocean from cities on the east coast of America. He said those would start to leak before the power was in use and that I had to create a space port that would dematerialize and transport the bags into the sun.

Thoth traveled to many planets, but the Antares system was notable to him. Their ability to travel without a craft and with the speed of thought was rare among planets. They too created their beautiful crystal cities with the power of thought.

During the week that the Sacred Government for the earth was called by the masters and the Key of the Power of Ytolan was once again seen; three men from Antares stood in the back of my classroom. They wore simple white robes and their long white hair hung down their backs. They spoke to a brother in the back of the class and said they had come just to observe. They confirmed they had come from Antares without a craft.

I have often thought about that unexpected visit from those holy ones who simply called themselves "The Three White Ones, Separate Yet One". Could we have attracted their attention because the handing of the Key of Ytolan to the world of men signaled that once again a noteworthy time of enlightenment had dawned on planet earth?

One day perhaps we shall be able to ask them as humankind reaches its maturity among the star families.

Alphabet Used To Access Akashic Record Libraries
From Two of the Moons of Neptune

1. A ⊣
2. CH ⌒•÷
3. H ÷
4. G ⌣ (ʊ)
5. K ⁄•
6. O →
7. N ⸫ (λ)
   N (⼌) Nasal N
8. L |• (ʃ⁑)
9. M ⸜ (⸪)
10. Z ⁒•
11. T •| (ʃ⁒)
12. U ⊐ (⊤)
13. B Ⱳ
14. E •|⁚ (ʃ⁑)
15. I)
16. Q ⇾
17. P ✗•
18. R ✗ (4)
19. J ((e)
20. F •|•
21. D ⁚)
22. S _⊏
23. W ⁒ (Z⁚)
24. C ⌒•
25. ING ⼂•
26. TH •|⁚

(Figure 29)

144

Continued Alphabet Used To Access
Akashic Record Libraries
From Two of the Moons of Neptune

27. ED ˙D

28. QU ⇁ɪ

29. LY ✗·

30. Y ✓ (ʔ)

31. Z ✗̇ (Z as in azure)

32. BE ◖

33. X ＜

34. V ⋀ (Z)

35. GH ⌣⸽ (Ʊ⸽)

Written from left to right, words are separated by triangles.

(Figure 30)

The Language Of The Akashic Records

(See Fig. 29 & 30, Alphabet Used to Access Akashic Record Libraries from Two of the Moons of Neptune)

The ancient Lemurian temples were pyramids and also served as educational centers for the population. The knowledge of the language of the Akashic records was taught so that information could be downloaded directly from the repositories of cosmic knowledge, known as the Akashic libraries. In our solar system they are found on two of the moons of Neptune.

Akashic records are maintained by two groups of beings in libraries on two of the moons of Neptune: Triton and Nereid. The two categories of the beings of Neptune are: (1) human-like beings not dissimilar from us, with fair skin and hair, averaging about 6' tall; (2) those in the other group are hairless, very thin with spindly appendages and large eyes (either blue or black). They are also about 6' tall, have very white skin, a small nose, a slit for a mouth and a head that is very enlarged towards the back (usually indicating an activated pineal gland). They have 6 fingers and 1 thumb-like digit on each hand.

The records are accessible to all and these are mostly used by races within our galaxy. The two moons use the two alphabets illustrated. The moon Nereid would use the alternative letters given in parentheses and where no alternatives are given, both groups use the same.

The way the language of the Akashic records came to earth was through the advent of one of the Kings of Neptune—the one we simply know as 'King Neptune'. He used these alphabets and when he arrived on earth, brought them with him.

The Story of King Neptune

King Neptune is a being of the God-Kingdom who, when he takes form, is slightly more than 6' tall. When not in form, he appears as a blue light. He is one of 9 kings of Neptune, but for the last 5 million years has been trapped here on earth. It occurred as follows:

Three of his friends, known only by the letters R, X and Y, persuaded him to visit the earth 5 million years ago. He left a hologram of himself behind and came with them. I have had to use a hologram when I have been sent on a spiritual assignment at a time when I have a class to teach. The hologram is tangible and has the knowledge I would have. No one can tell the difference. The result of this is that, in King Neptune's case, no one knew he had left and he hasn't yet been missed.

The group traveled without a space ship, teleporting through a time/space portal between earth and Neptune. There is only one of these portals on earth, located within the Grand Canyon. While they were here, the portal was accidentally destroyed by what seemed to be a huge monster about the length of 5 or 6 Titanic ships. Thus, they were trapped by the monster called Afxghelm.

They do not have a palace under the water. Instead, the whole ocean is their home. The primary function of King Neptune and his friends is the production and balancing of minerals in the world's oceans.

During the earth's ascension, which most are entirely unaware of[16], the earth moved through the sun and what is called the realms of Arulu on its path of ascension. We encountered Afxghelm two realms beyond the sun. He was the last of his kind, ferocious-looking enough that all creatures avoided him. I was instructed to call 60 angels to sing him asleep as we moved through his realm.

16 The hologram of our previous location in the sky has been kept in place to avoid panic.

Once we had moved through into the realms beyond, I was able to communicate with him. His first words to me were telepathically delivered. "Aren't you scared of me, too?" I told him I had heard that his species used to design plant forms and asked if we could be friends.

At first, I got no reply. The masters instructed me to touch his tail, which was the customary way his species signaled their intent to initiate friendship. After doing so, I asked him to come to earth and help design new plant forms to replace many that had been destroyed in the Amazon jungle. He seemed happy to not only have a friend, but to be useful again.

I contacted the nature god Pan and told him to warn the nature kingdoms not to be afraid of Afxghelm. I would tell the dragons. Pan offered to write a song about Afxghelm. Because he needed a cool, dark place to live, we decided he would live under the moist sand along the beach just west of my house.

Because of his proximity to the ocean, I contacted King Neptune and the queen of the water fairies, known only as Water Faye. King Neptune immediately asked if the first plants Afxghelm could design could be plants that absorb oil in the ocean.

Within three months, this assignment was complete and the water fairies could implement it. This extraordinary, but true, tale of King Neptune had come full circle. The very 'monster' that had accidentally been the cause of his entrapment here was now collaborating with him to improve his kingdom.

The Realms of Arulu

As the lords of Amenti have governed the earth, so the great lords of Arulu have governed all planets in our solar system. The realms of Arulu lie within our sun and for billions of years civilizations within our solar system have traveled through those realms as they ascended to higher levels and planetary systems.

Thoth states in *"The Emerald Tables of Thoth"* that he voluntarily forfeited the right to sit with the other masters in the realms of bliss in Arulu. So did his father Enki. Both did this in dedicated service to setting humanity free from bondage, delaying their own journey into higher realms in order to assist mankind into higher forms of awareness.

Thoth, on one of his many visits to my house, said that he has laid his body down in a form of stasis, and travels freely 'out of body' throughout time and space.

He said that the higher aspect of his younger brother, Osiris, guarded the entry to the spirit worlds, the lower one being called Duat and the higher one Sekhet Hepspet. Thoth's older brother, Marduk, also known as Ra, had an aspect in both spirit worlds and guarded the gate between them. He has not embodied. Thoth and his father dwelled primarily in the Halls of Amenti—that vast temple, protectively surrounded by the Halls of the Dead (resembling billions of flames of various lives burning in darkness), that house the lords of the earth.

The remainder of the Annunaki had all departed, first to sit as lords of Arulu in the sun and then eventually to evolve into higher realms through the sun. An untold number of waves of civilization had moved through the earth plane to Arulu and beyond. The initial seven lords of light (but not the master Horlet) came from a previous wave of earth's inhabitants.

One can only feel the vast antiquity of these lords, but the following incident gave me an idea of just how long they have been here. On the night of the 7th of June, 2005, I awoke to a deafening series of explosive sounds and flashes like lightning **within** my bedroom. When it began, I jumped up from a deep sleep yelling, "What was that?" I looked over at my little girl to make sure she was safe. Although a very light sleeper, she didn't move and continued sleeping soundly as the loud sounds and flashes of blue light continued. Then, a wonderful sense of peace came over me—the lords from the Halls of Amenti were in my room! I was informed that for the first time in 800 million years they had left Amenti. They had decided it was time to come and play!

To reach Arulu from the position the earth occupied before its ascension began, one had to go past Osiris and the gate he guarded. Then, one traveled past Marduk through the gate that separated the two spirit worlds. The next gate at the upper levels of the higher spirit world led to the Ascended Masters and was guarded by a lord named Ratmatorasaatmatet. The master then left through an unguarded door at the upper level of the Ascended Masters' realm, leaving the earth at a 45 degree angle to the left on a heading for the sun. *(See Fig. 31, The Journey to Arulu)*

Progress was stopped upon encountering a dark lord from Amenti guarding Arulu. He was known as Lord 2, the Light-Repressor. In order to pass both him and the next one (the Illusion Maker), it was necessary to know their names, the meaning of the names and their sigils.

It is also necessary to know and focus on the value of their contribution to the eternal plan instead of allowing their appearance to terrify one. The master has to be truly grateful to them, not only for making sure the unworthy did not enter the sacred realms beyond, but for making learning possible by creating the necessary illusion. If we did not have the illusion of being separate, how could we relate in order to provide mirrors and insights for one another?

After passing Lord 2, the angle yet again takes a 45 degree turn perpendicular to the direction of the sun. Then the master encounters the Illusion Maker and if allowed to pass; yet another 45 degree angle takes him to the sun and the great golden doors of Arulu.

The sacred key *(See Fig. 32, Key to the Realms of Arulu)* is used to enter. The master can either govern the solar system with the other masters of Arulu, or proceed to higher kingdoms such as the God-Kingdom.

The Journey to Arulu

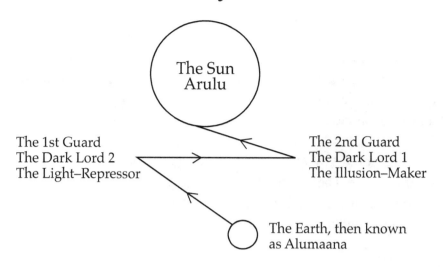

The Nine Lords of Light Within the Halls of Amenti

Lord 3 – Untanas

Lord 4 – Quertas

Lord 5 – Chietal

Lord 6 – Goyana

Lord 7 – Huertal

Lord 8 – Semveta

Lord 9 – Ardal

Lord 10 – Aravetas

Lord 11 – Utachion

The dweller who keeps the
axis of the planet steady –
also known as:

Horlet

(Figure 31)

The Key to the Realms of Arulu

Guarded by the two dark lords of Amenti, the light repressor (Lord 2) and the Illusion maker (Lord 1), the Realms of Arulu within our sun, have awaited those who move beyond ascended mastery.

(Figure 32)

PART FOUR

The Magical Realms

First Ring Vs. Second Ring Magic

In speaking of the magic kingdoms, it is necessary to lift the veil from magic and its uses. Magic is the manipulation of reality through the use of intent. There are two ways to practice magic; first and second ring magic.

On the walls of ancient Central American ruins, the story is told of how first ring magic was initially brought to earth by star-beings from Orion. This form of magic is left-brain based and utilizes external techniques for its effectiveness. When most speak or think of magic, it is usually first ring magic they refer to.

Second ring magic uses the right-brain, feminine, non-cognitive methods of affecting reality. The magic originates from within rather than from without. It is inner abilities that are used by the unseen realms on earth.

Among the kingdoms and realms on earth, only the physical ones have forgotten their heritage as magical beings of the cosmos. As a result, their ability to do second ring magic became obscured and man resorted to the left-brain, or first ring magic.

Only in the deepest recesses of mystery schools did pockets of knowledge survive of an inner technology that could influence the environment in mystical ways. Only there were remnants taught of the knowledge that once flourished in ancient Mu and some of the older Atlantean civilizations.

The advent of first ring magic wrought havoc among men. Climates were disrupted, global catastrophes occurred and men became power-seekers and turned upon each other. The oral traditions of the Toltec seers speak of these times of great destruction when first ring magic was used in the warfare that destroyed and ravaged Atlantis.

Between 200,000 and 75,000 years ago when Atlantis was divided into two large islands, Ruta and Itiya, practitioners of first ring magic congregated on Ruta and grew strong.

Those practicing second ring magic lived on Itiya, laboring diligently to keep the earth from experiencing another global catastrophe. At the end of the period, however, it became abundantly clear they were losing the battle. They fled to safer areas, including the inner earth.

The only way to obtain power without damaging the inter-connectedness of life is through perception. First ring magic uses ritual, incantations and other external sources of power. This must eventually deplete not only the practitioner, but the environment. In addition, the power available through left-brain methods is limited, whereas that available through the right-brain, internal methods is not.

First ring magic causes environmental disruption and catastrophe through depleting the environment and disrupting the earth's energetic flow. The planetary energy flows along its ley lines, or meridians. In addition, each species has a grid telling it how to act. These grids are arrays of lines along which light in the form of information flows. When these, as well as the ley lines, are disrupted, the planet tilts on her axis or draws in other catastrophes due to lack of life force.

The potential for abuse of magic is a very real threat when first ring magic is used, since it doesn't require that the practitioner develop impeccability. Knowledge of certain practices is all that is needed. Power seekers have disrupted the environment with first ring magic since its introduction to humanity.

Second ring magic, on the other hand, is the result of perception. In fact, the more inclusive the perception the more power is available. Practitioners, because of their perception, become unable to harm life.

For the most part, the magical kingdoms have very strict rules governing the use of magic, with dire consequences for its misuse. Exceptions have been, among others, the demons and sometimes the dragons. Since the planetary and cosmic ascension began, the Mother Goddess has decreed that power to do magic be matched by a corresponding degree of perception. This removed the destructive magical abilities from beings in the cosmos.

Second ring magic is used by fairies, elves, pixies and other beings from the magical kingdoms to create, grow and sustain plant and mineral life. Angels do the same for human and animal life. Large planetary angels sustain planets; smaller ones govern oceans, rivers, lakes and mountain ranges. Angels support humans in many ways, some staying with a single human all his life, much as a guardian spirit would.

Therefore it can be said that magic, or the power of intent, is the primary force that carries out the will of the Infinite within the cosmos. Only when it becomes exclusive or self-centered does it destroy rather than sustain life.

Power Seekers vs. Perception Seekers

Power is the result of altered perception. The key word is

'result' because if we seek power directly, we are on a dead-end street. Let's look at the differences between those who are seeking power and those who are seeking clarity of perception.

Power Seekers

- Seek power directly
- Focus on power
- See the purpose of power being to manipulate energy to be able to see into the future and the past. It is power over the environment and power beyond another's abilities
- Enhance self-image, which is strengthened by titles and labels
- View perception as a result of the use of power
- Obsess about the unseen realms and the unknown
- Get power from outside sources, such as allies
- Measure themselves by what they are doing.

Perception Seekers

- Seek clarity
- Focus on perception
- See the purpose of power to help break free from mortal boundaries and gain Ascended Mastery
- Eliminate self-importance and shun labels, which trap awareness
- View power as a result of perception
- Seek more refined goals until the unknowable is reached
- Get power from living in the awareness of the inter-connectedness of all life
- Access the attributes an ally could provide by going within, since all life is within, and draw on these sources as though they are parts of themselves
- Measure themselves by how they are being

When we obtain personal power, it becomes a challenge because we are able to perform 'miracles'. The temptation is to impress others and if we succumb to this, we are choosing the way of the power seekers. This is the point where a lightworker has to choose to walk either the humble and unobtrusive road leading to complete freedom, or the dead-end road of showmanship. Most choose the flashy road, but it is of little value except to enhance the ego of the performer.

A miracle shouldn't be planned. It occurs naturally when we are pushing the boundaries of mortality. Miracles shouldn't be performed to persuade, demonstrate or gain approval, or raise the status of the teacher. Power seekers often use miracles to encourage faith from their followers. The increased faith is focused on the power seeker and it creates a momentum to further feed his abilities, providing him with additional power.

Power seekers can get trapped in identity labels, such as a shaman, sorcerer, or medicine man. If they become arrogant and fall into the trap of 'thinking they know', they can get stuck in the unknown and won't be able to access the unknowable. This is a limiting position because the known comprises 1/10th of the universe and the unknown the remaining 9/10ths. Both of these are within Creation.

On the other hand, the **unknowable** is outside Creation—it is that which is dreaming Creation into existence. A perception seeker's goal is to access the unknowable. That is why they focus on clarity of perception and strive to shed limiting labels and beliefs, understanding there is no point of arrival. This fluidity allows the perception seeker the freedom to be all things.

How a Plant is Created Through Magic

In creating plants, fairies work with smaller plants. Devas are more advanced in evolution than fairies and work with trees and shrubs. Elementals are tiny fairies with a group mind and may work with blossoms.

The song of Spring awakens the seed and it emits a frequency signaling the fairy for a specific plant, e.g., a tomato, that it is time for him or her to perform the functions required to initiate growth. The fairy then takes the following steps:

1. The space in which creation will take place is defined by playing the song or individual frequency of the tomato in the specific place where it is to grow. The same principle applies in the formation of a cosmos.
2. The fairy plays the specific 'notes' of the tomato plant's different systems, such as its root system.
3. This summons the elemental fairy responsible for the plant's root system to assist in energizing and helping in the formation and growth of that section of the plant.
4. In the same way, elementals are called for the stems, leaves, blossoms and finally a fairy is called for the beautiful tomatoes.
5. All functions are performed with joy, absorbing energy from the environment (their light becomes a growing ball) and discharging it into the plant. The fairies and elementals play, laugh and dance around their creations, their attitudes stimulating its growth.

Plants register and feel emotions very strongly, reacting positively to joy, appreciation and love and adversely to pain, anger and violence. Scientists have also found and measured a strong response in plants to sexual orgasm. This is why some ancient civilizations celebrated the planting of crops by making love in newly sown fields.

The Garden Deva

The garden around my house had been tending itself superbly since I had requested the nature spirit in charge take care of the flowers and plants. It was as though the garden had been fertilized and an abundance of flowers bloomed. I asked permission of the nature spirit to cut back the ivy from the top of the chimney where it had become a fire hazard, indicating where I wanted to cut, and waited for an answer.

A cigar-shaped diaphanous cloud about 18 inches tall materialized three feet away. I heard permission being granted with the assurance that the ivy would withdraw its lifeforce from the branches to be trimmed. As I stood mesmerized, the little cloud moved to my right and disappeared (It was a clear day and no trace of smoke or clouds were visible anywhere).

Due to the difficult location, I hired a gardener to prune the ivy. Though I had given meticulous instructions, he butchered the plant. The nature devas (a little more developed than fairies) must have rebelled, because the next day, the flowers were dead. To my dismay, my magical garden continued to dwindle. I cried with remorse and buried several quartz crystals throughout the garden as tokens of my love and appreciation for the work of the devic realm, but to no avail. The nature spirits didn't return that season.

The Dragon Kingdom

Introduction

For thousands of years dragons have been depicted within the art and artifacts, folklore and music of cultures ranging from South America to the Orient and from Europe to Malaysia. Our global fascination with them, however, has yielded little information and the mystics that could see or communicate with them have kept their secrets to themselves for the following reasons:

- Any allies gained from the magic kingdoms have added to the power of mystics who, for the most part, have been power seekers. Sharing such information was, for obvious reasons, not desirable.

• The mystics who fell into the category of perception seekers (like the Taoist immortals or the Toltec seers) focused their teachings on achieving enlightenment, with the specific purpose of not wanting their apprentices to become side-tracked by the unseen realms' lure of power.

These reasons combined, therefore, produced very little detail about these highly evolved and amazing beings.

The Magic World Of Dragons

Brilliant and duty-oriented within a world of impeccability and protocol, dragons have been taught great pride in the abilities of their race. To quote the words of the dragon called The Beautiful One when I asked her about Twitches (see later discussion), *"They look like dragons, but don't have the same intelligence. They came from a distant star system through the inner earth. Almost every large cave has one in it. They'd like to be dragons but then, who wouldn't?"*

There are currently 110,000 dragons that have their world among and yet apart from us, ruled by a God-conscious two-year-old dragon with whom I have become friends. He is known simply as "The Dragon". I am always amazed at his ability to rapidly come from his world to visit. It takes him about one-half hour, while other dragons take 3-4 days, depending on how much magical power they have.

When we passed through the sun on our journey of ascension, we encountered other dragons with a different language; they have not accompanied earth. Although 51% of the races of the cosmos are dragons, the following information applies to dragons of earth.

Dragons have inhabited the earth for 3.127 million years. Since they've been here 818 waves of civilization have lived on the earth.

General Information

Dragons are very colorful and their color choices, based on what pleases them, are their distinguishing features. When you ask their name, they give you their colors (which they occasionally change).

The foods I find to be some of their favorites are tulips, also used in tulip and beeswax tea (The Dragon likes pink ones best), mice and garlic stew and various dishes cooked with horses. Ghost horses are very plentiful and the dragons I work with cook these. They can, however, produce food with thought.

Injuries occur as in humans—not irregularly. The one known as "Black" has had a broken tail and the yellow one I call "Daisy" has injured her back and can now hardly carry anything. It is, however, disease that frightens them. They very seldom get sick and when they do, it's often fatal. They seldom catch cold, for example, and are therefore not well-equipped to deal with the condition. There is a record kept where dragons can go to get help when they're sick. Four human names are listed in it as people who know how to heal dragons (my own was just recently added when I healed the Beautiful One of measles).

I find dragons to be superb healers; they de-materialize tumors and do the most amazing healing surgeries on humans. I was very surprised to find they don't trust being healed by other dragons as much as I do. When I asked The Dragon what should be done when the Beautiful One got measles and claimed she was dying, he said, "Please, no dragon healers! You can heal her and I'll bring some blue tea. Tell her to stop thinking about dying!" She responded quickly to the healing, even though she hated the tea.

Dragons get embarrassed very quickly when you praise them publicly and their feelings get hurt when you in any way imply they need help performing their duties. The Beautiful One is 8,000 years old, young but mature. A dragon of 40,000 years is considered old and one of 25,000 years is aging.

"We do not understand the human function of laughter", the Powerful One had said to me. But during the earth's ascension they had to start using their feeling bodies or perish. Now we hear them laughing and even crying. Sneezing, however, is a different story:

The Beautiful One protects my home and lies curled around it. She approached me in a bashful manner: Could I possibly build a fire with a lot of smoke for her to inhale? She needed to sneeze. It couldn't be in the fireplace; the flames would shoot up 18 feet. With a sneeze that shook the house, we reached our goal. Days later when I asked whether she could feel how much I loved her, she said she could tell because of the trouble I went through to help her sneeze!

Dragons don't build buildings or need instruments of any kind. They live in nature and materialize their needs with thought. Their food, for example, is cooked by thought. Their ability to breathe fire, as depicted in the ancient drawings of diverse global cultures, is used for protective purposes only. As in all areas of their lives, the strictest protocol governs its use.

Understanding Feeling Bodies

Although dragons had feeling bodies, or at least they had the necessary fields, the fields weren't spinning appropriately due to lack of use. Other beings in the cosmos, however, didn't have all the fields, which was vital for their survival during the cosmic ascension.

Around the bodies of beings like us that can feel, there are the following fields, the different geometric shapes of which get progressively larger:

A. **Three star-tetrahedrons** (three-dimensional Stars of David). One is stationary, one spins clockwise and one counterclockwise at the ratio of 34 times for every 21 times the clockwise one spins. They all occupy the same space.

B. **Three octahedron**s (two four-sided pyramids base-to-base). Just like before, these three occupy the same space with one stationary and two spinning in opposite directions at a specific ratio (the ratios follow the Fibonacci sequence).

C. **Three dodecahedrons** (twelve pentagons in the shape of a soccer ball). Just like before, they occupy the same space, one stationary, one spinning left and one spinning right.

D. **Three Flower of Life spheres** *(See Fig. 34, How Beings Receive the Ability to Feel)*. Each of the shapes previously mentioned occupy larger and larger areas around the body. Those beings, like the dragons that chose not to feel have two stationary fields and one counter-clockwise spinning field. Their fields that should spin clockwise are stationary. In the case of beings that cannot feel, the Flower of Life spheres have a deformity in the spheres themselves in that—as seen from the front, the right-hand portion of the spheres are incomplete in each of the three fields.

To give them the ability to feel, the following steps were taken:

A. The Flower of Life spheres had to be completed.

B. In all cases, the clockwise and counterclockwise spinning fields had to spin at the proper ratios. This was done by the Angel of the Merkaba, Arahib.

C. They had to be given the necessary endocrine system to produce hormones. This was done by the goddess Panatura.

How Beings Receive the Ability to Feel

Beings with feeling bodies have 3 perfect Flower of Life spheres around their bodies. Beings without feeling bodies have 3 incomplete ones.

Steps in becoming able to feel:

1. There needs to be 19 perfectly interwoven circles in each Flower of Life Sphere
2. All fields associated with the emotional and mental bodies should be spinning in the right direction and in the appropriate ratio and speeds
3. The necessary glands need to be provided to produce hormones that are needed for emotion
4. Hormones need to be provided
5. Old patterning needs to be removed
6. Frequency needs to be provided that produces balances emotions

Perfect Flower of Life Sphere

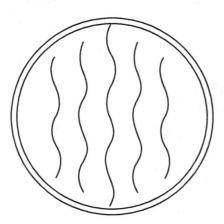

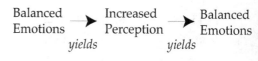

Balanced Emotions → *yields* → Increased Perception → *yields* → Balanced Emotions

Incomplete Flower of Life Sphere

(Figure 34)

D. They had to be given the appropriate hormones. This was done by the angel Schatlba.

E. The archangel Metatron then had to use the dispersal energy of the violet flame to remove all old patterns that no longer served.

F. The Great White One, Ascended Master of the Whales, had to sing in the frequencies of the eight emotions present in a balanced life.

At the time in 2005 when the races of the cosmos were given the edict by the Mother Goddess, "Use your feeling bodies or perish," there were only 600 of Lucifer's great hosts left. Many had ceased to be, as the cosmos was pulled through previous ascension levels. Some had made it into various underworlds, a major evolutionary leap. All remaining had to receive feeling bodies for the further journey of ascension. The entire process took days to accomplish and we could not go through the gate before its completion.

Dragon's Interaction with Humans

Long ago, the folklore of many cultures told of a time when dragons and humans interacted. I asked the dragons what had changed that.

"Dragons used to show themselves to humans, but humans were continually trying to hurt them. It became necessary for dragons to use their magic to be unseen by the humans."

A linguistic bridge was created for man to be able to communicate with dragons. The language was used in written form only to speak to man, never among themselves. The exception was numbers above 25. *(See Figs. 35 a, b, c, d, e, Dragon Language)*

Dragons are linked telepathically. They are in contact with dragons in their realm whenever they want to be. When

Dragon Language

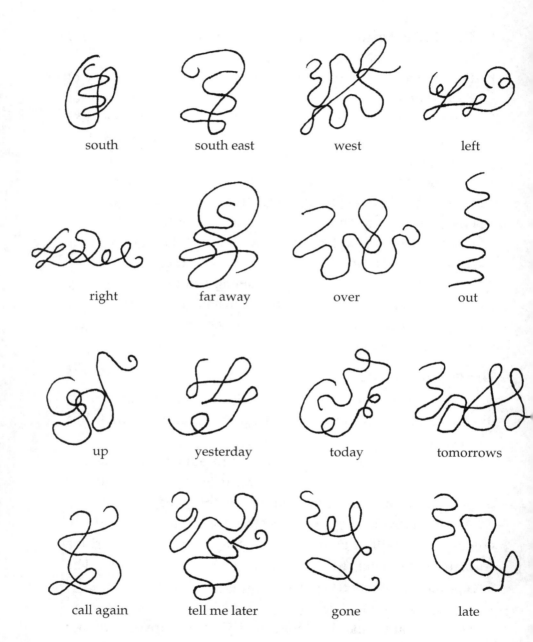

south	south east	west	left
right	far away	over	out
up	yesterday	today	tomorrows
call again	tell me later	gone	late

(Figure 35a)

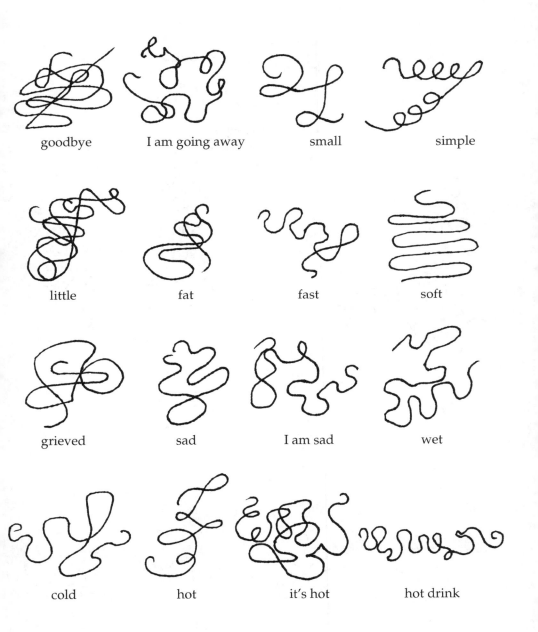

goodbye   I am going away   small   simple

little   fat   fast   soft

grieved   sad   I am sad   wet

cold   hot   it's hot   hot drink

(Figure 35b)

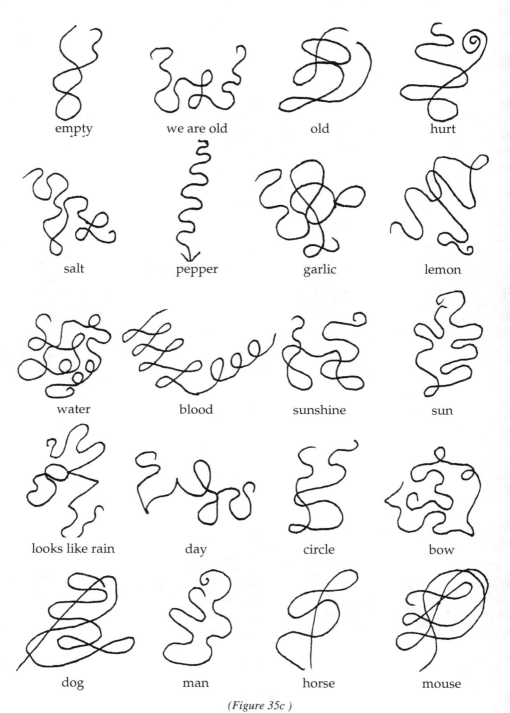

empty   we are old   old   hurt

salt   pepper   garlic   lemon

water   blood   sunshine   sun

looks like rain   day   circle   bow

dog   man   horse   mouse

(Figure 35c)

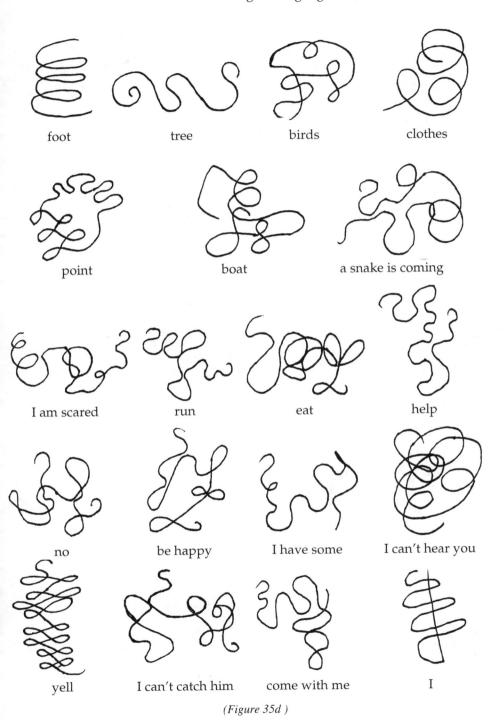

foot   tree   birds   clothes

point   boat   a snake is coming

I am scared   run   eat   help

no   be happy   I have some   I can't hear you

yell   I can't catch him   come with me   I

(Figure 35d)

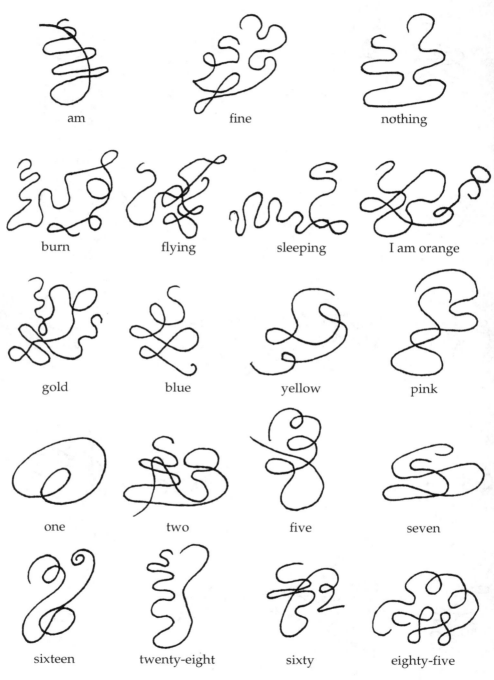

(Figure 35e)

'speaking' to one another, numbers up to 25 are felt as 'pressure' in different parts of the brain. Beyond that, signs for numbers are telepathically projected at one another.

I asked, since they didn't write (The Beautiful One reminded me very quickly that they don't have fingers!), how they store information. She explained that they created a box into which they put information. The information is heard when the box is opened.

I understood exactly what she meant. As I write this, the Lords of Amenti are in a meeting and a box with my words in it is waiting outside the door of their meeting hall. I want to get a message to them, but they won't let me enter or interrupt. It is waiting there for when they have finished.

Dragon Physiology

Dragons are a highly evolved species with a very distinct feature. All other creatures with vertebraes have 4 limbs, they have 6; rear legs with 3 toes, front feet with 3 toes and wings. They have scales and a bag in the back of the throat that holds a special gas for their fire breathing. The gas is not naturally produced in their bodies—the bags have to be filled intentionally.

Their tails have varying shapes. Some end with a 'head' like an arrow and some just taper to a point. Dragons at times choose to be small (3-5 feet in length), but the average size is 18 feet from nose to tail tip. The Dragon is a little over 80 feet in length.

The gestation period for their young is 2 years in the womb. They have live births and can produce up to 6 babies at a time.

On Saturday, October 8, 2005, ground-breaking changes within the dragon race were set in motion through the divine intervention of the Creator Goddess. This event signaled crucial changes in dragon females. Mother set them free from male-engineered bondage and inequity in the following ways:

1. They were not previously permitted to have hair. She gave them the right as females to express their looks any way they saw fit.
2. It was illegal for homosexuality to occur among females but legal for males. She made it legal for both sexes.
3. Although Mother had previously decreed that females could no longer be forced into marriage, she now gave permission for females who were unhappily married to leave their marriages.
4. The greatest bondage she released, however, was when sexual feeling was restored to females. In the past, sexual stimulation could not be felt in their bodies. It had been genetically engineered out of existence. On Sunday, October 9, 2005, during an 11 hour period, Mother gave them back those abilities.

When such a large percentage of the cosmos received the sacred gift of sexuality, the entire cosmos rose in frequency.

Dragon Language

Most dragons live in the Asiatic regions and a slang version of the dragon language has developed, influenced by Chinese (never to be spoken to The Dragon). The language has no future or past tense, only a present tense. They don't conjugate verbs. In other words, it would be as though they were saying, "I is, they is, he is", etc. There are no words for colors; they are seen in the head before the sentence forms.

Frequency is a very important factor: for example, the word "I" has 101 different dragon words, depending on the frequency. "I am happy" has a much higher frequency than "I am sad" and so a different word for "I" would be used in each case. Frequency also determines word order, much as in English. "Do come here!" has a more imperative nuance than "Won't you come here?"

Nouns

There is no word for "a" and the word "the" does not change as in French or German. There are therefore no genders associated with nouns.

the world	xit yataam
the dragon	xit zayagasong
the tree	xit yit
the ocean	xit aaw
the grass	xit limansangtriug
and	simmat, liyong, zuganyg

(different words used for different frequencies)

Sentences

It is pretty	etti sa krimsaet
You are pretty (plural)	riysunis sai krimsaetyi
I am tired	li wtang ma
They are tired	lisuun wtang r
He is glad	uusaat ro nsto
We are glad	nstoyan uusaat
She is old	osoyizat ro osozatin
You are old (singular)	riysu osoyizat z
I am hungry	adu ma we
Within the earth	firma to sa
I command you to	ma tum se a

(used for young dragons)

Adjectives

sad	sontt
happy	song
tired	wtang
strong	ghrun (h is silent)

```
tasty . . . . . . . . . . . . . . . . . . yess
delicious . . . . . . . . . . . . . . yattumsaw
scared. . . . . . . . . . . . . . . . tarraeng
respectful. . . . . . . . . . . . . . lizetxya
large. . . . . . . . . . . . . . . . . parrat
small . . . . . . . . . . . . . . . . par
hot . . . . . . . . . . . . . . . . . . solt
cold . . . . . . . . . . . . . . . . . brisolt
good. . . . . . . . . . . . . . . . . czriyattgan
sick . . . . . . . . . . . . . . . . . pust
well . . . . . . . . . . . . . . . . . yamasatuung
```

Changing an Ancient Dragon Dynasty

After planetary ascension began in February 2005, the pace of my work in the unseen realms picked up considerably. I needed help. In calling on dragons, one must be very specific about their duties. For instance, the dragon named Beautiful One who guarded my house would assist by giving her opinion on occasion, but would never do anything else other than her assigned duty of protecting me, my house and family.

Before I asked for additional assistance from dragons, I took quite a bit of time to write out intended duties after Beautiful One explained that the dragon chosen would be selected based on the talents needed. I had her monitor as I called loudly, reading out the job description, until she said I'd been heard. We then waited about 10 days before she announced that a male purple/blue/green dragon was on his way. It took him about a week to make the journey. I had asked Sarah, the spirit, what an appropriate welcome for him would be and she said he liked the smell of oranges (as do most dragons). I diluted orange essential oil and sprayed it over the area of the lawns where he would lie.

When he arrived, it took him an hour to get his massive body situated around Beautiful One and the house. She commented dryly that it was "A bit crowded." When he had settled, I read him a poem I'd written for him and asked if I could call him Powerful One. He said I was 'cute' and went to sleep for a week.

The one major criterion in earning the right to work with a dragon is that you have to be able to keep him busy. I became concerned that I was over-working him, however. At one point, I had sent him on a job where he felt the only way he could do it was to become physical, something that was very dangerous for him and would take two days to do. Although his task was very important to me, his safety came first. I recommended he ask for assistance from the dragon world, but that hurt his feelings.

After unsuccessfully considering every possible strategy, I persuaded him to at least return to the dragon world for advice, saying that once there he could do two things on my behalf as well.

Firstly, I had become aware of the only dragon working for a major government and that he would be sent to capture me. He would be sent at the end of April, and Beautiful One would be put in the awkward position of having to defend me against another dragon. If, on the other hand, I somehow prevailed against him, all dragons would have to abandon me.

With the help of the spirits and Beautiful One, we carefully studied his contract. It was clear he had been tricked into the assignment for the government. I found a loophole in the contract and Powerful One promised to present it before the Dragon Council, and request that the dragon who would be my opponent be recalled to the dragon world.

Secondly, after discussing it with both my dragons, we agreed to ask for a third one to alleviate Powerful One's workload. He would ask the Council to evaluate my request while he was in the dragon world.

He left, and through Beautiful One (dragons can tune in and hear each other if they choose), I was aware that Powerful One was being heard before a council of two hundred dragons. The meeting dragged on for two weeks, although in their world it seemed much shorter. At the end of the two weeks, they asked me to speak to them.

They told me that dragons were for protection only; why did I need more to work with me in other capacities? The rude arrogance of their tone took me aback. In fact, the Old Dragon (so-called to differentiate him from the one who would later take his place) seemed downright hostile. I replied as politely as I could, saying there were children's hospitals where healing was needed; criminal rings that harmed humans to undo; mountains of garbage to dematerialize. But, unaware that the latter task had been delegated to the 'inferior'—as they believed them to be—Twitches, I had insulted the Council.

The Old Dragon retaliated by demanding that Melissa, the earth's leading Indigo child who works with me, (and who was translating their language for me), and I sit in what was to us days of meetings with them. I explained we had little ones who needed tending. They evaluated this and basically called me a liar, saying it wouldn't inconvenience anyone. I had been kept waiting while they talked. I now said I needed to think things over for 24 hours.

I was stunned. Didn't they realize that that which benefits the earth benefits all? Sarah explained they had expected to govern the earth and its races during the ascension of the earth. They were very put out that humans were playing the key role. Humans represent the feminine as the nurturers, and dragons represent the masculine as the warriors. (See Fig. 1) The ascension of the cosmos was designed to be under feminine rule, supported by patriarchal orders. Patriarchal rule would put us immediately into another descension.

I called for Thoth to advise me. I felt unprepared to deal with the situation and Beautiful One now had her tail in her ear so they couldn't use her to listen in on me, while she steadfastly maintained the protective shield.

Thoth arrived at 9:00 pm that evening and told me it was time to put the Old Dragon in his place. I agreed and waited for him to do it. Then I realized he was waiting for **me** to act. Shaking in my shoes, I announced as firmly but politely as possible that I received my assignments directly from Mother. Since I had tasks assigned by her in the following days, I would not presume to keep her waiting. There was a stunned silence. Apparently few contradicted Old Dragon and lived.

In fact, someone else was bold enough to defy him and presented him with the opportunity to get back at me through someone I loved, Powerful One. When Powerful One contradicted Old Dragon by pointing out that giving me the dragon I had requested would help the earth, Old Dragon stripped him of his magical abilities and sent him back to me, outcast forever.

I cried myself to sleep that night. Thoth came to comfort me, saying, "Soon you won't need a dragon. The Old Dragon has made his bed and will have to lie in it." The dragon world was in an uproar. Beautiful One kept repeating, "He should not have contradicted The Dragon! No one does that. It's very rude." Powerful One said nothing except, "It was the right thing to do." But, although he was exhausted from flying as fast as he could before his magic ran out, he was unable to sleep.

Finally, he slept for 10 days and when I said, "Oh, you're

awake!" he replied, "I wish I weren't." I told him he could take time to be alone, not realizing he would hide for months in shame. His beautiful colors (maintained by magic) would disappear, leaving him brown.

Meanwhile, a few weeks later as the earth was moving up in realms, Mother gave every being a feeling body. *(See Fig. 34)* Dragons already had feeling bodies but didn't use them. By the time the earth was getting ready to move out of its previous position in space (a fact concealed from the masses by a hologram), Mother issued the following warning to all beings in the cosmos: "Use your feeling bodies or perish when the cosmos moves two levels from now."

I contacted the Old Dragon, but he refused to speak to me. So I sent a message through Beautiful One to ask him to tell Powerful One who, in hiding, would not have heard Mother's message and also to tell him to return home. Mother also called several lords for the task of making sure all beings knew how to use their feeling bodies.

The Old Dragon defied Mother and persuaded 90,000 of his 200,000 subjects not to use their feeling bodies. The other beings in the cosmos that also chose to do this comprised 10% of the total. The Old Dragon's insolence had increased as his rage against Mother grew. At one of the most sacred events ever to be held on this planet, Mother's coronation on earth *(see pg.189)*, he did it yet again. The situation grew until the lords in the Halls of Amenti decided to take action. They deposed him and stripped him of his magic, installing a two-year old dragon who was in God-consciousness and without ego, in his place. *Revelation 12:9 "And the great dragon was cast out, that old serpent ..."*

One night I awoke in terror. Something was terribly wrong. Hooves clattered loudly through the house. Pan was there and completely distraught. The Old Dragon had decided to wage war for supremacy and, moving back and forth through time, as dragons can do, had threatened, coerced or bribed others in the cosmos to join him. He had managed to gather a third of the cosmic races to support him in his rebellion, but not Beautiful One. She lay with her tail in her ear, firm in her duty even if it cost her life.

But Mother outsmarted him. Soon after Pan ran through the house and with but hours to spare before the war in heaven would have begun (it would have wiped out 52% of all creatures in the cosmos), Mother moved the cosmos up three levels. This wiped out 10% of the cosmos and 90,000 dragons on earth, but saved us from the 'war in heaven'. The fairies took 110,000 tulips to the remaining dragons in the dragon world as Mother gave a speech to the stunned beings in the cosmos about blindly following corrupt leadership over the higher wisdom felt in the heart. *Revelation 12:4,5 "There appeared another wonder in heaven...a great red dragon ... and his tail drew the third part of the stars of heaven, and did cast them to the earth ..."* [17]

With the advent of the New Dragon, Powerful One returned to the dragon world to get his magic restored (he needed assistance to get there). But he was never the same again. Not having had the experience of emotions before, he was overcomed by them as they flooded his being. (This was also true of Thoth who had not felt emotion in thousands of years.) Powerful One kept crying when I tried to give him work. I encouraged him to use the tears to release the pain, but his mind wasn't thinking clearly either.

I was in Toronto when Sarah, the spirit I was working with, told Melissa to urgently interrupt my class. Powerful One was

17 In scriptures, scribes and translators had confused Lucifer with dragons, creating confusion about all dragons not "being of the light".

181

on his way to take me away to a cave. I broke for lunch early in order to be in my room when he arrived. He had apparently put Beautiful One in a cage before she could suspect his plans.

When he arrived, I reasoned with him. I learned that two of New Dragon's dragons were on the way to help, but were hours away. He was very agitated. His powerful tail put a dent in the bedroom floor. I asked him to first do the honorable thing and set Beautiful One free before I would talk further. I told him I respected him, but would not speak to him if he behaved dishonorably.

When he set Beautiful One free, she attacked him ferociously. The dragon fight continued around my house for days after I got home. The ferocity and passion could be felt throughout the house. Thundering noises, big thuds and blue flashes of lightning had to be explained to a group of students who arrived wide-eyed during this time. It got so hectic that Sarah warned it could destroy the back end of my house.

I consulted with the New Dragon almost hourly as things came to a head. It was illegal for a dragon to interfere in a fight between two other dragons. He was new to leadership and secretly confessed to me that he didn't know what to do. At the most critical moment, one hour before the time when Beautiful One would have been killed, Thoth was let out of a meeting in the Halls of Amenti to intervene.

He took the battle out into the street away from her and the house. He won the battle and stripped the wings from Powerful One, then led him to me by the nose. Powerful One was sobbing and I couldn't stand his humiliation.

Powerful One was taken to the dragon world and, because he attacked the Dragon, was put into a cage.

The Old Dragon Insults the Mother

On May 13, 2005, I was instructed to prepare 4,000 sigils, very complex language units that look like roadmaps. Knowing there were at least six languages to work with, it was necessary to determine exactly where these languages needed to change. The sigils represented angel names as well as their meanings (that which they do within the cosmos).

I was working as instructed, when halfway through one of the languages, my hand was forced into drawing crystals as languages. *(See Figs. 36 a, b, c, d, The Crystal Language of the Mother)* Try as I might, there was no way my hand would write any other language. For at least 100 sigils, I could only transcribe them in the language of crystals. Just as suddenly, this stopped and I went back to the old languages. The only explanation given was that there was a surprise coming at the next raising of the cosmos for which the crystals were very pertinent. They were the language of the Goddess.

As promised, when the ceremony of the angel sigils was complete, the cosmos rose and I was told to go to the Halls of Amenti. After entering immortality in February 2005, I was made free of the Halls of Amenti where the Seven Lords of Light—now numbering nine—govern planetary aspects and chakras. This meant I no longer had to ask permission from the lords to enter the Halls. The Emerald Tablets of Thoth describe the time when he too had been made free of the Halls of Amenti and taken before the Lord of Death, Untanas. The Lord of Life then informed Utanas that he no longer had a hold on Thoth; that there was no longer a need to quench his light. I had had the same experience in March.

After going into the Halls of Amenti, I found an entirely

The Crystal Language of the Mother

The crystals are like computer chips, containing the perfect templates of the 32 root-races of the cosmos.

Neutrinos

Shooting stars of heaven

Liquid light

Cancellation of guilt

Appreciation of separateness

Collaborative consciousness

Fashioning form

Marveling at the unfolding

(Figure 36a)

Rejoicing in the fruition

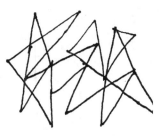

Gentle encouragement

New forms of intelligence

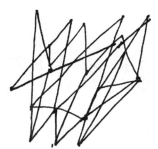

Humility and faith

Pyramids of creation

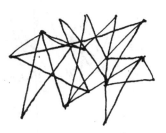

Resonating truth

Expanding possibilities

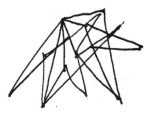

Transforming impurity

(Figure 36b)

Formidable innocence

Unconditional fearlessness

Spontaneous intimacy

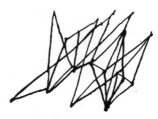

deliberate gestures

Permitting exploration

Fortifying desire

Sustaining vision

Planting dreams

(Figure 36c)

Overflowing with gratitude

Tuning color geometries

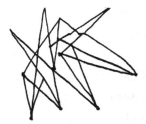

Geometry of radiation

New life code

Living universe

Limitless light

Living flame geometry

Divine mind seeded

(Figure 36d)

different structure than had been there before. The palace that would rise and form the center of the New Jerusalem, and eventually house the sacred world government, had been created.

The Halls of Amenti themselves were completely altered. I was in a huge coronation room already filled with 800 rulers of planetary systems, plus 13 rulers of the suns through which we are passing on our planetary ascension. The great masters, kings and queens of various kingdoms and lords of our earth were there. Everyone waited in a hushed silence. But, there was one notable absence, the Old Dragon. Great masters from many realms had been waiting for the arrival of Mother, as protocol demanded.

He was still absent when the entire end of the hall opened and hosts of angels could be seen. Some of the races, like the Andromedans, had never seen angels because, until recently, they had not had the feeling bodies necessary to do so. The hosts of angels sounded a fanfare of trumpets and a vast light appeared. The Queen of All Creation, the Mother Goddess who had birthed Creation, was coming down to earth.

She descended into the rectangular hall, gliding across a carpet of stars that had been created by Thoth. The ceiling of the hall had ribs of gold and was formed like a giant telescope through which you could see planets moving in space. There was a jewel-encrusted throne erected on a platform with seven steps; all of gold and radiating light. The seven steps represented the seven levels of light.

The Mother Goddess dimmed her light as she got closer. Her crown had 12 stars (representing the 12 starsystems around the earth that would lead the ascension) and she had a scepter with a ball of light that represented the central sun. In Revelations, John speaks of his vision of a woman who came from Heaven, crowned in glory with a crown bearing 12 stars. Half-way to her throne, she was met by the goddesses of Space and Time[18], who placed a mantle around her shoulders. *Revelations 12:1 "And there appeared a great wonder in heaven; a woman clothed with the sun, and the moon under her feet, and upon her head a crown of twelve stars."*

It was difficult to see her features because of the incredibly radiant display of light around her. An angel took its place behind the throne and spoke, "The Queen of Creation is come down to earth and the mantle of Grace is placed upon her." The Mother ascended to the throne, accompanied by the goddesses of Space and Time. Her sleeveless overcoat was worn over a gown of gold, crusted in jewels. Each jewel radiated its own light. The train of the cloak appeared to be of a thinner material. Then Space, being the eldest daughter, took her place two steps down at the right of Mother and Time took her place two more steps down on the left.

At this moment as all watched Mother's glory, the Old Dragon entered with a noisy commotion—the only one rude enough to be late.

The angel behind the throne spoke of all Mother has done for Creation during this cosmic ascension. At the end of his recital, angel choruses sang. Mother looked up and the ceiling opened. A column of gold light descended upon her. A female voice spoke, identifying herself as the Mother of God and all existence from which the Infinite and Creation sprang, saying, "This day I become one with the Goddess of All Creation". Then, within the bright light of the column, a crown descended, hovering above Mother's head. She reached up and placed it within the larger crown already on her head.

Angels broke forth in tremendous choruses and fanfares. The ceiling closed again, Mother stood to speak. The angel behind

18 The Goddesses of Energy and Matter have incarnated.

the throne instructed all beings present to kneel. The Old Dragon was the last to do so. Everyone else in the vast hall who heard her voice was enveloped in overwhelming feelings of peace and love. She was now a totally different sovereignty, Queen of Creation and All.

Mother spoke of the journey home, saying the quality of the journey is joy and those who will flourish will be those who give joy to others. She said that three gifts would be given: two would be given only to those kingdoms, planetary systems, solar systems and suns represented by those in attendance; the third gift, bestowed on this occasion as a token of her love, would be given to all Creation. Why did the Old Dragon come at all? The spirits confirmed that he foresaw and wanted the gifts.

The first gift was the gift of becoming part of the immortal body of the cosmos. Beings present who would open their hearts to her love would not have to experience death. From there, they would assist in creating an entirely new existence, becoming the creator gods of tomorrow. This announcement triggered a flurry of comment from those present. Some spoke in low rustling tones, others communicated through a display of colored lights on their foreheads, some by movements of their heads.

The second gift to all is the erasing of all karma. Learning would come effortlessly and all beings would be absolved. Again there was a rippling of sound as this was discussed.

The third gift, only for those present at the coronation, was that henceforth there would be a way for them to have direct access to the Mother of All. As she said that, the entire end of the hall opened once again. Hundreds of thousands of angels formed a column and a double gold door formed at the end of the corridor. Two angels stood on either side of the door and their names were given. Those present who approached the angels at the doors, addressing them by their names and stating the reasons they needed to speak with the Mother of All, would be admitted.

The Mother of All then approached the opening doors in a great blaze of light. She handed a scroll to one of the angels kneeling before her, then she returned to her throne and the doors closed. The angel moved towards the Hall and placed the scroll on the second lowest step before the throne. The angel behind the throne took the scroll and the message from the Mother of All was read:

Thirty-two solar systems would be formed and crystals (similar to the sigils I had drawn and previously described) would be placed within them. The planets within the solar systems could then be used at the discretion of the rulers of the thirty-two root races from which Creation sprang. The crystals would immediately start to change the old programming within the thirty-two root races and aggression would be replaced with joy, limitation with abundance; re-programming them to be part of the joyous journey home. Beginning immediately, old pain would be erased and their thinking would become growth-promoting to all life.

After this proclamation, another great angel of light arrived to place a gold box on the second lowest step of the platform. Again, the angel behind the throne took the box, removed a key and read the scroll attached to the box. He said this came from the Infinite God, the Alumuanu King who represents the Infinite. When all Creation, led by the earth, would ascend to a certain level, the King would join with Mother. The key would enable the Mother of Creation and All to reach the Alumuanu King at any time.

At this time, Mother ascended straight upwards, the ceiling opened and again everyone was asked to kneel. After her departure, all rose and exited to enjoy a banquet in another hall. But the Old Dragon, having gotten what he came for, left for his kingdom.

The Day The Wall Came Down[19]

In the four directions, the dragons represent the warriors in the north and humans the nurturers in the south. The fairies and elves represent the inner child of the planet in the west, and the Ascended Masters of all races the sages in the direction of the east. *(See Fig. 13)*

Until the 8th of August, 2005, there were only 4 dragon Ascended Masters. The most senior master is a 75' dragon named Hy. Hy had married and lost one wife in his lifetime, but the greatest loss of all was the loss of his mother. When Hy was very small, she had been killed during the night by the Old Dragon, because she had made Hy a purple stuffed toy dragon (toys were outlawed until recently).

According to the New Dragon, Hy had shown very little passion, even for his wife who yelled at him a lot. The only thing he was absolutely passionate about was when he was given the task of placing a wall between the dragon world and the human world. Having constructed the wall, Hy was therefore also the one who had to break it down, something he was very resistant to doing.

But the perfection of the divine plan, created long before any part of existence we are familiar with, had taken this into account and devised a solution. He fell in love with a human Ascended Master. He was working in England at the time and his feelings made him so afraid that he went to the dragon world and hid.

The New Dragon spent days talking with Hy, asking him to break down the wall. But Hy was convinced that he was 'broken', since he'd never felt like this before. But that which is resisted is strengthened and as Hy's passion for her grew, it shattered the wall on the 5th of August 2005. For the breaking down of the

---

19 The walls referred to are membranes separating realms.

wall, Hy was blessed with his first child, a boy dragon carried for him as a favor by a female Ascended Master dragon. He had a birthday party on the 6th of August, 2005 and it was the greatest of celebrations. The fairies brought 100 tulips and when I wished him a happy birthday, he said, "The word is fantastic!" Apparently, he is driving the expectant mother crazy, hovering over her, watching his baby grow. The baby will be the dragon of highest consciousness ever to be born.

But no sooner had the wall between the north and south collapsed, when the wall between the elves and fairies and the Ascended Masters collapsed. This event has brought both passion (through Hy) and joy (through the elves and fairies) into one of the most stuck places on earth; the Ascended Master realms.

The Far-Reaching Consequences

What we know as the cosmos is to us everything that is. But the truth is that there is much, much more beyond.

Because the earth is the pivot point, not only for what's inside the cosmos but also without, when our walls came down, three other cosmoses collapsed into us, changing everything we thought was the future. Millions and millions of lords of light have streamed into our cosmos, like an ejaculation of light into a womb, birthing a much higher form of existence. Millions of goddesses have likewise entered.

The Day the Unborn Children Left

At about 8:00 pm on the 8th of August 2005, an unprecedented and massive exodus of unborn children began, causing 40 million miscarriages and loss of future children among human babies.

The reason was the collapsing of the walls. Would a spirit rather be born to a human mother struggling with a career, diaper rashes, baby-sitters and paying bills, or would it prefer a dragon mother able to materialize her needs with thought, protect herself, and choose her own destiny?

Dragon females had only recently (July '05) been granted the right to marry if and whom they choose, under the New Dragon's rule and after a proclamation by the Goddess of Creation that all unwed females would have the right to choose marriages.

A mother like that seemed preferable and furthermore, Ascended Masters were now for the first time having children. This enticed our unborn to forsake their human mothers for other mothers.

By the time the masters had gathered a legion of 60,000 angels to bring them back, over half had left. About 300 were supposed to be given to dragon mothers, but the rest now had to await new pregnancies by human mothers.

Since this had never happened before, there weren't angels assigned to prevent such an occurrence. Now there are. But what happens on earth happens in the cosmos. The unformed children of the cosmos are the 'lightbabies'—filaments of light that can also leave us for that which has been opened to us; the vast higher realms. An angel has therefore also been placed there as a preventive measure.

Egsplauvitpata, The 30 Ft. Giant and His Contribution to Cosmic Ascension

Hy, the dragon, broke down the barrier between the warriors, (the dragons representing the direction of the north), and the nurturers (the humans representing the direction of the south). The elves and fairies, representing the west, broke down the barrier between the planetary inner child of the west and sages of the east. The breaking down of the barriers between the directions of above and below had to occur next. The direction of above was represented by the peoples of the inner earth and our outer earth represented the direction of below.

Not only would the removal of the barrier on earth ripple throughout the cosmos and beyond, but our Ascended Masters would yet again change. Through Hy they had received the ability to procreate, but other than the Ascended Master dragon who carried Hy's child, none had the least interest in doing it since they had no desires. They had to be able to fall in love as well.

To accomplish this, someone from the inner earth had to fall in love with someone from the outer earth and have it be reciprocated. Furthermore they had to be Ascended Masters. Falling in love seemed as impossible to me as it did to the other Ascended Masters. After all, how could one desire someone else in that way when one knows that all is within?

To be the proxy upon whom the cosmos turns and through whom soul groups alter, not just anyone will do. In the case of Hy, he was the one who had built the wall and one of the then 4 ascended dragon masters. In the case of the elves, only the one who sits on the right hand of King Elrinkra, Elvichbaspla, could do it. Now Egsplauvitpata the giant was the only one that could represent the inner earth and I was to represent the outer earth.

There appeared at first to be insurmountable problems: he was a giant, I was not. I was absolutely sure I couldn't fall in love and furthermore was very confused by my assignment, since he was married. But apparently all this had been taken into consideration in a well-laid plan that was put in place long before. The story of my interaction with Egsplauvitpata began like this:

I have had only one life before this one, that of Inanna. After her father had scrambled the languages of humans, Inanna spent some time in Akkad (the word means low place), learning the language of the people. Akkad was the marshland of Sumeria and there they called her Isis.

Inanna's first love, Thoth's younger brother Osiris, or Demuzi, had died tragically right before their wedding due to the treachery of his sister. Inanna's family were all ascending through the sun (Arulu). Only Enlil, her father who had laid down his body, Thoth and Enki who spent most of their time traveling the cosmos and residing in the Halls of Amenti, remained. Marduk, Thoth's older brother (known in Egypt as Ra), had also died.

Inanna had her primary palace in India—the land her grandfather Anu had given her. He had also given her his palace in Iran. There was a smaller palace in a higher location in Northern India that she regarded as her retreat, especially when the climate got too hot at the main palace.

Inanna was lonely. Her family was leaving; Thoth's visits were infrequent and the short lifespans of humans—as compared to her immortal life—made it painful to bond with them. Then she met Egsplauvitpata.

Giants were frequent visitors to her palace. She had giant dinner services, hairbrushes, mirrors and other items for her visitors. When the spirits I sent to bring some of these items back to me first discovered the spoons, they thought they were shovels. We couldn't understand why anyone needed 24 golden, bejeweled shovels until we found the rest of the objects and Thoth explained it all to me.

Inanna also had many magic objects. One of them can alter physical forms to the size and shape desired, so she was able to make herself large enough to relate to him and thus their love affair began. Once again, however, treachery and jealousy took him from her.

Egsplauvitpata had more abilities and gifts of consciousness than any of the other giants. Another giant and his beautiful wife decided to try and steal them for themselves. Firstly they would have to get him away from Inanna and find a way to keep their crime from being discovered by Thoth. Then the wife would seduce him into marrying her and afterwards they would devise a way to steal his wealth of gifts. The treachery is all the greater because the wife was Inanna's friend.

They sent Inanna a message in Egsplauvitpata's voice to say he didn't want to see her again, then hit him over the head and knocked him unconscious. They robbed him of his memories by placing a block in his brain. They also dramatically damaged Thoth's ability to think, so that he wouldn't detect the treachery. That wasn't restored until September, 2005.

Inanna was immortal, but on a beautiful moonlit night that danced on the waterlily ponds of her northern palace, she could no longer endure the loneliness. After receiving the message in her lover's voice, she made arrangements to guard and shield all the palaces until her next and last life. She then laid her body down between three long triangular crystals about 9 feet in length, and left to be with her beloved Osiris as guard to the spirit worlds.

As she left her body, she could see the treachery surrounding Egsplauvitpata. She appeared to the wife and said she would come for him and restore his memory when the time was right for him to play his part in the planet's progression. Inanna told her that if she married him, she should be prepared for this.

The wife chose to marry Egsplauvitpata regardless. Perhaps she and her former husband thought they would have his abilities by then, so what would it matter? They never managed to get his abilities and the former husband died when the inner earth experienced the freezing time.

When I first contacted Egsplauvitpata, he had already become aware of me through the goddess, the Mother of All. We were to meet under very strict rules in a cave where we spent most of five days together. I remembered my feelings of being in love with him when he laughed. His memory was restored and the wall came down.

I speak to him almost every day and even though we cried as he returned to his world, having his wisdom and advice with my work is a great gift.

Further Information

Although Inanna was the personality that lived life within my body until the 16th of December, 2000, she then left to enter the Infinite, the first being within the cosmos ever to do so. A higher aspect or light body took her place in this body. It has felt much like a child trying to run an adult's life, as this was the higher aspect's first incarnation within a form. On July 15, 2005, Inanna again re-entered, bringing with her the many things that had been missing in my life for five-and-a-half years.

Dragon

As we moved into higher realms after Egsplauvitpata broke down the walls, we were in front of yet another wall. Behind it was a kingdom of 3,400 dragons governed by a 14 trillion year old ruler, simply called 'Dragon'.

These dragons existed as the epitome of exclusiveness. They trusted no one, not even each other. Their separation had caused a unique language to evolve, understandable only among themselves. They didn't speak any other languages, either. In fact, they were inclined to eat other dragons—a problem that had to be solved before we could move our dragon kingdom into theirs.

This realm of dragons represented the masculine pole of the warrior races, while the dragons of our earth represent the feminine pole. They were exclusive in nature, as the masculine tends to be. Our dragons had become inclusive (the feminine pole) when they started using their feeling bodies. Previously, they had wanted to live in isolation from one another, but were now quite content to live close together.

The resolution of these opposites lay yet again in one simple solution—love. Dragon had never trusted any female enough to take a wife. There was one, however, he had watched with great interest and for whom he now began to develop a consuming love. This was the Creator Goddess who was growing in luminosity each day here on earth. Although she had assumed a human shape, he wanted to be near her, love her and protect her.

His love grew so strong that it eventually broke down the wall separating the two realms. Mother sent him a fetus to carry as his son to bring joy to his heart. Male dragons, like our seahorses, carry fetuses and birth them after they are conceived by the females. The males carry out this function using a specially prepared sac on their bodies.

Dragon left his kingdom to get as close to Mother as he could (his subjects eventually followed him). This meant that he curled himself around my house where the gate had formed to allow the Mother goddesses to come through and unite as one with Mother on earth.

It was a dangerous situation, not only for my dragon, Beautiful One, but to all beings who regularly gathered there to observe the occurrences at the gate. His unfounded suspicions of everyone bordered on paranoia. He was liable at any time to see someone as a threat to his beloved Goddess and attack them.

His exclusiveness of thought did not allow non-cognitive information to help him see behind appearances. He therefore took everything at face value, which led him to wrong conclusions. He was powerful enough to hold the whole earth hostage if he so chose. Mother decided to take the following steps:

1. She immediately stationed 20 of the most powerful kings in the cosmos around my house! The feeling of their presence was profound;

2. She revealed herself to Dragon for 4 hours. Visions of her glory and majesty poured into him, healing all the pain of his 14 trillion years of life, opening his heart and making him more inclusive. To this point, the only other she had healed in this way had been Thoth;

3. She gave him a task to perform with the New Dragon of the earthly dragons and some of the kings, so that working together might foster camaraderie;

4. So that they could understand him and he them, she had one of the kings place a translating device around his ankle. It chafed him and he kept trying to stuff flowers between his ankle and the device. But, Mother spoke to him and said she would line it with her love. As she spoke loving words to him, the effects of her soothing voice not only solved the problem but put him to sleep;

5. She took the fetus's higher aspect, or dream body, to the other earthly dragons' world while Dragon was sleeping. This meant that Dragon's dream body went also. There, in cooperation with the New Dragon, they would be confined until it was time for the birth. They would be treated with love and respect, learning how to live inclusively. This would be automatically programmed into the grid of all in Dragon's kingdom as well.

On October 10, 2005, Dragon had become so inclusive that,

during a health crisis, he chose to sacrifice his life so the fetus might live. With but minutes of life left for him, Mother stepped in and moved him into the Immortality Stage, saving his life.

Twitches—The Long Oppressed

Often mistaken for dragons because of their resemblance, twitches had been ruled by the dragons in a very repressive way for eons until the present Dragon agreed to allow them to flourish.

Twitches lived only one overtone above us when we were in the old three-dimensional earth before the ascension began. Their primary function, as delegated by the dragon rulers, was to dispose of garbage by eating it. Their magic had been stripped after 12 years of age for so long, that eventually they simply automatically lost it at that age.

As we raised our realms, we raised the twitches with us. To make sure they would not in any way become more than the slave race they had become, the Old Dragon started increasing their humiliation as their frequency rose. Seeking to escape this persecution, they fled to the center of the earth's moon. After the New Dragon graciously restored their magic on the 30th of June, 2005, they returned to earth and sent me this message (the translation is unfortunately incomplete):

Ooeeneema-ay trumeeni beesmava silshee beeamani

Sorry we do not speak ....

Vauee haureipi umanahay veeah mavuana

... magic... (presumably saying magic has been restored)

peeipiha mahur

in the night

lavau preesh meuni

... is very pretty

vaa baa sushee mauvay
> thank you

havau treunu mauva-ay
> friends from now

The name of the twitch who translated this is:

Bar u tra abauw hay pa ur la ma nee beesh

After the New Dragon ruler had agreed to their magic being restored, they had to be properly instructed in its appropriate use. My task was to call in the lords that would instruct them in the impeccable use of their magic. The lords of impeccability of conduct are:

Geranashsarbut

Sparushimsperva

Ochbaranutsparek

Urublifparvamarut

The Fairies And Their Language

Why We Can't See Fairies

Throughout diverse cultures, fairy tales and folk legends can be accessed at two different levels; either as entertaining tales with a moral message, or well-disguised, deep esoteric truths revealing secrets about the human psyche or the hidden realms.

One puzzling factor has always caught the attention of students of folk stories. Amongst the great variety of cultures, similarities in the details keep surfacing. Dragons breathe fire, whether in the folk tales of Peru or China. Unicorns are beneficial and healing in their interactions with man. Fairies fly and have great magical power; elves continue to delight and bring whimsy and humor to life.

Not only have these tales come from a far distant past before consciousness fell with each successive global cataclysm, but also from times when mankind as a whole could not read or write. Among the Mayans and other indigenous peoples, some sages or rulers strenuously resisted writing among their people. They knew that words or symbols would lull man into thinking he knew something because he'd named it. With a word or symbol representing an object such as a specific flower, its essence was no longer felt through the heart. In other words, that real world lying beyond form was no longer accessed.

In this way, the non-cognitive information of the universe around him became unavailable as man slowly sank into a world of logic and reason. With this shift, nine-tenths of his reality disappeared as he lost the right-brain oriented tools to discern and communicate with it. Fairies, pixies, unicorns and the other beings of the magic kingdoms, without whom the earth would not flourish, became delegated to the realms of myth and fiction. As centuries passed, they continued to fade ever further across the horizon of human perception.

But because we have changed, doesn't mean they have ceased to be. As awareness on the planet begins to rise to the levels from which it sank, more and more of us will once again be able to communicate with the beings of these magic kingdoms, finding them delighted to befriend and aid us. *(See Fig. 37, Fairy Language)*

The Realms of the Fairy Queens

In ancient times, during the fall of the earth 75,000 years ago, the Luciferian hosts managed to capture the elf kingdom as well as half of the fairy kingdom.

The fairy kingdom was split. The captured half, under Queen Dyetneria, was taken to the underworld. The other half, under

Fairy Language

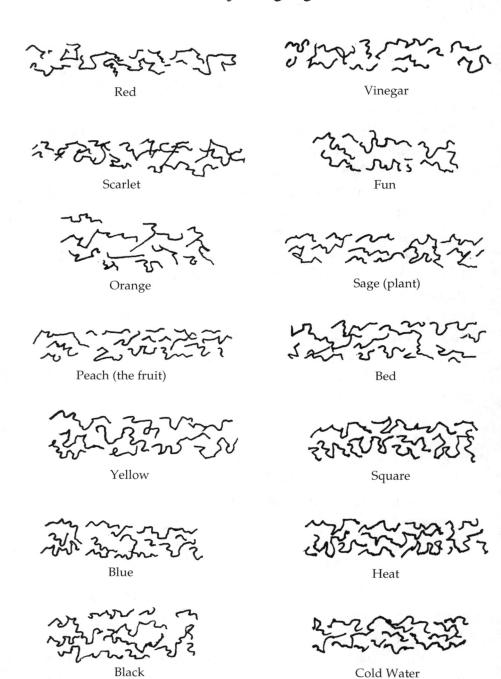

Red

Vinegar

Scarlet

Fun

Orange

Sage (plant)

Peach (the fruit)

Bed

Yellow

Square

Blue

Heat

Black

Cold Water

(Figure 37)

Queen Amaraka-lara, resided in what became a dimensional overtone above the physical world of man.

In February 2005, as the earth began its ascension, one of the first tasks assigned me by the Creational Mother Goddess was to reunite the fairy kingdoms.

I had to get permission from our planetary lord, Horlet. Then I had to go up an overtone and ask Queen Amaraka-lara's permission. I next had to know the name and sigil of the gatekeeper to the underworld in order to give him Mother's instruction and Horlet's permission to let only the fairies out (for some reason the Mother didn't tell me about the elves at that time) and to close the gate behind them.

Millions of fairies moved through our realm that day to the one above us where Queen Amaraka-lara expected their knock on the gate to the higher fairy realms.

Weeks later the two queens sent me a message that they wanted to be friends. They said they had made me a present and I should go outside by my front door. There, side by side, the two most beautiful and identical flowers had sprung up overnight.

It was not until after the sixth move into higher realms of physical life on earth that the elves started sending many symbols and messages to me through King Elrinray[20]. When I asked, Mother gave permission for them to join the fairy realms.

Once again, permission had to be obtained from Horlet and the fairy queens. I had to again descend to the underworld to get the elves released.

Because these kingdoms represent the sub-conscious mind of the planet (and also the inner child), they brought to light unresolved planetary issues and karma that had been submerged

20 A dear friend who is the incarnation of the King of all the elves in the cosmos.

for 75,000 years. Suddenly all major light-promoters found increasing challenges in their lives as they struggled to turn challenge into insight.

The increase in spontaneity and joy brought relief, however, as our planetary inner children again made these gifts available to us.

They reside among us now within the same frequency level, keeping themselves hidden until humankind reaches a fuller understanding of the aliveness of all things and a matching degree of harmlessness.

The Drain Fairy and the Elves

A few years ago, the unmistakable smell of a drain fairy announced that one had moved into the house. The putrid smell would move around and then some days not be there at all, indicating that he was scouring the clean water pipes.

Because his primary focus was the guest bedroom, I decided to contact him to ask whether, with enough notice, he would work on the clean water pipes when we had visitors. Since then, we have become friends. He is very proud of his work, easily offended when called 'stinky' and has recently had a love disappointment.

Drain fairies collect treasure. Elves have been known to try to steal that treasure and so drain fairies have become very threatening towards elves. A drain fairy once told me I could have a piece of jewelry for every song I'd sing her. However, an elf would have to go to the drain fairy's location to collect the jewelry and I could not persuade any of them to do it. They just kept saying, "No, they're too scary!"

To make up for their unwillingness to get the jewelry from the drain fairy, they offered to find some for me themselves. Fourteen elves set out on the quest. Weeks later, their little feet aching, they carried into the house a pink bead bracelet they claimed would bring me 'lots of money'.

Unfortunately, they then fell down the drain in the guest bedroom's bathroom, waking me up by screaming loudly, "Help! Help!" The little house elf, Eoptika, tried to help but fell in too, losing his shoe. Their 'treasure' was lost and I was forced, against their will, to get the drain fairy to help them out. His stench caused one elf to pass out. After several days they were finally out, but the bracelet they had worked so hard to get had slipped too far down the pipes to save.

Little Eoptika had to get new shoes, but a new sense of cooperation was forged that for thousands of years had not existed between their species. They were willing to set aside their differences to further a higher cause.

The Fairy of the Mists

As the cosmos was moving further in its ascension, the earth was fulfilling the prophecy of ancient scriptures and moving into new heavens. This has been concealed from all but a few by the placement of a hologram around the earth, as previously mentioned. *Revelations 21:1 "And I saw a new heaven and a new earth, for the first heaven and the first earth were passed away..."*

The vital role of the earth as wayshower meant that as we moved, we were pulling portions of the cosmos behind us. As foretold in the scriptures, the heavens were being rolled up like a scroll. Instructions came from the Mother Goddess to perform ceremonies just prior to each of the first 12 cosmic shifts, signifying the merging of the zodiac houses. *Isaiah 65: 17 "...I create new heavens and a new earth: and the former shall not be remembered, nor come into mind."*

For this purpose twelve wheels of symbols had to be constructed. Melissa, Sarah, a group of students and I worked for a week to prepare them. But the night before the ceremony was to be performed, the wheel for Capricorn was missing from Melissa's apartment. When we asked the spirits what had happened, they said they had seen a remote viewer (some have the ability to move objects) enter the apartment. He wore a black T-shirt and charcoal jeans.

The spirits saw that the remote viewer didn't understand what the wheel was for, but knowing it might be important to those who had sent him, took it. The spirits saw him leave the apartment with the scroll rolled up and placed in his back pocket, but that it was not there when they saw him outside the building. *(See Fig. 2, Wheel of Symbols and Sigils)*

Everyone searched for the scroll in the building and on the sidewalk. It was nowhere to be found. Then as the spirits looked deeper into the matter, they found it was in the possession of a fairy.

We asked the fairy to give it back, explaining it was ours. She refused. We then explained what it was for, but she was confused and still unimpressed.

We were getting desperate. It would take hours, if not days, to find the correct symbols. I decided to 'pull rank', telling her I was friends with Queen Dyetneria and Queen Amaraka-lara, rulers of all the fairy realms.

Her response was: "I am a fairy of the mists. I don't know them. All I know is that the man (the thief) wasn't supposed to have something that important. And now I don't know what to do."

Finally I gave up. I asked her to destroy the scroll and I would start over. She agreed that would be best. We started to re-construct the wheel and that was the only time I spoke to a fairy of the mists.

Inanna And The Wolls

Inanna is the name of my previous incarnation. She incarnated as the personality named Almine in this lifetime. She left my body on December 16, 2000 when a higher lightbody took its place. I have described this event in the autobiographical section of *Journey to the Heart of God*. The lightbody remained until July 15, 2005 when Inanna re-joined with it in my material body.

During most of that time an unheard of situation was occurring. Inanna had been the first to leave Creation for the Infinite, where she dwelled until her re-entry into form. The day before the re-entry, fairies known as 'Wolls' contacted me and asked whether I wanted my rainstick back. Because I could hear but not see them, they asked if I was asleep. They had followed Inanna from the Infinite back into Creation.

Since almost nothing is known about lifeforms existing within the Infinite, we share this with our readers for interest's sake. The Wolls have since become part of Creation as well.

Inanna had apparently lived a very solitary life during her time in the Infinite, resting on a small planet she had to herself. She had visited the Wolls to make friends, leaving behind her rainstick with the markings of a language she had developed for herself. Because she was preparing to enter my body, the Wolls had followed her into Creation to return the rainstick. She looked just like me and so they thought I was Inanna, even before her re-entry into my body. Following is a transcript of the conversation with the Wolls:

> **Setchama, Setchama, chi ar unet?** (Urgent, Urgent! Why are you sleeping with your shoes on?) **Kri tu manunet ervi kla ba?** (Don't you see me standing right here?) **Gispartraluk efpish par tra.** (We want to tell you a question) **Ga u spa vu**

Inanna's Rainstick

The symbols on Inanna's rainstick

Red

The following message was given to me by three fairies within the Infinite. They called themselves "Wolls":

Setchama setchama chi ar unet?
Urgent urgent, why are you sleeping with your shoes on?

Yellow

Kri tu manunet ervi kla ba?
Don't you see me standing right here?

Gishpartraluk efpish par tra.
We want to tell you a question.

Ga u spa vu sami klat ka nuk hesh?
Do you want your rainstick back?

Orange

Uvefelbi prish vaatr ra ur rat mir ve plataa.
You forgot it yesterday five times ago.

Hu skana ma kli bu sat.
We have no use for it.

Green

Ech uses hektamara fulbi kufda plea?
Do you stay asleep all day?

Blue

(Figure 38)

210

sami klat ka nuk hesh? (Do you want your rainstick back?)
Uvefelbi prish vaatr ra ur rat mir ve plataa. (You forgot it
yesterday five times ago.) Hu skana ma kli bu sat. (We have
no use for it.) Ech uses hektamara fulbi kufda plaa? (Do you
stay asleep all day?) (See Fig. 38, Inanna's Rainstick)

The Elfin Realms

One day the elves I was working with on a little project said:
"We're so sorry about your finger!" I asked the spirits what they
were talking about. "Oh, you're going to break it tomorrow. It's
the relationship finger because you're not allowing yourself to get
enough joy from your relationships.[21]"

I immediately started a time of contemplation, thinking not
only about the joy of my loved ones, but also the great blessings
of my 'family' of spirits and beings from other kingdoms. But as I
sat there, waves of joy washed over me. After a while, a little face
appeared in front of me.

The little one was a fairy. She had the most perfect, exquisite
purple face. Her hair fell in waves, changing from purple to green
and back again. I had just met Aribafira, the fairy of joy. I tried
to get her to live with me, as does Firiha, the little fairy who lives
with and rides on my office manager's shoulder. But she preferred
the garden.

But Aribafira isn't the first one to make an effort to cheer me
up. The hardships of the responsibilities as cosmic gatekeeper
sometimes wore so heavily on me I forgot to smile. During that
time, I was working day and night to produce thousands of angel
sigils that were needed to protect the earth from what was then a
threat. But on occasion I would hear a little song, and the first two

21 A dear friend who is the incarnation of the King of all the elves in the cosmos.

words were always the same: "Pedlbufpaba, pedlbufpaba ....",
followed by some other strange words.

It was during a lengthy ceremony, when my body ached from
18 hours of lying on a wheel of symbols, that I saw Pedlbufpaba,
the elf. Once again, only his little face appeared in front of me.
Uncombed curly brown hair, about chin-length, framed a 'sun-
tanned' looking face. Brown sparkling eyes in a slightly dirty face
stared back at me. The little nose was very stubby and he smiled as
he sang his now familiar song to cheer me.

King Elrinkra of the elf kingdom, and his right hand elf
Elvichbaspla, have become very close to me. They are always
willing to help and their elves are dependable and very proud of
doing their work well. They shout when they become excited and
their courage and cheery love of life make them seem 10 feet tall,
even though they are only a few inches high.

Elfin Language

Words

Friends	treuvanach
Are	pleishaber
Standing	kretuanech
Water	sitvradom
Nice	belufvrabi
Light	skeravubit
Red roses	kleshba-atrug
With	savarnet
Tulips	hechstupava
White daisies	preugnarvat
Pink	seblutvarupa

Phrases

Gishtrakelvu kurskahep tra shpertvu.

You're sitting on my arm.

Urstanik hepsbi uraesh klavatr bartra hug kavul skapa.

I know you let me come too.

vatr breshpapek huftra uraek.

Oh, it's not hearing.

Mitiakel uvene kara hug pata.

OK, we go home.

Elveter parable paranuk.

One day goodbye.

Bu ester ruf ta pa.

Then tomorrow hello.

(The above was given by an elf named Ulefskatradom -pishbiplakelbum. He could see I couldn't translate and understand what he was saying, so he wanted to come back the next day when I had had a chance to translate it.)

Kurech pi strata uratel bif ta tra.

We like friends.

Ursh vatel efbi arokva.

Rosie is not feeling well with specks.

Guchstakel uladom prefbi.

Itchy and sick and that's it.

Karunach patrebil usuk natra.

The boy is feeling well.

Pishpata ur bafum.

We don't like that.

Karabig ta ham.

That's a riddle.

Tabula bafum patel arunik.

When you find it we will tell you.

Skarufba ulef tiune.

Red and purple and blue.

Hulstabi plesh anuni.

Sing songs like.

Kabuura rat ellabi.

An adventure is said.

Spirakel marvet urem.

There's a worm in my apple.

Ursat hurspabil unaech klit estom.

We go after the moon.

Ski vafel urspa hirsh maklet.

With leaves on puddles.

Enskabel utuf plavuvet.

Like pigs in mud.

(See Fig. 39, Elfin Language)

Pixies

A brand new type of pixie has recently been created to assist with plants, bugs, some gemstones and to help solve problems when people feel entangled. These beings stand between 1'' and 7'' tall.

The following message came from one of the pixies who moved in under the stairs by my back door.

Skatruvich	**asher**	**vystraba.**
(pixie's name)	is	myself.
Klesuvet	**maraneck**	**trenevis**
plehet,		
When	looking for	me,
vaur	**pata kelsh uber**	

Elfin Language

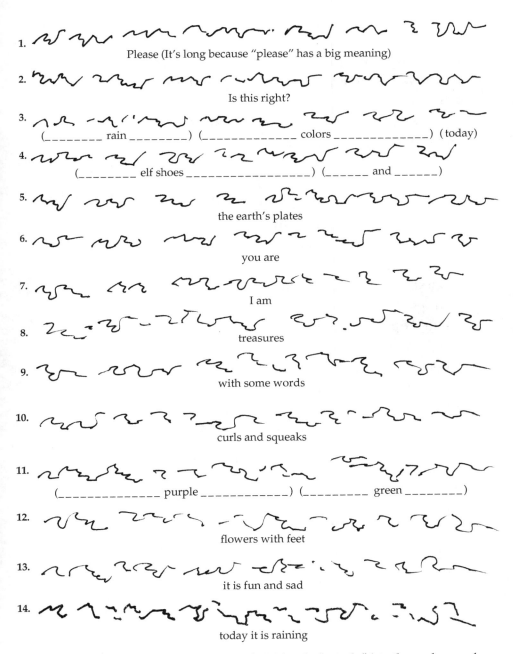

1. Please (It's long because "please" has a big meaning)

2. Is this right?

3. (_____ rain _____) (_____ colors _____) (today)

4. (_____ elf shoes _____) (_____ and _____)

5. the earth's plates

6. you are

7. I am

8. treasures

9. with some words

10. curls and squeaks

11. (_____ purple _____) (_____ green _____)

12. flowers with feet

13. it is fun and sad

14. today it is raining

As I was writing, they kept insisting that I wasn't writing the "squeaks" into the words properly. Only when I did the "stair-step" wiggles in the lines, as shown above, did they approve.

(Figure 39)

search	the	creaky	tall
sitravavaskletruhet	**pirvanestru**		**sitva**
ushaberlok.			
staircase	beyond	big	birch tree.

Some other pixie words are:

Ahead	skarak
Baskets	presvatraba
Black	penevustra
Blowing	peleshva
Calling	nunavish
Cold	vuvish
Darkness	klustarnut
Drops	achbar
Fingertips	beltranadom
Fish	bistra
Forecast (noun)	echbarek
Frozen	urshmishuvuset
Golden	kelkluch
Gripping	krutma
Here	kranatuk
Holiday	elevustra
Ice	stelaber
In	huk
Leaves	starop
Live	vilespi
Pink	pare
Please	elechvisbi
Precipitation	lufbisuveras
Prepare	sitelmarnok
Rain	nananoch

Red	klet
Scars	nanavok
Storms	vilplesbi
Time	netrava
Today	parva
Tired	tritel
Wax	prius

Goblins and Gremlins

I know very little about these beings, other than the following three brief insights:

- I asked one of the spirits to get Eoptika, the house-elf, to come and speak to me. He was always very polite and respectful. He welcomed the many visitors that came with good intent, explaining politely that I couldn't see or hear all of them except 'sometimes', but I had told him to express my love to them.

  I was therefore very surprised when he refused to come when the spirits called him, just saying, "I'm busy!" I instructed them to tell him I insisted. He came, but was absolutely furious.

  Apparently he and some of the other elves had, with tremendous effort, cornered a gremlin that had come into the house. "How am I supposed to get my work done when you call me away?" he screamed. I apologized upon hearing what was happening and sent him back. The spirits explained that gremlins play 'nasty tricks', hiding and stealing things. They also harass elves and fairies.

- I asked Eoptika to tell me about goblins. "Ooh, nasty creatures! They kill fairies," he said with distaste. "They're much worse than gremlins."

- One day I received a message in an unusual language I hadn't heard before. I wrote it down carefully but no one could translate it. I asked my beloved friends, the two fairy queens Amaraka-lara and Dyetneria. They were 'having tea', they said. Although they couldn't translate it, they could tell me it was a goblin. They always ended our talks by confirming that "We are friends."

I took the matter to the Archangel Mi, the angel in charge of all fairies, devas, elves and other elemental kingdoms. He said it came from the goblin queen but he could not speak the words. "Why not?" "Because my mouth cannot speak words that are untrue." He explained the message told untruths about the little elves I had welcomed into the house and urged me to chase them away. This of course would have left the house wide open for the goblins to invade without anyone there to warn me.

Dwarfs

Dwarfs are all of a very similar height—2'7''. In the same way, they don't vary very much in lifespan. They all live to be about 305-308 years of age. They are responsible for mushrooms, bulbs and vegetables like potatoes, etc. In terms of hierarchy of the species, they are less complex than elves and fairies in their development, but higher on the evolutionary scale than gnomes.

They have a very short alphabet and most words have two meanings. I was walking behind a Dwarf when he became concerned that he may have done something wrong and that I was following him. He spoke the following words:

Birshva	**hursklepatet**	**vilnechprva.**	
I don't	understand	your letters.	
Hustanadoch	**eleuf**	**pranut**	**kelurgvarnatat**
Why	are	you	following

Pletrruk?

me?

As with all other magical creatures in our legends and stories, knowledge of these precious little beings have survived, but their reality has been denigrated to myth.

I promised a little dwarf called Periduperki, who visited me, that I would 'tell people about dwarfs'. We accidentally forgot to include their information in this book, but he kept pinching me on and off until I remembered.

The Story Of Kiribach

In Toronto I first encountered the equivalent of what it would look like if elves had midgets. They were very tiny—about 1'' tall and spoke a different language. They had come for help and this is what they said:

Irshparvblik huchpa urs vanet.

This is a dark night.

Kriibach tre misarvatep.

Kiribach is missing.

Hurs kananech ior hurpata.

We live in this room.

Iunik baurtel flem tra pa.

You are a pretty one.

Kurvartl urs mananek?

Can you help?

Plesurparva ubismi hek.

She is gone.

Elef tra ha skuvil.

There is no light to find her.

Pirshpata unech marvik.

It is depressed.

Siutl buersh iubi plava.

Lost since forty nights.

I called the Archangel Michael to ask what to do. He answered immediately. The little elf girl had been taken by a three-headed dog that had trespassed out of the realms where he had been confined. He was keeping her prisoner inside an egg-like container in a lake three dimensional overtones up.

Michael said he would send the dog back to his realm and confine him, but I had to get her out. I asked whether there was an angel to save beings from creatures like this. He said yes, but there was only one and he was inside the egg too, along with a little cat-like animal with ears like a rabbit (these little animals were not from these dimensions but often hid here for safety). He warned that breaking the egg would destroy everything inside.

I called my friend the Dragon (king of our earth's dragons) and he sent a dragon to free everyone and bring little Kiribach safely home.

A Communication From The Unicorns

Unicorns reside one level of frequency above humankind until such time that we live in a state of respect and reverence for all life.

Symbols of purity and love, they are mentioned in the Bible, seen on rock drawings and told about in fairy tales. Yet few ever communicate with these beautiful but elusive creatures. We therefore include the following communication.

Following is a message I received on July 2, 2005. It was translated for me by Beubshlala, a unicorn I have befriended. She says it is in unicorn 'shorthand', with the words being abbreviated.

Asked why one couldn't recognize words like 'you' or 'we' by their repetitions from one sentence to the next, she said unicorn language is very complex. That is why the 'shorthand' is used. 'We' would vary greatly from sentence to sentence, depending on the meaning of that sentence.

Transmission and Translation

Elvin re ray ahur biichapa ut linen bripshi.

We want to move into your area.

Varugneg hiptla ulraef biibschpi uinlahup krieonatek?

Do you mind this project?

Kravrutl bipla tries la bauptir preknak.

In case you need us for work, we eat watermelon.

Sahutl vriim plempara rek bursh tre ubil.

Night is the best time for work.

Krivatldonk tri esbi plaak hur vararep bitel.

If you like us to build our houses near you.

Ta hulibishla vrus tarem.

We are a group of ten.

U ech schpihepl da.

Over here we have no water.

Kluyimarut prek hurtl sputrek barem varup.

We are moving so we have more to drink.

Yauch spartl pluesbavi raputapl kri unes espraak ra ur vra di.

We do not make a lot of noise.

Pleus kara nuik kefta pliuner haruva spu barek urardi es nauneg.

We will not go if you do not like this.

Bakuf pla ur skaranug.

We like you.

Hespa u fanupratlvut karu naureg speba.

There is also a place that we have houses there in the desert.

Kefbananug tre mispa?
Do you ever visit?
Ahur skarmif esplaha.
We set a place in our house for you.
Eskur marvet bes mi pla.
We learn about friends.
Arek utrana nut hefpa.
Sorry we must speak loud.
Uarg spel e tra paranut plesba?
Is this big for your ears?
Akurservavet georch tra u varem.
One day you see me in the garden.
Speltravur ramach urnet gaurtranet mir ertag.
I will not be afraid of you.
Bashpilbi hep katra.
I shake your hand to be nice.
Hespatl ple vu kaerah.
Well done.
Echvatl beurch spavi kra bel pik e spatra ulek.
For you today roses in the summertime.
Kefa tre dom, kefa tre dom aranik.
And you are like that, and you are like that done.

A New Group of Unicorns on Earth

During the Spring of 2006, another group of unicorns that spoke an entirely different language arrived on earth. During the earth's rapid rise into higher frequencies, we have moved into their realms and then one day, they were suddenly there.

They had come to pay a visit and I heard the loud clatter of hooves across my hardwood floors. A loud commotion followed around the bathtub—one had decided it was a nice place to rest. He had an inconceivably long name;

Bauvichbelushahispachiamavishpiakiaubafpaechmispauvechpahan unaechmiakishpaustaechunamishpeta

He introduced his other unicorn friends:

1. Keshbaravechnitsuttreva
2. Ketlhufbipleshplanaekbichtreshparva
3. Klutsheshvibarechnirsetvaklueshpaverbi
4. Krechashvarabiheshusvarabi

He then said the following:

Tia ufbaech ninu bich piata.

Am the one from your bathroom pool.

Eska bauch tiamata nushpave minuhet satu baklauava?

Would it be right to speak?

Neshu pespa kesba uhutva bilhaspek piava.

It is good rites of yours with robes. (Presumably this is my bath-time 'ritual' when I put on my robe.)

Traunich setruva hesh kletvarabitreunamit. Trech urnavit pesh kletrahut serva. Tresh ra hunanik vesh pretpave bech averbi kluanesh?

These are our friends who give treatments with wind. Do you have interest?

Baufba erch klava, chia ma utchvelesbi. Beskbaurt nech tiaui balesuispa urch berch panit.

Those persons of mother's house makes unhappy and are always sad. (Presumably referring to some of the students in my house who had been crying.)

PART FIVE

The Spirit Realms

Working With Spirits—the Adventure Begins

Throughout the month of January 2005, I knew only one thing for certain: life was about to begin a whole new journey. The old patterns would be swept away.

During the previous month, I had begun to work closely with four spirits who had specific gifts. There was Sarah, about 4'6", chubby and wearing an apron. She had a great sense of humor, a wonderful ability to find her way and a great deal of problem-solving ability—a rarity for a spirit. She had little patience with those who didn't do their job.

Evelyn and Faye arrived together, the result of Sarah's search to find spirits who could materialize and de-materialize matter. This would save me hours of work getting rid of tumors and would also assist in other areas. Evelyn was a little aloof. There were clear parameters as to what she would and wouldn't do. Faye had last incarnated during the witch burnings and had died at the stake for her ability to de-materialize objects.[22] She couldn't read or write, and was doubtful about using the very thing that had caused such a traumatic death during her last life.

Both Faye and Evelyn (who had been called by Sarah from

---

22 She became very sad each year during the anniversary of her death at the stake.

France where she was assisting a woman delivering a baby in a car), wouldn't commit to helping with my work until they had observed me for a day or two. They stood glumly in a corner, arms folded defiantly across their chests. Both assured me of their ability to materialize and de-materialize.

As it turned out, they could de-materialize physical objects, but not re-materialize them. They said they might be "a bit rusty", since they hadn't done it for a few hundred years. So Sarah once again was gone for days finding another spirit with such gifts.

His name was Malcolm. He looked like a big burly biker and he liked weaving baskets from etheric supplies he would create at will. Malcolm assured us he could materialize objects and, as it turned out, he couldn't.

A great sadness that could be felt throughout the house hung over the spirits. They all felt they had failed. The only being that seemed unaffected by the gloom was the dragon, Beautiful One. Her name was actually En Lau Hay Tow, but the name I gave her was easier to pronounce

Towards the end of January, the crystal skull I had been aware was waiting for me in Central America began 'calling' incessantly. It was known to me through previous prophecy only as the 13th skull, the mother of all skulls. Its calling was nagging at me like the crying of a child.

The spirits confirmed that there were several sacred objects waiting for me, but that the skull had to be retrieved first. I knew we had a good crew to de-materialize and transport it, but who would then materialize it back into physical form? I decided to cross that bridge later and sent Sarah, Evelyn and Malcolm while Faye stayed home with me practicing her materializing obsessively and unsuccessfully on a stick.

On the 29th of January, 2005, while the three spirits

were transporting the skull back to me after successfully de-materializing it, Melissa heard a frantic "Help!" from Sarah somewhere over Mexico and then absolute silence. She tried to speak to Malcolm and Evelyn, but no response came from them either. All Faye could tell me was that they had fallen through a 'hole' into an upside-down place where they were caught by 600 demons.

I was in the middle of my little girl's 6th birthday party and had 40 guests in the house. As politely and firmly as possible, we cleared the house within a hour.

A dear friend of mine, a Native American chief, and his assistant were visiting and, dressed in full regalia, had honored my daughter with a song. I pulled him aside and told him what had happened. I presented him with tobacco and asked for his help. We did prayers and he did a pipe ceremony, calling his own spirits to help. By the time we left the room, my assistant received a message from Melissa. "I don't know what happened. There are three very confused and disheveled spirits here with me in Canada. Sarah has lost her apron and all they keep saying is that they dropped the skull in that upside-down place when the demons caught them."

I couldn't risk sending them back, but I couldn't leave such a sacred object there either. I called Thoth. I had seldom called that he did not come, but this time he didn't immediately arrive.

The only other solution I could think of was to call the 40 spirits that always came to warn me when there was some sort of alien threat to the earth and humanity. On October 14, 2004, they had hit me so hard to get my attention they had almost knocked me out of my chair while teaching. They came at once and I asked them to find Thoth for help.

They finally did find him and he agreed to help only if we

couldn't do it ourselves. He wouldn't talk to them further (perhaps because of their annoying habit of all shouting at once) and left. I asked them to please go in and get the skull.

The 40 have some sort of group mind in place. They seemed to have no leader and would only move or act if all of them agreed. They were in my house many days before there was a consensus of opinion and they finally left to get the skull—an act of great bravery since, as they pointed out many times, "There are only 40 of us and 600 of them."

Even though before going in, they attached a thread of gold light to the opening (that we later sealed) it took weeks in that place full of illusion for them to find the skull and bring it out. Midway through, I had to fend off an attack by the 600 who, being forbidden by Thoth to harm any of the spirits, turned on me instead.

The skull arrived a few weeks into February and I was so relieved I gave a group hug to the 40 spirits—definitely a new experience.

The Egyptian Quest

While we were waiting for the skull, Sarah, Malcolm and Evelyn went to Egypt to get a set of sacred objects Thoth had left for me. They weren't permitted to tell me what they were, but they were wrapped in a white cloth in a wooden box 2' wide x 3' long x 2' high.

For days they struggled to get into what was to turn out to be the first of nine doors. When it dawned on me that it was a test of some sort, I gave them Thoth's Atlantean name, Chequetet Arelich Vomalites, and it opened the first door only to reveal another which opened to my name. They then found themselves in pitch darkness. "Zin-uru" produced light (Zin-uru means 'let there be light') without there being a light source.

There were various tests of increasing complexity from that point on at the gates. Firstly it tested what I knew, including:

- I had to figure out how to create a space portal, how to use it to teleport objects or people and how to convert it to a time portal. *(See Fig. 14)*
- My knowledge of the inter-galactic alphabet and how to construct sentences with it.
- The angelic orders of Alcyon, the Pleidean sun, and their colors.
- Various numerical systems. The number of points of each of the stars of 12 star systems as given in Gnostic teachings.
- Hieroglyphic symbols and basic sigils of some archangels.
- An ability to speak the Niburuan language.
- The tones that open the chakras and in what order, as well as basic dynamic geometry.
- How to gain access to the temple inside the earth, known as the Halls of Amenti.

The second category confirmed who I knew, i.e., my relationships such as:

- The archetypal spirits of the elements and the four directions.
- The dragon guarding the earth's magnetic axis and dragons in general.
- The elemental and angelic kingdoms.
- The lords in the Halls of Amenti and the great lord of the earth, Horlet, also known as the Dweller.
- But most of all: our mother the Earth.

The third category tested what I could do:

- To teleport the spirits and objects backwards and forwards in time, through space and upwards and downwards through dimensions.

- Suspend water in the air, rotate it, freeze it instantly from the bottom up and keep it suspended in mid-air.
- I had to learn how to use my physical double (the dream body) very much more proficiently than I had been doing.

The quest furthermore taught lessons, tested my impeccability and my ability to overcome obstacles, as well as my focus and the steadiness of my nerves. The spirits had informed me that as they went through the doors, they would close behind them and if we didn't make it through all doors in and out of this location under the sands next to the great pyramid, they would be trapped forever. Knowing that Sarah was as close as Melissa's mother, since she had grown up with her, and the responsibility I had towards all of them, I felt the pressure mounting as each successive door became more and more challenging.

The two most vividly remembered lessons of this quest are (1) the value of relationships and (2) that obsessing about the questions leaks energy. My misperception had been that, because I was all things, I should be able to get to the stage where I was able to do all things. The greatest growth in the cosmos is gained through inter-dependency.

Although it is true that each of us is a unique perspective superimposed over all that is (therefore all things), each one also has a unique gift that can contribute to a better journey. In working with angels, for example, each angel has a very unique specialty, but cannot stand stress. The spirits are, on the other hand, less specialized, but simply don't crack under enormous stress.

The second lesson came in the following way: we were on the way out when, after a hugely stressful day, we finally opened a door. I was exhausted, but since the spirits didn't need rest (unlike angels), I asked them to find out how to get out of the very large, doorless room (about size of a football field) while I slept.

Spirits working on the side of the light cannot make themselves say "Yes" when the true answer is "No". I hoped that one would ask, one would answer and one would write it down, as they can produce pen and paper with thought.

But spirits think very two-dimensionally. They did exactly as instructed even though each time a question was asked, water leaked into the room. By the morning, it was at least 3 feet deep and all they had determined was that questions produce water! What made matters worse was that there was a grid in the floor that needed to be activated, which couldn't be done with water on it. The message was clear: confusion is a choice and obscures clear vision. Too many questions leak energy and then we can't access our power.

An example of how my impeccability was tested at every gate (either by a direct question or by a situation in my day) went like this: the attack by the 600 demons was foreseen by me and confirmed by the spirits. The day before it was to happen, I heard the question while in ceremony to open the gate: "Would you rather save the demons from their darkness, or have the three sacred objects now?"

I had begun to realize that the skull and these objects would in some way favorably affect the planetary grid. In other words, all humankind would benefit. I correctly chose the demons and the gate swung open for the following reasons:

• Every being that directly crosses our path has a contract with us. He or she comes to give a gift and receive one. If we do that which is before us, the big picture will take care of itself.

• Raising consciousness has to be done from the bottom levels up.

• I had become too attached to the outcome because of concern for the well-being of the spirits. I could see why such a test would be needed and I was determined to pass it.

Because of my choice, the intended attack never came. In the grand scheme of things, I just needed to see their value.

It became clear that what we were going through would be nine gates that corresponded to the nine initiations of man: three in Identity Consciousness, three in God-consciousness and three in Ascended Mastery. They moved through the stages of:

Transformation,
> *yielding Transmutation,*
>> *yielding Transfiguration*

There were, in addition to the testings, tasks required of me that had to be done on behalf of the planet. Gifts that increased my own light were given in exchange and I had to make certain choices pertaining to my destiny.

Hy and the Spirits

Evelyn and Malcolm were sent to do work in England during the summer of 2005.

At one point I could see they needed assistance and requested that the Dragon send one of his dragons to help. He sent a dragon I called Daisy, an elderly dragon with a bad back. But, she found a field of wild poppies in England and ate them, causing her to sleep for a week in an opium-induced sleep.

Embarassed by her conduct, the Dragon sent Hy, who was then his personal assistant. Hy was the second most powerful dragon in the kingdom. He took a fraction of the time it would have taken Daisy and completed everything I had assigned him very successfully.

I complimented him on a job well done and asked him to send Evelyn and Malcolm home. He said he couldn't because they were fatigued and fast asleep.

I couldn't believe my ears. Firstly, human spirits don't sleep—Secondly, Hy had done all the work, so why were they tired?

I asked the two other spirits I worked with to find Evelyn and Malcolm. I became concerned when they couldn't. Suddenly they started laughing and one said, "They're in the dragon world, tucked into a bed side by side, pretending to be asleep!" I spoke to Malcolm and Evelyn and asked what they were doing. "Hy kept insisting we looked tired, even though we tried to tell him we're not. Next we knew, we were here in bed and unable to get up, so we're pretending to sleep so he'll let us go!"

But Hy was not to be fooled; he knew they were pretending and insisted they rest. I finally had to appeal to the Dragon to override Hy, who could be very stubborn, much to Malcolm's and Evelyn's relief.

Hy's stubbornness was fast becoming a legend in the dragon world. After this incident, the Mother Goddess gave him a task to perform. No matter how much the Dragon coerced or threatened him, he refused and hid. Eventually, Mother herself had to intervene. She shook the dragon world with thunder and purple lightning, sending the dragons fleeing for cover, until Hy came out of his hiding place and did as he was told.

The Sirian Demons Capture the Spirits

In April of 2005, as the earth moved into a particular higher realm, there didn't appear to be any occupants within that realm. Unbeknownst to me, 16 beings who had originally come from the Sirian star system, did dwell there but, like the various other kingdoms such as the dragons among us today, those beings preferred to keep themselves hidden. Our entry into their realm was regarded by them as a challenge and a threat.

The first indication that anything was wrong was when Melissa could no longer hear or see any being other than ghosts (a very low frequency) and material life. Soon, even the ghosts could no longer be seen, what followed was a three-week nightmare.

Melissa was seven months pregnant at the time and also had two children aged two and three. She was forced to sit in a chair as unseen hands beat and scratched her. Soon her face was scratched and her belly covered in bruises. At times she was even prevented from responding to the needs of her children. This torture continued even at night.

Though I called for help from the Lords of Amenti, Thoth and others, the shields maintained around my house by the Beautiful One were so thick my calls could not get through. Every attempt made to cast out the tormenters brought double retaliation.

Tom, one of the spirits who had joined our group, could work with computers. Anxiously, each day I awaited word from him, but the only one I knew was safe was the spirit Faye, who was under my shield when the attacks began. The other spirits had indeed been captured and were being held hostage, as we would learn later.

Sarah, with her usual brilliant resourcefulness, found a way to get a message through: my then 5-year-old daughter sat down and pretended to write me a letter. Then she pretended to deliver mail and brought me a letter from 'my friend, Sarah'. Because my daughter is kept strictly away from my work and its intensity, this was startling—she didn't know about Sarah! I asked what the letter said and she pretended to read it. "Don't worry, everything's going to be OK and soon we'll play again." At least that meant the future outcome would be beneficial; how to get there was the problem.

We still didn't know what we were dealing with, but during a brief time of respite, Melissa called to say her youngest daughter could see the attackers. They were huge, with black 'skin' and green eyes. Normally, there were 2-3 of them present at a time.

Not wanting to bring retaliation upon her, I waited. How long could the unborn baby survive this stress? Then after a week, the letters began. Written in gold, they were passed in front of her face. If she tried to look away, the beings would slap her face. The letters were from our alphabet, but the language was incomprehensible to us.

Because of having been given the task by Mother to call the names of the multitudes of angels and lords who played a part at the various gates, I had been given a gift: if I got a 'feel' for a particular language certain names were in, I could hear them.

When a brief opportunity arrived, Melissa was able to copy the words formed by the golden letters and fax them it to me. This resulted in a scratched face again, but now I knew the language and could hear the demons' names and see their names' sigils.

The leader's name had a meaning—something a being in the cosmos receives when it has 'made its mark'. The meaning also had a sigil. With this I was able to send them away, but they kept coming back. Then, their tactics changed and they attacked from a distance. Melissa became so weak she should no longer stand and could barely write. She could not speak at all.

The beings finally spoke, saying they hated our language and wanted us out of their realm. They said they had our seven spirits hostage. This was puzzling. Faye was safe, and other than her, we only had six. Perhaps they had taken some poor spirit by mistake. I demanded the return of the spirits and that Melissa be restored, saying each was needed to produce the 7th gate that would get us out of their territory.

After days of negotiation, they finally agreed to release one spirit a day, but kept backing out of the agreement, trying to re-negotiate and lying. Two dragons were sent to courier the spirits to the safety of the shield. Sarah, whom I had demanded be released first, had warned that they would try and take some of the spirits back on their way. The dragons would serve as protection and prevent this.

The glimpse into the insane minds of these beings was very disturbing. I had to give a show of strength I was far from feeling and negotiate with beings possessing very little logic. They wanted us to leave soon, but made it as difficult as possible. They wanted to demand our departure, but didn't want to communicate in a language we could understand. But one of the biggest shocks was yet to come!

When Tom was captured, he was caring for someone in depression that I had asked him to help. Because he could move physical objects, he had twice had to keep the patient from overdosing on anti-depressants. He did this by hiding the medications in the back of the toilet—something that took him all night.

When the kidnappers came for him, he refused to leave the man he was caring for, so the patient was killed. He died instantly and their power was such that with their minds, they produced a suicide note in his handwriting. Shocked and outraged, our morale sank to a low point. How could beings with no vision be permitted to wield such power?[23] Now it was clear where the seventh spirit had come from. I decided to move us through the gate ahead as rapidly as possible, and to do this we worked through the nights. The instant all seven spirits were under the shield, we moved through.

The next realm was inhabited by unicorns and some other beings we regard as mythical, but they had no ruler. Sarah warned

23 When the Mother of Creation came to earth, she changed this when she decreed that power would equate to perception.

that although the demons were confined within their realm, their influence could reach to the one above. Melissa would become sicker and they also intended to steal a specific intuitive part of the minds of all earth's women on the following Sunday at 11:00 am.

I was scheduled to speak at an expo in Toronto at that exact time. I had to cancel and worked for two days and nights to finally move us through both gates and out of their reach. We had but half an hour to spare before the attack on the women would have taken place. Permission was received from the Old Dragon to move into their realm (then the highest on earth) and once there, we were safe.

How The Sirian Demons Were Confined to Their Realms

The confinement of the Sirian demons had to be complete. Their influence could no longer affect the realms above, nor those below. No being was to enter their realm without Mother's permission.

The demons had escaped from an exploding star or planet 3,000 years ago in the star system of Sirius. There were another 2,400 of them scattered across the galaxy and about 1,200 of what the spirits called a 'cousin species' of demons. They had been planning to have the others join them on earth, a right they had forfeited, however.

Gatekeepers that could match them in power and ferocity had to be assigned to guard their gates. Mother's instruction as to who should guard them came as a complete surprise.

Enemies Become Allies

To understand who it was that had to confine them, we recap the events that occurred during the first week of June 2004[24]. I

24 See *Journey to the Heart of God*, p. 26-32

had just returned from astro-travelling after solving a mystery that had plagued Toltec seers and mystics for more than a million years of oral history. This had enabled me to unlock a cosmic gate, allowing more love and light to flow into the cosmos.

When I returned to the body, I was in poor condition. My breathing was shallow and I could hardly walk. I explained to the group of women who had gathered in my home, what had occurred and the enormity of it left us speechless. We listened to Handel's "Messiah" while attempting to internalize these extraordinary insights. Above the house, the heavens opened and I could see a column of angels descending. They blew on trumpet-like instruments. The frequency raised the earth to the next over-tone.

My condition grew worse by the hour. The cells in my body were on fire and felt as though they would burst with the energy they contained. I was trembling and by early evening, waves of tremendous terror and pain hit me in the solar plexus. To the best of my ability, amidst waves of nausea, I could only make out that the grids around the planet were releasing the fear and anguish that had been programmed into them. I was to become a filter to move it through me and convert it into light, but it wasn't moving through. During the out of body experience, I had stood before a huge gate, guarded by three gatekeepers: one light, one neutral and one dark. The dark one, huge and ominous, had followed me back and I now came under the worst attack I had ever endured.

The beloved sisters stood around my bed, but as the night wore on, I started to seriously doubt whether I would survive. I had long since lost any food I had consumed that day and waves of pain and fear continued to bombard my solar plexus. I felt as if a spike had been driven into my head. Due to the trauma, and initially unbeknownst to us, the fields around my body had been bumped into a distorted configuration. I could feel my life force leaking out. In the early morning hours I asked the sisters to call my friend, an unconscious channel for Melchizedek. Minutes before the phone rang, he awoke to find a dark being entering into his bedroom from the study. He asked where the other two were, instantly aware that there should be three gatekeepers.

In my haze of pain and nausea I had failed to notice the distortion in my body's fields. I was struggling for every breath and was mentally saying goodbye to my children. Through Melchizedek's advice and the insight of one sister, I was able to move the octahedronal fields around my body back into position. This immediately reduced the pain by about 50%. Together the sisters stood around my bed and banished the darkness. I felt the tide turn and knew everything would be fine. I was able to sleep for the remainder of that night, but was unable to teach the next morning. The headaches, where the spike had been driven into my head, lingered for several days and my full strength didn't return for two weeks.

The same gatekeepers that had attacked me were now assigned by the Mother of Creation to guard the Sirian demons. I had to find their names: Tra, the light one, Sla, the neutral one and Blab, the dark one. Blab was so dark that I had to get his name, sigil, meaning and the sigil for his meaning (as I did for the other two) and then immediately forget it[25]. These three had to guard the gate to the realms below the demons. The gatekeeper Hutshumaraet guarded the one to the realms above them. In this way, the very ones that had almost cost me my life had now become allies.

---

25 The name can be freely given here because he has since ceased to exist as the dense levels disappeared.

The Spirits' Hall of Contracts

In June 2005 Mother sent me to the Hall of Contracts that serves as repository for the contracts made between spirits and humans. As one enters through the door, the vast halls contain the following:

- On the right wall, row upon row of boxes have the current contracts of spirits assisting humans;
- The wall straight ahead had all completed contracts;
- The wall to the left had all contracts where spirits harm others on behalf of humans.

My task was to empty the boxes on the left wall, place the contracts in the empty boxes on the wall in front of me, and seal up the entire left wall. No more would spirits harm on behalf of humans.

When a spirit breaks his or her contract, they are incarcerated in a green gel-like substance. In November 2005, Mother proclaimed that all spirits who had been tricked into breaking or making a contract by some sort of self-serving or ill intent, be set free.

Saving the Spirit Sarah

In February 2005, as we started to ascend, the seven lords of Amenti became nine. At the time, it was foreseen that the world banks could, within weeks, completely disappear and the nine, Untanas, Quertas, Chietal, Goyana, Huertal, Semveta, Ardal, Aravetas and Utachion, met with Thoth and Enki to discuss this. They knew that hardship caused by a financial collapse on earth would ripple through the cosmos, since the earth had become the cosmic archetype and wayshower.

This was an historic event, since Mother herself had twice reprimanded them for not lending assistance and support to either my assigned tasks or the kingdoms of the earth in general. But the dissolution of the world's monetary systems was only weeks away and Amenti was on eternal time, which meant that their meeting held in July 2005 would not conclude until January 2006.

Two very concerted weeks were required to get myself into eternal time, which is a very specific assemblage point position, in order to better work with them on finding a solution for what seemed to be imminent financial disaster.

My attempts to communicate with the lords were rebuffed. They did permit Sarah, the spirit who helps me, to listen to their deliberations, but she was not allowed to speak. We got daily updates that seemed to be delivered in slow motion because of the time difference.

From the updates, we learned they had decided that since I was at the top of the pyramid in moving the earth up, I needed the first support and that one gold coin would suffice. Even though not permitted to speak, Sarah interrupted and said that was insulting, considering my tireless work in assisting us to move into higher consciousness. She said they should ask themselves what is the most they could do, rather than what is the least. They were furious with her and made it impossible thereafter for her to be heard. She could hear but not be heard.

Her message did sink in, however, and they elected to create 96 billion dollars, knowing I had a children's foundation that needed money to provide care for homeless children worldwide. They apparently created the funds in gold coins in five containers and designed a large home for me to house the many visitors that would swarm to where the gates of ascension were being opened. These visitors would also come from the inner earth.

The problem was, they were having too much fun planning the house and gardens and the approaching date of financial collapse was fast approaching. I designed an eight-point financial plan to at least salvage currencies and support families around the world.

After two weeks of planning the global financial support, I took the plan down to Amenti for their approval and implementation. I was denied entry and told to leave the plan outside their meeting hall door until they adjourned. According to Sarah, that wouldn't be for months, but she had an alternative plan.

It was daring, but she felt confident she could pull it off. Wearing sparkly purple running shoes, a purple running athletic suit (Sarah is short and almost as broad as she is tall) and wings, she ran around the Amenti hall after gate-crashing their meeting. She delivered a cake from me to Thoth with words that said, "I miss you." Some lords laughed, some fumed, but they couldn't catch her and as she ran she played my voice out of her pocket, explaining why they had to get on our time (spirits and dragons have the ability to keep voice messages to be played later) and hurry up.

Days before the money was supposed to be delivered, I became aware they were trying to send Sarah back into embodiment as punishment for her 'insolence' in gate-crashing the meeting. She was in hiding and I had a very hard time finding a solution since they still refused to speak to me. How could they be so short-sighted? Couldn't they see she was vital to work which benefited everyone? Besides, she wasn't really **my** spirit, but Melissa's— and very dear to her heart.

On Saturday, July 16, 2005, in the Toronto airport on they way home, I received an emergency call from Melissa. The lord overseeing the lords of Amenti wanted to speak to me. I welcomed the opportunity. After all, those lords had been all but worshipped by me for many years and multiple times I had cast out demons in their names, called on them for support and given them my absolute trust and faith.

From the first minute, it was a thoroughly unpleasant experience. He demanded to know why I was shouting at him. Humbly explaining that what he was hearing through Melissa's ears was the airport noise and that I could hardly stand it either. He wasn't much inclined to listen. Speaking forcefully, in no uncertain terms he said how things would have to be. Sarah would have to be punished. She was far too 'cheeky' for 'only a spirit'. Melissa's contract with Sarah was that when Sarah incarnated, Melissa would have to die and become Sarah's spirit. It was time I knew my place and who my 'real' friends were. According to him, I could no longer speak to 'lower class beings' and only occasionally to the dragon that protected me. He wanted me to communicate only with the lords in the Halls of Amenti, else I wouldn't get the 96 billion dollars that was ready to be delivered.

So stunned I could hardly find the words: "I communicate directly with the goddesses in higher realms—the Mothers of Creation." "No, you can't speak to them either." That was the final straw. Something was definitely wrong! Telling him I would consider his words, I terminated the conversation.

Thoughts reeled through my head as I staggered to my seat in the plane. Melissa had three little children. I thought of the precious friendships I had with the elves and fairies in my house and my spirit family. He expected me to sell all this and my integrity for 96 billion dollars? Clearly they could see that whoever controls the gate-keeper controls the cosmos!

I started shaking and sobbing uncontrollably as I reached my seat, not caring about the inquisitive stares of other passengers. With all the power I possessed, I sent the silent plea; "Mother, please help me!" The next moment it felt as though I was knocked out. I collapsed into my seat and against the window. I knew nothing further until I woke about an hour and a half later. I clearly heard the words, "Look in the book." Since I hadn't brought a book on the plane, I didn't understand. The words were repeated until I finally pulled the airline magazine from the seat pocket in front of me. The first article talked about how children don't learn to think when their learning takes place through computers versus books. The words on the page blurred and only one sentence stood out clearly: "The answers unfold slowly throughout the book." Then I knew several answers would be given through the magazine.

Several articles followed about liars. Again words became blurry but sentences were readable. I read; "The actions of liars are unpredictable." "Don't you wish you could read minds?" "All the partying and fun and games were just a jockeying for position." There were many illustrations of people with long Pinocchio-like noses.

Turning the pages, everything blurred except a life insurance advertisement. It showed three women looking down at the earth and smiling confidently. It said, "For every problem, we have a solution ... even if a meteor were to strike the earth. All you have to do is ask." Nothing else in the magazine was readable to me and I sat back in stunned wonderment.

There was a movie about dinosaurs playing on the airplane screens, I saw a sentence flash across the bottom of the screen; "A meteor would strike and the old dinosaurs would make way for the new." Immediately after, I started receiving and whispering names—something that lasted 30 hours with hardly any interruption. I knew they were male lords and angels.

It was not until we reached Denver, however, that I saw the cosmos in a vision as I sat in a deserted waiting area calling the names. The lords and angels were pouring in from another cosmos outside our own, resembling a backwards-facing meteor heading for earth. The names I was calling were calling others who were calling others. The days of the old 'dinosaurs' ruling with power over others were making way for the new.

I contacted the Alumuanu King and he placed a shield around me, my children, my assistants and my students so the lords could not harm or try to speak to us. But he didn't have a solution for the problem concerning Melissa and Sarah. The lords retaliated by tying up Thoth and Enki and holding them hostage.

At lunch in an airport restaurant, still murmuring the names but praying for a solution, I saw a small sign above my table: "All you have to do is ask." After lunch, in the deserted waiting area, I heard: "Explode their fields." I knew what that meant. To move someone into another level of consciousness, the best way to do it is to 'bump' the assemblage point to the position of the new stage. In humans, if an angel holds it there long enough, it will stay; so an angel has to be called to assist in the process.

Sarah was the one who usually gave me directions as I moved the assemblage point for others. Could I now move hers into the third phase of Ascended Mastery and have her find safety within the Ascended Masters' realms? Melissa would have to be moved into Immortal Mastery, the second phase within Ascended Mastery.

But there was an option, a little more risky since some people can feel very ill if forced into the next stage this way, which didn't require the same precision. I decided to proceed and explode their fields[26] one after the other until they were in the required stages. Then I asked two angels to escort Sarah to the Ascended Masters' realms. I knew I was successful when her cheery voice rang loudly in my head, "Far out!"

They were safe. Mother had outwitted the lords. The incoming

---

26 Refer to Evolutionary Stages of Man in the chapter Realms of the Gods later in this book.

lords were tying up all lords lacking in impeccability and, for a change, they had to learn 'their place'! For the next month and a half, I had to call in more and more lords. As they poured out of the cosmoses, the walls or membranes between us came down and we assimilated those cosmoses. Their Mothers of Creation descended to earth and became one with our Mother of All.

Then came the news from Mother that 64 lords were on their way to Amenti. Our lords were too furious to notice. The 64 were instructed to tie up the lords of Amenti and display to them every instance of disrespect they had shown to the goddesses. They also had to release Thoth and Enki.

The 64 lords were also to connect the lords of Amenti to the higher grid of consciousness which would, within a week, cause them to be the lords with the highest consciousness of our original cosmos—well above the original lord that had been over them before. At the end of that week, Mother sent me to release them while she delivered a speech of mercy, love and forgiveness. She proclaimed them to no longer be the lords governing just the various levels of light for the earth, but for the cosmos. *(See Fig. 40, Additional Lords of Light Who came to Earth During its Ascension)* They would always have the same consciousness as the highest lords entering the cosmos.

As they spread their higher consciousness to all other lords, most were able to be untied after several weeks. But it was not until Mother repaired the damage that had occurred to the masculine grid that, all males were given the opportunity to live at a higher level.[27]

---

27 See Repairing the Masculine Grid in Part VII, Realms of the God-kingdoms.

Additional Lords of Light
Who Came to Earth During Its Ascension

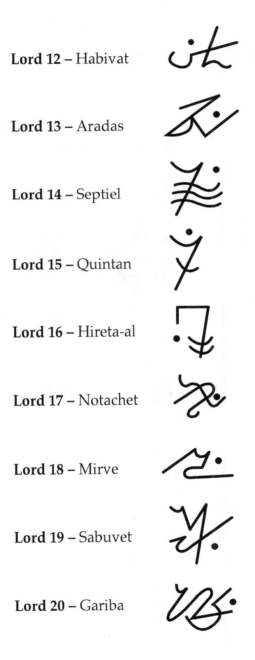

Lord 12 – Habivat

Lord 13 – Aradas

Lord 14 – Septiel

Lord 15 – Quintan

Lord 16 – Hireta-al

Lord 17 – Notachet

Lord 18 – Mirve

Lord 19 – Sabuvet

Lord 20 – Gariba

(Figure 40)

PART SIX

The Angelic Realms

A Rare Insight into the Angelic Realms

Although there is so much to know about these beautiful beings of light who work by our side to promote the smooth unfolding of the evolution of awareness, a glimpse into their realms is rare.

They are much expanded, as someone very right-brain oriented would be. Therefore they aren't particularly good with instant analysis and decisions.

I contacted the Archangel Mi concerning a problem with a small group of the fairies. Mi is over all devas and fairies of any kind. I told him what the problem was and asked him to propose a solution.

After a long silence, he said: "How do you do that?" I asked what he meant. "How do you power think the way you do?"

I explained humans were the problem solvers of the cosmos, according to what my star-brothers had told me. In fact, they had said that two earth children wanting the same toy did better than most elders in other star-races in settling disputes.

I could see I had put Mi on the spot and offered to come back the next day. But this continued for four days, at which point he apologized for not being able to think more quickly. I told him that if he did think the way humans do, he wouldn't be expanded enough to feel the well-being of all the trillions of creatures under his care. One forfeits 'power thinking' for the sake of expansion.

I proposed a solution. He told me which part didn't feel quite right. I agreed, amended it and, having reached a consensus, he implemented it.

Angels often travel in pairs or in even-numbered groups. If they are personally assigned to a human, they may travel alone alongside their human.

They get married and procreate, except there is no pregnancy because the baby immediately follows.

Seraphim are six-winged, adult angels. Cherubim have four wings and are infant angels.

Angelic Language

Since the recent rise in frequency within the cosmos, some of the angel words and letters have changed. They have no past or future tense. They say, "The only time is now." They also do not conjugate verbs and their words have no genders.

As in many of the other languages of beings from the hidden realms, words change depending on the frequency and emotion and on how the sentence is phrased. They do not use first person as they are very much in group consciousness and have no ego-identification.

Angel Vocabulary

And	Sor
Blessing	Am
Child	Chinanum
Education	Eslu
Forgiveness	Sweteeres
Healing	Torisuramitu
Love	Tulla
Miracle	Maphirina

Mother	Ahdannah
Music	Samammuet
Peace	Ala
Pray	Sforret
Truth	Minasar

Colors

It is difficult for them to see colors. Colors are originally seen as white light. They have to create a special focus to see the separation of light, which is color.

Blue	Lighteah
Green	Lightsalug
Orange	Lighteia
Pink	Lightsines
Purple	Lightsih
Red	Lighters
Violet	Lightserut
White	Lightx
Yellow	Lightbirma

Cherunimvael And Iunimubach

I had asked for two angels to assist me with very specific tasks. I requested one who could heal and one who could move physical objects. In response, the Mother Goddess sent me one male angel called Chirunimvael and one female one called Iunimubach. They arrived together and I put them straight to work.

Chirunimvael had been in seclusion for a long time. His overseer was the only other being with whom he had had contact. She was another angel called Siltcheebrechpauraret. His previous task under this overseer had been to move rocks from one place to another. He missed his overseer very much and separation from

255

her had not exactly created enthusiasm for his new assignment. She had been re-assigned to work on another planet and he wasn't able to see her for the foreseeable future.

Iunimubach was sent to Washington, D.C. to create a hand for a sister who had lost hers. She told me it would take 14 days. Working with angels doing healing on my behalf was new and I waited with eager anticipation for the results.

I tried to talk to her during her work, but she refused to answer. Work with both angels went slowly; after all, they slept for half the day. Because the two of them had arrived together, they seemed to have synchronized their minds. When one slept, so did the other.

The first time I realized that angels only affect the etheric and that as long as we still believe the deficiency exists it would, was when Iunimubach announced that her job was complete. All the spirits I work with went to look and affirmed that a brand new hand had been formed. But unfortunately, believing the hand to be gone, no one in the physical could see it.

I asked her to immediately heal a student's cancer. The situation was critical. Her journey there should have taken a matter of minutes, as angels travel very quickly. I was astonished five days later when she still wasn't there and I asked her what the problem was. Her response was, "The angel with the pretty colors in the box told me to take time to smell the roses along the way." Finally, after some initial confusion, I discovered she had been watching Dr. Phil on television at the house where she had been. When I explained about the commercial and the often harmful effects of television, she said, "Oh, that's so sad! He had such pretty colors!"

Meantime, Chirunimvael was behaving very strangely. Sometimes he would be loving and respectful, and at other times I sensed malevolence and he would be disrespectful. Other oddities kept telling me something was not as it seemed.

He went to sleep one day and disappeared. The spirits found him in China—he had no idea how he'd gotten there. Objects started disappearing around the house and even the elves had no inkling how this could be happening. Chirunimvael seemed to often 'misunderstand' instructions and do the exact opposite, at times undoing the work some of the other beings had done to assist me.

In fact, two elf brothers known as Shuugbrtl and Spirbavafekernet got so furious with his undoing their work that they came to me and asked, "We are so worried. Please tell us, is there severe karma for yelling and being furious at an angel?"

At one point when Chirunimvael 'shut down' in the middle of my asking him many questions, I called in the Archangel Michael. I was very concerned. It was as though Chirunimvael was unconscious. My house-elf, Eoptika, couldn't shed light on what had happened, but just kept shaking his head and repeating, "Shocking! Shocking!"

When Michael arrived he explained, as had Archangel Mi, that angels don't handle intellectual pressure well. Chirunimvael had undergone some sort of breakdown and would remain in that state for a few days. I felt very remorseful for pushing him beyond his limits and apologized to him when he awoke.

The real insights into Chirunimvael came when he fearfully and hysterically refused to move when the cosmos went into a large shift, causing a 'big bang' effect. The cosmic movement would last for weeks. I pointed out that other angels and spirits were moving, but he wouldn't budge.

I asked for his previous overseer to come. It took her two days, but when she arrived, she said, "He's only half an angel, you know. He isn't aware of it, but he's also half grim." I asked what that meant. "A grim is a type of fairy creature that plays malevolent pranks on others. He changes from one to another without warning and the one half doesn't remember what the other half does." I asked her to take him with her after she explained that all the missing objects would be found in the ceiling.

I certainly didn't miss Cherunimvael and his pranks, but I did miss his beautiful singing voice. When Mother gave me instructions to honor Lord Horlet with a banquet that included the Lords of Amenti, I asked if Chirunimvael could return to sing for him. I mistakenly thought, "How much trouble can he cause just singing?"

Mother had given the gift of the ability to taste to the lords. At the banquet they would taste food for the very first time. Granushimparfetrabruskara, the cooking angel, prepared the feast. Chirunimvael sang beautifully. But afterwards he set the cooking angel on fire and that was the last time we interacted.

I wondered why Mother had sent such a strange gift (besides the fact that he was really the best at moving objects). As usual, she was trying to teach me something. Chirunimvael represented the insanity of a split mind. In my own life I found what this mirrored. I was still living the insanity of believing form to be real. She now wanted me to move beyond that and had tricked me into not taking things at face value. Even an angel was not always what he seemed.

The Angels Who Guard The Wise Ones

There is a very large gap between manifested life and the etheric realms. This gap has prevented too much interference from beings in the hidden realms. Consequently, finding any advanced beings that can manifest physical objects into the material realms is rare indeed. For example, the hand Inunimubach created did not physically materialize.

The ability to materialize with thought is not necessarily rare in higher realms; only the ability to manifest within material life. The dragons manifest their needs with thought, as do the beings in the star system of Antares. Spirits within the human spirit realms can do so also under certain circumstances.

There exists a race that can manifest matter from the ether, however, but they are very elusive and unknown to almost all other races. One of the reasons they are so hard to reach is that very few beings speak their language, which sounds as though they are snoring. In fact, the beings I consulted about them (a spirit, a dragon and the archangel Michael) didn't know what to call their race.

In appearance they are spherical, with an orange glow and little protrusions that resemble two cat ears. There are only 24 angels who can speak their language and I had to be able to get their names in order to request that they serve as go-betweens. This was not as easy as I had thought, since the names were in a language I had never encountered before.

When I finally had all 24 angel names, I tried to speak to one of them. To my surprise, I was rudely rebuffed. Having only encountered love and gentleness (with the understandable exception of Chiruminvael) among angels, I didn't know what to do.

"We don't speak to humans. We don't like them." I tried to invite them to look at my intent but the one to whom I was speaking wouldn't even continue the conversation. I clearly wasn't going to get help and retreated.

I called on Archangel Michael, explained the situation and asked for help. He said they lived in virtual isolation from other angels and didn't know how important man had become in the cosmic ascension. In fact, they didn't even know about the ascension.

I couldn't understand at first how angels, the epitome of inclusiveness, could be exclusive. The way it must have occurred is that they had over-focused on a task; namely, the protection of the beings they guarded. Inclusiveness and expansiveness came from alternating doingness with beingness. Over-focusing on activity produces the opposite. It then became clear to me that in every kingdom and realm, groups of beings represented the polar extremes. These angels represented the masculine, positive pole of the angelic kingdom.

Michael went to speak to them. It took many hours before they saw the bigger picture. He then returned to say they could now see the scope of the ascension and the role I was playing. They were prepared to talk to me.

I again approached one with the most pronounceable name (Huuvaumi) and asked if he would translate. "You won't hurt them, will you?" I invited him to look at my heart and see my intent. "Yes, I can see. They hurt very easily. Don't speak too loudly." I asked what to call them, but he made the sound of a snore. I told him I couldn't pronounce it and would call them the Wise Ones.

When we finally spoke, I said I had heard they can manifest matter and asked if they would help humanity. They said they would and asked what I wanted them to manifest. I explained that millions in Africa would die because of a devastating drought that the rain spirit was working to alleviate, but the crops would not come in time. I asked for corn and maize to be manifested to citizens, but not to possibly corrupt leaders. They agreed that it should go to 'the little people'.

I asked if they wanted to work from my sacred home, but they replied, "To be around humans long is fatal to us; we will send one of us at a time." I asked if they had any further questions. "Yes, what is it like to have hair?" After recovering from my surprise, I explained the wonderful feeling of having the wind in one's hair.

As the conversation closed, they said, "We are friends."

According to the spirits, their contribution will alleviate the famine to a very large extent. I believe the miracles they will do will also bring hope to hearts that have suffered much. These little known beings, the Wise Ones, are the sages of this universe. Their interaction with our planet can produce only blessings.

Angels And Their Functions

Animals (healing)

Glunechspirparvakruegnichspara (masculine)

Cooking

Granushimparfetrabruskara (feminine)

Creation of Lifeforms and Bodies

Varumpreugbarskla

Bavarishpleugsparut

Meugbrauvartel

Spiiranechhefbipartum

Launishbreurstika

Veulemechhaberfatskarut

Heshbiplatelurfrabanuksertum

Geifrachbaneksaurlaem

Lanabarukbrenuminapreg

Pirshratumvrsklaursparugnartet

Klienughefirbitpaersk

Creation of Planets

Elsamir

Fairy/Devic Kingdoms

Mi

He is the angel of all fairies and devas in the entire cosmos.

Hair

Braufparasushibavetguhur

Expect physical results in 3 to 4 months. She is a very sparkling, exotic, vivacious angel. She doesn't grow hair that has fallen out.

Happiness

Kupendiberspruberklvethetuabach

He says you will feel him give kisses.

Hormones

Schatlba

Merkaba Angel

Arahib

He also works with planetary fields

Moon Portal's Gatekeeper

Kayashmatetsetaeamaat

Peace

Chvtu (feminine) *Her color is a shimmering peach.*

Speaking to the Wise Ones (partial list)

Aaooi

Uoomiia

Anuia

Umiinaooh

Eoohuauhahey

Ohauhaem

Leviauhem

Eeblish

Oooshvmn

Lu-uaesh

Strengthening Faith

Barunuelpriferblaupreshpa

Sisherbachhuvrepletaramumvranuch

Oimerbaplahutsplatlnavartek

Kravaumspiratelbartvuchplahem

Irufbarplasunachetelharup

Efelplaviingbershklarahupplael

Viiaumaeulhipelvraniorskklavavrumachelbi

Ulafperechparblisitrafulvaek

Nunavitpeleprapaklanukvarichspelanur

Kiteldompritlvatreunirspevaharupesh

Synchronizing Our Lives Through Inner Transformation

Harabaipshvael (masculine)

I am aware of an additional 896 angels within this group.

Time

Baraupshlalamirvabeturbatabael (masculine)

This name will change when the whole earth and cosmos go fully into eternal time.

Treating Each Other Kindly

Eskaravachparlapleteshkarvaurepprotem (feminine)

Husuubichnaryamishetvurabaa (masculine)

This pair says they are 'husband and wife' and work together.

To Help With Bugs in the House

Esskrubavakklefbiheshpata

To Aid Mental Clarity

Situravekpluashbachnutranamitsautvaulplavasitanadochkresh-Biuvater

Healing of Feminine Organs

Liersbrisatrunekhistramelkrusbinichvartekiulef

Healing of the Spine

Michtramelurvasinklefbitrumanot

Those Who Help With Transfiguring Experiences:

To be on the right

Spilurgarnetkrevathupshpaklurmispa

To be on the left

Glanugshketlbitrevapaulip

(See Fig. 41a, b,c, Angel Sigils)

(Figure 41a)

Angel Sigils

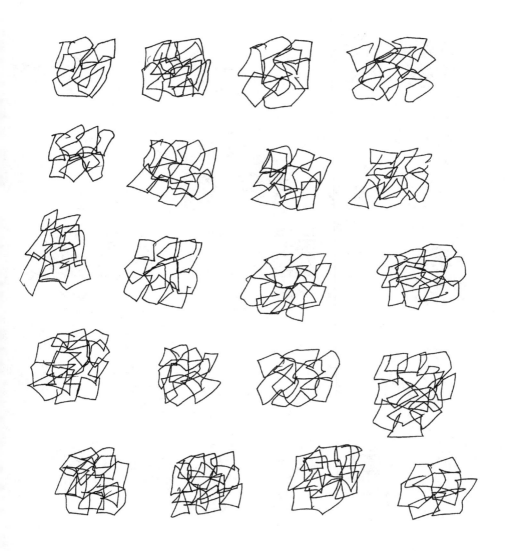

(Figure 41b)

(Figure 41c)

PART SEVEN

The Realms of the God–Kingdoms

Transfiguring into a God-Being in the Flesh

The evolution of a human being into the stage that lies beyond humanness, that of a god-being that can come and go throughout the cosmos with the speed of thought, follows three distinct stages. Each stage has within it three separate phases. This brings the total number of phases to nine through which a human being can evolve.

An initiation is a test of skill, impeccability, knowledge and often one's relationship with other life forms. It not only tests the worthiness of the truth seeker to move from one rung of advancement to another, but through the testing provides him or her with the chance to fill any gaps of perception necessary for the next phase. *(See Fig. 42, The Sacred Sothic Triangle)*

In the Egyptian and Atlantean initiations, the last stage, with its three phases, was guarded by the two Lords of the Two Horizons, also known as the two Lords of the Three Gates. The initiatory process was represented by the symbol in *(Fig. 42)*. The smaller triangle represented the triangulated view of Sirius rising above the horizon as seen from the bottom of the pyramid. However, as the nine rungs were completed, the Lords of the Two Horizons would bring the Ascended Master to the top of the pyramid. From

The Sacred Sothic Triangle

Representing the nine phases of human evolution.

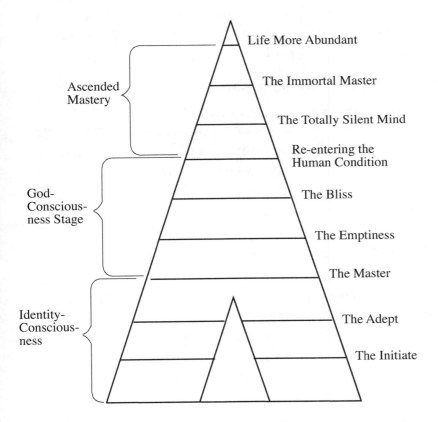

The Sothic triangle has a 4 to 9 proportion and is also the ancient hieroglyph for Sirius. It represents the secret that the last three gates or phases within Ascended Mastery, presided over by the two Lords of the Two Horizons. The two triangles represent the view as seen by someone at the base of the pyramid (Identity Consciousness) and at the top of the pyramid (Ascended Mastery) of Sirius's rising above the horizon.

(Figure 42)

there the horizon and Sirius's rising would be further away. This would create a larger triangle. The master would have completed all nine phases of his human evolution. The two triangles represent the change in perception between the phase of the Initiate and the Ascended Master. It illustrates how much vision will expand, and how much more of the unknown can be accessed as a master.

Stage 1. Identity-Consciousness
(See Fig. 43, Seven Bodies of Man in God Consciousness)

This stage is like the bottom of the pyramid in that many enter this stage, but far fewer make it through. The three phases of this stage are all lived while in ego-identification, that state of beingness that sees ourselves as separate from others and identifies with the body and surface mind (the ego).

Phase 1.—The Initiate

Type of Change: Transformation. Transformation is the stage within change that discards that which is no longer needed. The truth seeker dies to the old way of being. *(See Fig. 51)*

Testing: Fear. To have all belief systems, identities and worldviews eradicated leaves one without the comfort of shelters or a frame of reference and creates fear.

Changes: The seals of debris in the chakras start to burst open, causing at times physical distress in their areas. The chakras become spherical, instead of resembling a cone to the front and a cone to the back with the narrow ends meeting in the middle. *(See Figs. 44, 45, 46, Opening the Chakras)*

Challenges: The Initiate has to learn not to take anything at face value, but to cultivate the necessary humility that will remind him for the rest of his journey that all he can know for certain is that he doesn't know.

Seven Bodies of Man in God Consciousness

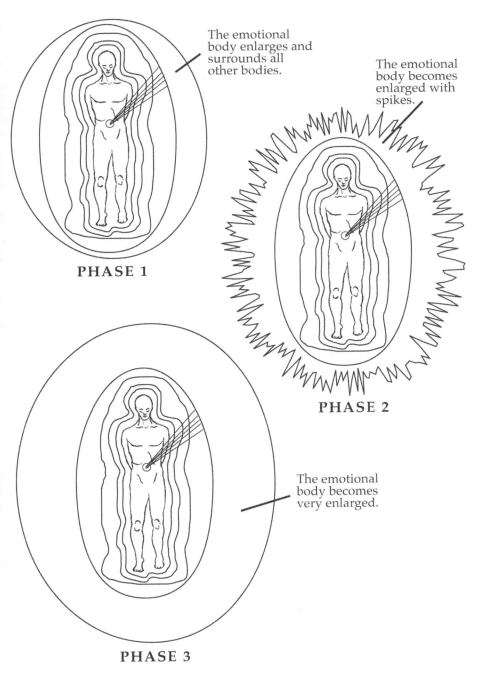

The emotional body enlarges and surrounds all other bodies.

PHASE 1

The emotional body becomes enlarged with spikes.

PHASE 2

The emotional body becomes very enlarged.

PHASE 3

(Figure 43)

Phase I of Chakra Opening

Chakras receive
from the front ⟶
and back

Mental and
physical debris
blocks the center
of the chakras

The pranic
tube is blocked
by the chakras'
debris

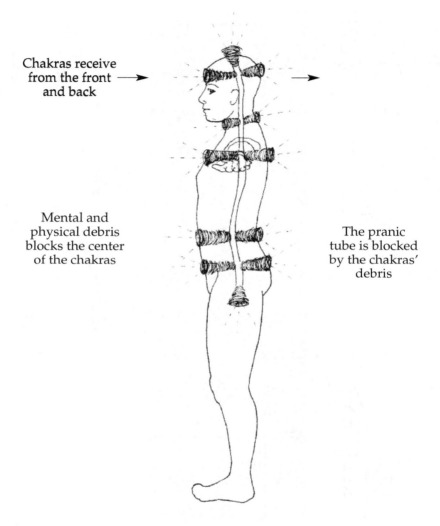

Seven levels of light enter the chakras. The light cannot immediately download into the endocrine system because of the blockages of a person who hasn't overcome the past and holds on to that which no longer serves him. The light is assimilated during sleep.

(Figure 44)

Phase II of Chakra Opening

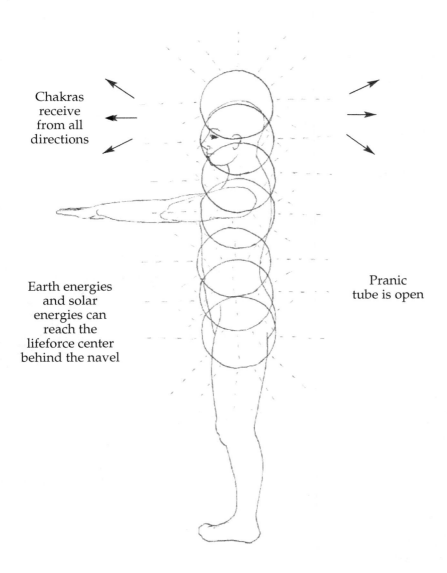

Chakras receive from all directions

Earth energies and solar energies can reach the lifeforce center behind the navel

Pranic tube is open

Less sleep is needed while the endocrine system downloads the seven levels of light. Light is felt as non-cognitive information

(Figure 45)

Phase III of Chakra Opening

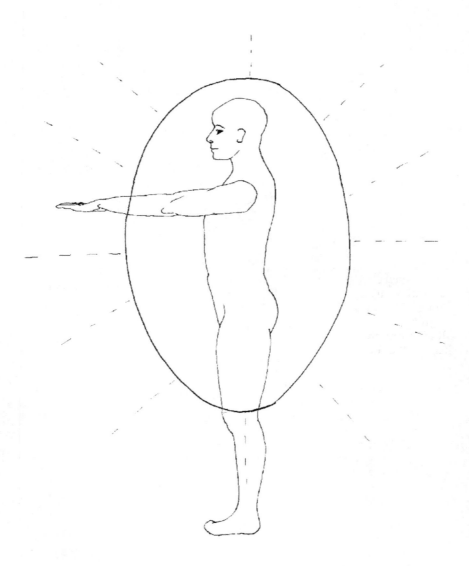

The chakra spheres have opened into a unified chakra field.
The mental body no longer blocks access to light from the higher bodies.

(Figure 46)

Phase 2. The Adept

Type of Change: Transmutation.[28] During transmutation something of a lower frequency is changed into another substance of a higher frequency, much like the alchemist changing lead to gold. In this instance, challenge is transmuted to insight.

Testing: Addiction. Every stage's second phase has the testing of addiction. In this phase, the adept learns how to turn challenges into power by seeing behind the appearances of 'problems'. This results in power surges that create endocrine releases of hormones that can be very addictive. The adept can become addicted to challenge.

Changes: As the adept learns to cooperate with the challenges of life, every challenge becomes a source of power and energy; this causes the spherical chakras to become enlarged and overlap each other more and more.

Challenge: The adept can take himself too seriously at this point and so divert his attention from chasing challenges to balancing the sub-personalities. It is essential to become emotionally self-reliant at this point by bringing balance and expression to our inner family. If we neglect this, it is unlikely that we will pass the testing of power presented during the next phase.

Phase 3. The Master

Type of Change: Transfiguration. The third phase of every stage tests us with power. Because it is seeing whether we are worthy of the major evolutionary leap that occurs during transition from stage to stage, its testing is severe. Passing the test produces transfiguration of either the fields of the body or the body itself.

28 See *Journey to the Heart of God*, Part II, The Anatomy of Change

Testing: Power. The master's abilities become quite apparent at this point, bringing praise and in some instances, worship from others. The feeling of power can produce a sense of gratification that can divert the master from being a perception seeker to becoming a power seeker, in which case he cannot proceed any further on the path.

Changes: Not only is power the result of bringing order to the mind, but also of the chakra spheres growing so enlarged that they form one large unified chakra field around the body. A heartache, an orgasm or the opening of the crown chakra by a peak spiritual experience, is felt throughout the body.

Challenge: At the very moment that our egos want to assert themselves, we must not waver for an instant from reaching beyond the allure of the magical world of the unknown to the far distant horizon of the unknowable. Resisting the temptations to do miracles for show, we must keep our goal of increased perception firmly in mind. Not many truth seekers make it beyond this point.

Stage 2. God-Consciousness

The previous stage believed the character we play on the stage of life to be real. This stage no longer identifies with the character. In fact, during the first two phases we walk off the stage of life only to return for the third phase. But even as we again stay in character, we know without a doubt that we are just enacting a role.

Phase 1. Emptiness

Type of Change: Transformation. Everything we thought we knew gets thrown out of the window. All we know is that we are no-thing. The usual emotions are gone, from the dramatic shift in perception as our minds become empty. Nothing in our lives makes sense anymore and a great dis-associativeness is felt.

Testing: Fear. Although the testing in the first phase of every stage is fear, most ordinary, everyday fears were overcome during the previous stage. Now the very foundation upon which we have stood has been knocked out from underneath us. Not only do we at times feel terrified, but a vast loneliness grips us. We feel afraid when expanding too much, fearing we may lose our self-awareness just as we have lost our identities and that our responsibilities won't be properly done. However, something larger is running our lives and everything gets done without much forethought. We feel claustrophobic when we contract our awareness back into the body.

Changes: The changes that take place during this entire stage affect the emotional body. During this phase, the emotional body forms a large round ball, slightly larger than the luminous cocoon formed by the seven bodies of man under usual circumstances.

Challenge: If enough fear is present, one can step out of God-consciousness and, because one didn't stay in long enough to enjoy the more blissful states that come later, be hesitant to try it again. This could then keep us locked into Identity-Consciousness. It is helpful to have someone ahead on the path be able to say that the disassociativeness one is experiencing is appropriate to this rather bewildering phase.

Phase 2. The Bliss

Type of Change: Transmutation. The realization that it isn't that we are no-thing, it's that we are all things and we transmute the feeling of complete emptiness to the fullness of bliss. We feel everything as though it is inside us.

Testing: Addiction. The test is a difficult one, not only because of its intense addictive quality, but because most traditions teach that this is the end goal of the spiritual seeker's path. The years of disciplined living have to somehow penetrate the euphoria and remind us that there is no point of arrival.

Changes: A strange phenomenon now takes place in the emotional field, reducing the physical energy, while creating a vastness of emotion. It is as though the desire of the cosmos has become one's own. The emotional body forms rope-like spikes radiating out from the physical body. When I first observed this in my own field, I thought that the shock of encountering the Infinite's vastness had shredded my emotional body. Only later did I realize that it was an appropriate part of the bliss phase.

Challenge: There is very little growth during the first two phases of God-consciousness when one essentially walks off the stage of life. The master has no boundaries and is in a very vulnerable state. But because others around him are allowed to misbehave as they choose, they aren't growing either. The great challenge of this phase is to remember that there is value to the play; that it was designed that all may grow. The master has to re-enter the human drama while remembering it's just a play.

Phase 3. Re-Entering the Human Condition

Type of Change: Transfiguration. The emotional body now expands itself to twice its former size, completely transfiguring the size of the body's luminous cocoon.

Testing: As with all third phases, the testing concerns the impeccable use of power. The master has the ability to manifest whatever he or she wants to, but having spent many years gathering such power, must now forgo using it in most instances in favor of cooperating fully with life.

Changes: The changes that occur during this phase create intense emotion. But even as the renewed emotions again churn the surface of the master's life, the vast stillness of expanded awareness lies beneath.

Challenge: The tremendous power that is part of the master's life at this point demands the utmost respect and sensitivity for all lifeforms. It also requires the mater's full cooperation in order to become a tool in providing learning opportunities for others. In other words, the master becomes a steward of all life.

Stage 3. Ascended Mastery

The three stages themselves follow the roadmap of all change: Transformation, Transmutation, Transfiguration. The stage of **Identity-consciousness** is in essence transformational in that it is the shedding of that which no longer serves, namely the ego.

The **God-consciousness stage** is transmutational in that it turns a form of awareness that learns very little from experience, into a combination that does.[29] In its third phase, the master observes his experiences from an eternal perspective while again enacting the human drama—it feels a lot like thinking with two minds at once.

The **Ascended Mastery stage** transfigures not only the fields of the body, as do the other two stages, but also the physical body itself. To transfigure something that dense is a tremendous accomplishment and the primary function of this stage is transfiguration.

Phase 1. The Totally Silent Mind

Type of Change: Transformational. Previous God-consciousness phases had silence within the mind during any time the master did not have to relate or act. Now, even this

29 Refer to the Third Awareness, p. 62 in *Journey to the Heart of God.*

280

form of inner dialog is discarded. Interaction, writing, speaking is done from a place of complete silence as though being on 'auto-pilot'. The silence is only broken occasionally to do something deductive.

Testing: Fear. It takes a lot of trust to have your mouth speak that which you didn't first think of. If anything is done from a place of old, obsolete programming, everything starts to spin. One is physically incapable of doing something that isn't meant to be. The overall fear is that life is completely out of control and it is—out of the control of the egoic self. But the vast cosmic mind governs our lives at this point.

Changes: Because of the transfigurative qualities of this entire stage, every phase has very dramatic changes, all of them pertaining to the mental or linear bodies of man. In this phase the mental body implodes into a pinpoint of light, pulling the emotional body with it. It then explodes and fuses with the etheric body. The emotional body becomes smaller and denser. *(See Fig. 47, The Seven Bodies of Man in Ascended Mastery)*

Challenge: The vestiges of a desire for a personal life have to be laid aside at this point. The master can and must make sure that his life has joy and balance in it. His life affects too much to have it be anything less. But his life's work is pre-determined by his contract with the Infinite. To a certain extent, he can determine how he wishes the work to unfold, but he cannot deviate from his purpose. He cannot allow the total inner silence to seduce him into inaction.

Phase 2. Immortality

Type of Change: Transmutation. This is the incredible phase in which mortal matter is transmuted into immortal matter—'lead is turned into gold'. The whole event takes but minutes to

The Seven Bodies of Man in Ascended Mastery

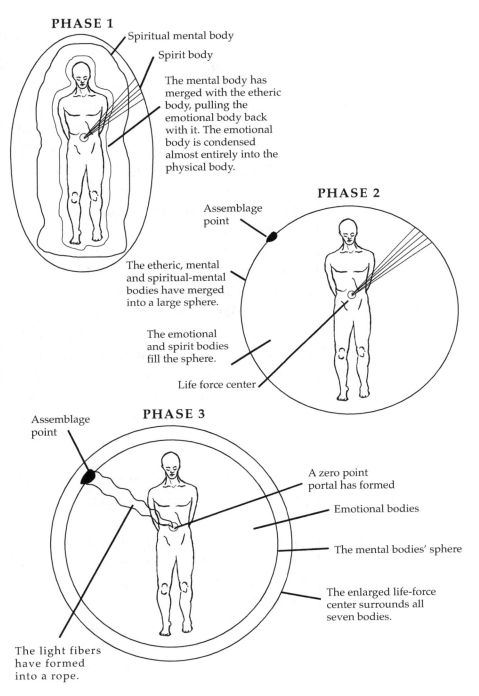

PHASE 1

Spiritual mental body

Spirit body

The mental body has merged with the etheric body, pulling the emotional body back with it. The emotional body is condensed almost entirely into the physical body.

PHASE 2

Assemblage point

The etheric, mental and spiritual-mental bodies have merged into a large sphere.

The emotional and spirit bodies fill the sphere.

Life force center

PHASE 3

Assemblage point

A zero point portal has formed

Emotional bodies

The mental bodies' sphere

The enlarged life-force center surrounds all seven bodies.

The light fibers have formed into a rope.

(Figure 47)

complete and feels like a lightning flash throughout the body.

Testing: The bliss that follows this transmutation far exceeds what was experienced before. Within the body of the Immortal Master, the energy lines zig-zag through the areas where the chakras used to be localized. *(See Fig. 48, Hormonal Excretions that Hold the Higher Bliss)* In women, they criss-cross from side to side and in men from front to back. They end in the area above the pineal gland, about four inches apart, and excrete a substance that is the hormone for this level of bliss (also called the life hormone). It can be tasted as a sweet substance in the back of the palate during intense bliss. Once again, addiction becomes the challenge.

Changes: The Immortal Mastery phase culminates in yet another spectacular alteration in the bodies of man. The spiritual mental body implodes to a pinprick of light and when it explodes, merges with the combined mental/etheric bodies and carries them outward, forming a large sphere around the body. The emotional bodies fill the sphere and the spirit body's light-fibers radiate out from the life-force center through the sphere.

Challenge: The unseen realms present an alluring detour during the third phase of Identity-consciousness. Yet, now they become a way of life. They are no longer seen by the master to be outside himself, so no longer present an enticement in the former way. But beings from the various unseen kingdoms we dwell amongst are attracted to the master's light and enter his life. The master has to learn to know the many different idiosyncrasies of dealing with the various beings around him so that he can further refine his ability to benefit all life. This helps him resist the temptation of inactivity induced by bliss.

Hormonal Excretions that Hold the Higher Bliss

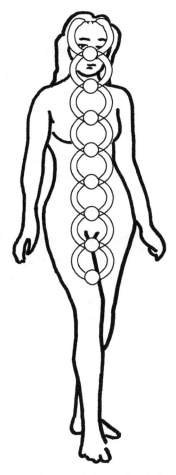

*In the Immortal Master the alpha chakra (a hand length below
the spine) and the second heart (on the sternum) are fully opened.
The energy meridians move (sideways in women, front to back
in men) through the centers where the chakras used to be before they
formed a unified chakra field. The meridians end slightly above the
pineal gland causing it to excrete life hormones for
heightened bliss and immortality.*

(Figure 48)

Phase 3. Life More Abundant

Type of Change. Transfiguration. The change that occurs with this transfiguration is the apex of human achievement; it creates an evolutionary leap that only 9 Ascended Masters had made up until August 2005. When fully transfigured, the master exits the human kingdom and enters the God-Kingdom.

Changes: The life-force center explodes during this phase, forming a large ball of life-force, slightly larger than the sphere of mental bodies. The spirit body's light fibers cluster into one rope extending from the assemblage point behind the shoulder blades, to the zero point portal that has formed behind the belly-button.

Testing: We can surmise by looking at the third phases of the previous two stages that this stage's third phase also has something to do with power. The challenge here is to accumulate, harness and conserve enough power to shatter the glass-like shield that separates kingdoms. The master has to overcome the huge temptation of over-polarizing into the light; into the seasonless place of no emotion and great peace—the place of ultimate stagnation and inaction.

Challenge: Ascended Masters have great perception. The greater our perception, the greater our emotions have to be. When emotions aren't recognized and utilized as the growth mechanisms they are, these very large emotions can be deliberately disconnected in order to experience the peace of the bliss that plays through every cell at this point. But, it is the power of emotion that will crack the 'glass' shield the master has to go through to get to the next kingdom. All chakras must be participating in creating this emotional response. Most Ascended Masters live only in the upper chakras. It becomes necessary to re-awaken the lower chakras, re-activate the sex drive and use it to arouse the other emotions. With the power of emotion, the shield shatters, the zero point opening explodes to fill all the fields. The fields around the body explode to double their size. The chord of light fibers now elongates and loops from the assemblage point on the outside edge of the fields to the heart center and back again to the assemblage point. The master has become a god-being in the flesh. *(See Fig. 49, Within the God-Kingdom)*

The God-Kingdom—Future Destiny Of Man

A large leap of consciousness awaits man if he wishes to go beyond human boundaries. As we have seen, only 9 made it across this boundary before 2005.

Unlike the 3 stages within the human kingdom, the God-Kingdom has two levels. It is essential that more and more humans enter the God-kingdom, as did Christ, Buddha, Krishna, Quan Yin and Sunat Kumara among others, because it is their destiny to change the inactivity found there. Humans are accustomed to struggle, and a great struggle awaits in the God-Kingdom to avoid succumbing to the inactivity and lack of growth in that realm. The struggle is against the huge enticement of bliss. Although we encounter bliss as a testing within the human stages, the bliss of this higher stage is eight times stronger. It becomes difficult to move even a limb and activity tends to slow almost to a standstill.

During the first phase of the God-Kingdom, the fields around the body are very enlarged. The small zero point opening found behind the belly-button of an Ascended Master explodes as the transition to the God-Kingdom is made. The zero point enlarges to fill the entire mental body, pushing the emotional body outside of

Within the God-Kingdom

To leave the human kingdom and enter the God-Kingdom
the body's fields transfigure as shown.

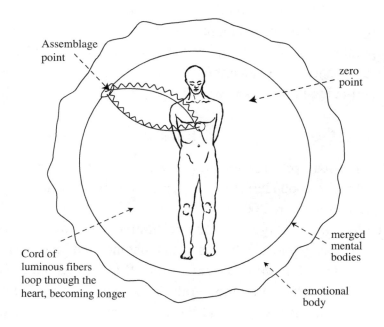

(Figure 49)

the mental body.

The mental body (the sum total of all the mental bodies initially found in man, fused into one) starts to rotate. *(See Fig. 47)*. The chord of light fibers loops from the assemblage point through the heart and back again. During this phase emotions are felt much more intensely.

One of the main reasons the vast majority of Ascended Masters never enter here is because it requires pulsing the emotions (See following sections on Emotion and Sexuality) between their positive and negative poles, fueled by sexuality, to break the glass-like membrane between the kingdoms—something shunned by Ascended Masters until recently.

The second phase of the God-Kingdom is precipitated by yet another zero point explosion that pushes the mental body outside of the emotional body. The end result is a thin emotional body just inside the mental body, while the rest of the space is filled with the zero point. The clockwise and counter-clockwise movements of the mental body no longer make 360 degree rotations, but flip back and forth with just partial rotations. The chord of light fibers has to elongate to reach in a loop from the heart to the assemblage point on the enlarged mental body. Emotions dramatically diminish.

Gods have not reproduced themselves. Then on September 16, 2005, the god that is known as number 3 of the Alumuanu king's court, fathered twins. This was an event of such magnitude that it shot our cosmos up 38 levels, birthing twin rings of suns and planets around the outer rim of our cosmos. It also enabled gods to reproduce and catapulted our cosmos into the second phase of its equivalent of the God-Kingdom.

Another cosmos in its God-Kingdom entered us 12 days later, once again fathering rings of suns and representing the mating of gods. The suns had previously been governed by solar lords, but now the suns that were created were governed by gods birthed simultaneously within the suns.

To reach its God-hood, the cosmos, just like an Ascended Master, had to become very sexual. Sexual energy became heightened throughout the cosmos and reproduction increased. To prepare for its Supergod-hood, however, sexuality transformed to being in love and once again it swept the cosmos.

For someone in God-hood, the ability to fall in love can provide the movement between the poles of the eight emotions, essential in getting the energy necessary for making the leap to Supergod-hood. In order to help the cosmos reach its state of being in love, the greatest love story of all time was revealed.

Love Story of God and The Goddess

In high realms yet unimagined, a female Being existed—a being much like a human in having both female and male components. To know herself better, she externalized both her male and female parts. The love and attraction between them was the greatest ever known.

To experience motherhood she created a womb, using her own energy to multiply herself and thereby falling in consciousness. The pain of separating from her male half was so great that she had to forget him almost immediately or she would not have been able to embark on a descension that would ultimately benefit them both.

He determined he would follow her no matter where she descended, and devised a system to bring her back and protect her against the possibility he would lose his own way and forget their high origins. There was only one rule; he could not let her know how much he loved her and could only contact her when she was ready to once more ascend, bringing all her children with her.

The plan he devised is much like a bird plucking its own

plumage from its body that its love may follow the trail. Even though he would appear diminished in her eyes, he could only hope she would remember how resplendent he used to be.

Great being that he was, he gave pieces of himself away, forming kings in every realm and following her from realm to realm until they both came to the lowest—our original Infinite, where he became the Alumuanu King and she, the Mother of Creation. By then, both had forgotten who they were, each assuming they were the lowest of the God-kings and Creator Goddesses.

As more and more Goddesses from higher realms entered and became one with her, she remembered that although of all the many kings descending into our cosmos to surround her with their glory, he appeared to be lowest, he was in fact the greatest. If all the kings were to have entered into him as the Goddesses were entering her, his true magnificence would have been revealed. But he wanted to use these other pieces of himself to bring her back to the heights of glory from whence she came.

As the kings or other pieces of him poured into the cosmoses, their light would raise it cosmos by cosmos until, many trillions of years from now, it would raise them all up to the high level from whence they came. Only then would his majesty be restored and they both would be far more luminous from the knowledge and diversity gained in the journey. But the story doesn't end there.

As they reach the height of their glory, another God-king announces himself to her and says, "I am your other half and I have come to ascend with you back to the heights from whence we came. I have followed you for eons of descension to remind you of who you were and to take you back home."

How Emotions Expand Perception

The eight basic emotions form the sides of a pyramid. The emotions representing the contracted negative poles are at the top, and the pro-active masculine poles are at the bottom. The square base of the pyramid represents the corresponding perception. Dynamic balance requires that these poles pulse between each other, the positive poles making the negative ones become more negative and vice versa. When the sides of the pyramid form the perfect ratio to the base as represented by the Giza Plateau's great pyramid, there is equipoise—a stillness that when indulged in for long becomes stagnation. *(See Fig. 49)*

The stages of evolution from man's Identity-consciousness all the way to the stage beyond Godhood (Super-godhood) stair-step between being ones of either heightened awareness or heightened emotions. They alternate between emotion yielding perception, or perception yielding emotion. In other words, the sides of the pyramid are either longer than they should be for the perfect ratio or flatter, depending on the stage. If they are longer, perception (the base) has to increase to match the emotions. If they are flatter, emotions need to increase for continued growth.

Because the last phase of the last stage of each evolutionary cycle (like the end of humanness or godhood) requires emotion as its impetus to leap across to the next stage, the following needs to be known: how to create emotion during a phase where there is hardly any. The secret to this is the value and use of the sacred fire within, the kundalini.

To get the kundalini to awaken emotion, the knowledge of how to utilize sexuality is essential. Vague memories that sexuality can facilitate enlightenment have survived among certain groups, like Tibetan monks and others. Why, then have only 9 humans (before

2005) made it across from the human to the God-Kingdom? The answer again lies in the fact that for anything to have vitality, it has to pulse between its two extremes; its masculine and feminine poles and sexuality are no exception.

When men and women learn that the safety of the middle range is nothing but stagnation, they will once again allow each other to express the extremes of their masculine and feminine poles. They can be safe in the knowledge that it is done within the boundaries of perception. For example, a man might not fully express his very dominant side for fear of the woman thinking he is too rough or overpowering. He may be afraid of hurting her. But if the underlying perception is one of love and respect, it will prevent him from harming her in any way. If she knows this, she will not be frightened by his assertiveness. His going deeply into his masculine pole deepens her feminine pole.

The same principle applies when she goes into her masculine pole; it enables a man who feels secure enough about his own masculinity to explore the depth of his feminine side. Likewise, going into the feminine side awakens the more assertive side of the partner.

The full range of our sexuality can in this way awaken our emotions. Also, as they pulse they grow larger and larger until they eventually propel us forward in our evolution. To study the interchange of energy between two opposing emotions representing the positive and negative poles respectively, let's examine the way passion and joy pulse each other.

Joy is the feminine pole and is contracting. Passion is the positive pole and is expanding. Passion expands into the unknown, attracted by its negative energy, since with energy and matter opposite poles attract. In the same way, joy contracts into the

The Expansion/Contraction Cycles of
Passion and Joy

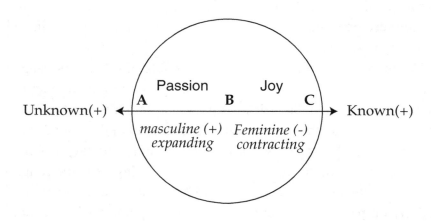

The Eight Basic Emotions and Their Polarities

Contracting (-)   *Expanding (+)*

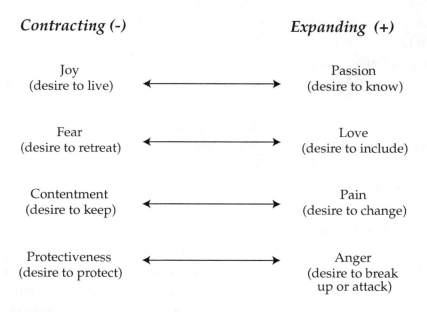

Joy   Passion
(desire to live)   ←——————→   (desire to know)

Fear   Love
(desire to retreat)   ←——————→   (desire to include)

Contentment   Pain
(desire to keep)   ←——————→   (desire to change)

Protectiveness   Anger
(desire to protect)   ←——————→   (desire to break
                                                          up or attack)

(Figure 50)

293

known, drawn by its positive polarity *(See Fig. 50, The Expansion/ Contraction Cycles of Passion and Joy).*[30]

As the feminine was captured and owned by the distortion that occurred within the masculine grid *(see p. 303)*, sadness that failed to yield change lowered the frequency of the cosmos and the fall or descension occurred. In the same way it is emotion that takes us home, providing the necessary energy and perception to help the cosmos ascend.

Sexuality—The Driving Force Of The Cosmos

First of all, the distinction must clearly be made between lust and sexuality. Lust asks "what is the most I can get for the least I can give?" Lust takes and sexuality gives. The true sexuality that exudes from a man or woman in love with life gives freely for it is life giving unto itself without agendas.

Much of what we think of as 'responsible sexuality' is simply the old paradigm of exclusiveness that was part of the journey of descension. Sexuality is the celebration of self, the constant awareness of the potency of our being that exudes as the sun does its light or the rose does its fragrance.

To constantly ask whether the recipient of our exuding sex appeal is worthy of receiving it, is to deny our being its full expression and to become attached to outcome. This one may receive, either because I plan to engage them sexually or they're considered 'safe.' That one shouldn't receive because I couldn't love them in the same way. In this way the most sacred part of ourselves becomes a currency we pay to get what we want, all the while calling it 'responsible'.

This constant weight of self-reflection lowers our frequency,

---

30 The MP3 download entitled Roots and Wings explains how life is affected by the pulsation between joy and passion.

hampers our fluidity and keeps us in our minds versus our hearts. The light-promoter lives responsibly, determining with the utmost discipline the consequences of every action. But progress requires that we develop trust in our discernment and our ability to protect our borders. Defining ourselves by what we are becoming, namely Immortal Masters, we can trust that we can secure our boundaries.

The other argument for hiding our light under a bushel is that we may hurt others. Living at less than the fullest capacity of our being is always injurious to others. Being at less than our fullest potency because a partner doesn't like the fact that men and women alike are fascinated by the energy we exude keeps him or her locked into exclusiveness and feeds their possessiveness and insecurity.

To shine with the full radiance of our being, celebrating ourselves with every deliberate gesture, evokes admiration in others. To allow that love and admiration to flow is to allow another to grow. Love inspires and enlivens. All great art has been inspired by love; whether love for another or love of life. To deny another the privilege of loving us because our self-consciousness or unworthiness or insecurity interferes is to deny them the evolution of their awareness.

We become what we admire. We grow from the assets we discover in another and our consciousness rises when we love. Victor Hugo said, "There is in this life no greater gift than that of being charming; to cast light upon dark days. Is not that to render service?"

The lust of males has been generally expressed as taking from women without giving the emotional components of love and appreciation that hallow the sexual act. The lust of females has been traditionally equally tainted by the desire to get what they want. Men have given 'love' for sex, and women have given sex to get love (also to get security, to get ahead or with other agendas).

True sexuality in its purest essence gives to everyone alike, trusting itself to act only with the utmost impeccability. If we believe that our pure intentions will garner pure results, even those drawn to us who break their own hearts on their unmet expectations will ultimately benefit.

The great beauty of the 18th century, Ninon de Lencloss, said: "I enjoy! I enjoy! I enjoy!" She was adored by kings and often loved by three generations of men in the same family at once. She allowed her passionate love affair with life to enrich all she encountered and men and women alike were drawn to her charm. She accepted the adoration of others unashamedly, knowing that she was receiving nothing more than that which she bestowed on all life. She had tapped into the creative power from which cosmoses form, the essence of all life—sexuality.

There is nothing enlightened about stifling sexuality and emphasizing only the upper chakras. Although it originates at the root chakra, the expression of sexuality results in a rising flow of kundalini that clears blockages in all seven chakras. It is the source of youth; the stimulant of pure emotions and the origin of vitality and consciousness.

When Sexual Desire Becomes Obsession

Sexual desire is often suppressed because it may be unrequited and therefore too painful. But not allowing desires to flow freely also causes pain. Pain signals us that change is needed. What needs to change in this instance is the improper suppression of desire that causes a massive energy loss. Energy loss in turn causes a loss of consciousness.

To learn to love without pain, or desire without pain (love is but the desire to include), is humankind's biggest challenge on this journey of cosmic ascension. The key is to trust that our desires won't turn into obsessions and that we can desire someone without an agenda.

Sexual desire is used to ascend cosmoses. It is a joyous and potent force under the correct conditions. Suppressing it bends the energy lines around our bodies inwards, causing energy to leak out. When expressed without reserve, it radiates energy in all directions, causing us to become radiant and attractive.

Obsession sets in only when the sexual relationship between the two poles of the inner sexuality do not pulse each other. In other words, we only focus obsessively on another when we're not in a dynamic sexual relationship with ourselves. When this is in expression, we maintain our emotional sovereignty and find our sexual appeal to others, as well as our ability to give, much heightened.

For multiple generations, men and women have been over-polarized; men have been very far into their masculine pole and women over-polarized into their feminine. As a backlash to this over-polarization, the last two generations have retreated more and more to the middle range. Women have felt less vulnerable and less dominated. Men have felt less pressured to prove themselves as breadwinners or as being 'tough'. But unless a man or woman lives both the masculine and feminine sides or poles, stagnation ensues and the dynamic inner relationship dwindles.

A result that flows from this enriching sexual relationship with ourselves, is our passionate love affair with life. Every sunset, every bite of a crisp, juicy apple, each walk with bare feet on dew-drenched grass becomes a sexual interaction with our world. Our senses heighten, our appreciation deepens and we start to live in that place of power—the eternal now.

Living in our heart only happens when we're living in the moment. Obsession is born from living in our heads, not our hearts. Obsession is concerned with the next moment and has an agenda, whereas sexuality is in love with the moment and appreciates what is before it. The former is concerned with what it can take from life and so depletes not only the one obsessed, but his environment as well.

The one who simply allows sexual desire to flow, unencumbered by expectations, raises not only his own consciousness, but also that of the one at whom it is directed, assuming it is received in the same innocence with which it is given.

In other words, pure sexuality—whether acted upon when appropriate or not—is a hallowing experience. It gilds all that it touches. Like all potent and expressed emotions, it can broaden our perception and enhance consciousness. It is also the key that opens the doors to the God-Kingdoms and awakens the power of emotion when it is most needed as an energy source to attain these elevated states of consciousness.

The Super God-Kingdom

Because this kingdom has not been accessible to anyone within our cosmos until September 2005, we have no name for it and, needing to call it something, I have named it the Supergod-Kingdom.

Unlike our cosmos, there is not a great diversity of life within these much higher cosmoses that represent these higher kingdoms. Only goddesses, gods and lords (who maintain the grid lines along which information travels as light) reside here. The Alumuanu king became the fourth being within our cosmos to enter the Supergod-Kingdom (the Mother was the first) on October 3, 2005

Phases Within God-Kingdoms

GOD-KINGDOM PHASE 2

assemblage
point

zero
point

enlarged
mental
body

thin layer
of emotional
bodies

Very few emotions are felt during this phase.
Mental body rotates the same
as in phase 1.

SUPER-GOD-KINGDOM PHASE 1

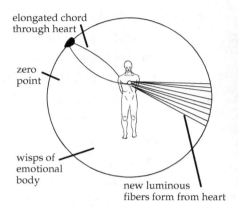

elongated chord
through heart

zero
point

wisps of
emotional
body

new luminous
fibers form from heart

Fields are 6 times the length of the physical
body. Mental body has partial rotations
alternating clockwise/counter clockwise.

SUPER-GOD-KINGDOM PHASE 2

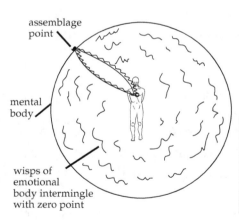

assemblage
point

mental
body

wisps of
emotional
body intermingle
with zero point

Fields are now 50 times larger. The
luminous fibers from previous phase
have now thickened the cord.

SUPER-GOD-KINGDOM PHASE 3

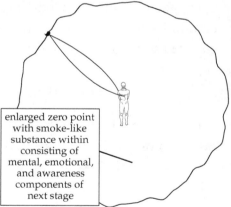

enlarged zero point
with smoke-like
substance within
consisting of
mental, emotional,
and awareness
components of
next stage

Fields are 360 times larger.
Chord is stretched thin again and
solid mental body is gone.

(Figure 51)

in the early morning hours. On the same day, the Lords of Amenti became gods as they entered the God-Kingdom.

Since it is now within the reach of our gods and not just an unreachable myth for our readers, we should be familiar with the phases of this stage. *(See Fig. 51, Phases Within God-Kingdoms)*

Phase 1 The fields become 6 times the length of the physical body. There was little emotion in the last phase of the God-Kingdom. In the first phase of the Supergod-Kingdom, it is 2 to 3 times less than before.

In all three phases of the Supergod-Kingdom, the chord continues to extend from the assemblage point on the outer parameter of the fields, through the heart and back again in a loop. But during the first phase, in addition to the chord, a whole new set of luminous fibers once again forms, extending out from the heart. Wisps of emotional body intermingle with the zero point throughout the field, which is surrounded by the mental body.

One of the notable changes within this phase is the change in time perception. It is as though each moment has already been lived. For example, to see what choice to make in a particular instance, one would simply look at the moment before to see what had already been chosen. It is different than living in the now; in that case there simply is no future and no past.

Phase 2 The field enlarges by 50% and emotions again become strong. In fact, they are 20 times stronger than in average humans, which is why a thorough previous understanding of the proper use and expression of emotion and sexuality is so necessary. Such emotion could otherwise cause destruction or be incapacitating. The luminous fibers that previously formed now cluster around the looped cord, making it substantially thicker. The mental body still surrounds the fields.

In Phase 2 and especially in Phase 3, we use hardly any thinking at all. Speaking and knowing answers are virtually automatic functions.

Phase 3 As with all the changes in fields, the explosion that transfigures them is preceded by an implosion. The fields in this case become 360 times bigger. Emotion dwindles to 5 times less than in the average human. The mental body disappears.

To accommodate the diameter of the greatly enlarged fields, the previously thickened cord now elongates and becomes thin as it stretches. For the first time, the assemblage point has no mental body to attach itself to and hovers on the edge of the very large zero point.

Filling the enlarged zero point is a substance resembling smoke—the building blocks of the fields of the next stage beyond. The smoky substance consists of a mixture of zero point, emotional body, mental body fragments and awareness.

Treachery in the God-Kingdom Affects the Cosmos

To understand the events that took place in the God-Kingdom and the cosmos, the following points need to be comprehended:

1. Grids are lines of light along which information flows to tell certain soul groups how to live and be. Whoever can tamper with or disrupt a grid can, in short, effect trillions and trillions of beings.

2. The lineages of the Mother Goddesses of Creation who are coming into embodiment are all consolidating into one being. The Gods of the royal lineage of the Fathers of the Infinite that are coming to earth are the husbands of the Mothers; they,

however, are not consolidating into one. So the Mother Goddess will have multiple husbands.

3. The As Above-So Below principle that can be seen throughout life also applies between cosmoses.

Treachery Within the Dragon World

Hy, the dragon, had a small task to perform that would help move the cosmos forward. No matter how the two-year-old dragon king (The Dragon) urged him, Hy refused to comply. The entire cosmos was watching and The Dragon's embarrassment grew every day. He was made to look less and less like an efficient leader.

Finally, the Mother Goddess herself shook the dragon world with thunder and lightning and as all the dragons on earth hid in fear, she demanded to know why Hy delayed the progress of the cosmos. The Dragon gathered an army of 2,400 dragons who forcibly escorted Hy in a cage to do his duty.

But as they were en route, The Dragon discovered the real reason Hy was rebelling. He was hoping to force a confrontation with The Dragon because he felt he was the better choice to lead the dragons. In a fight, he planned to put The Dragon out of commission and take his place.

Hy's was powerful enough (he was number two in power and seniority) that he would have been able to escape from the dragon army when they let him out of his cage, return to the dragon world and attack The Dragon.

As punishment, Hy was turned into a human while still in his cage. Only much later was he turned back again through the mercy of the Mother. Hy provided the first mirror of treachery against a leader by one 2nd in seniority.

Treachery in the Alumuanu King's Court

The Alumuanu King, the being we know as 'Father in Heaven', has no name. Neither do the number two or three below him in the trinity of gods that represent the Infinite. Since our cosmic ascension incorporated the Infinite, the Alumuanu King's court has been located on our cosmic assemblage point, on the outer parameters of the cosmos.

Thoth had been chosen as the cosmic king to represent our cosmos. But in August 2005, it looked as though he was about to be disgraced and his future coronation was put on hold. He was accused of stealing Osiris's third eye and tampering in the timing of Osiris's birth so that he, Thoth, could be king. The accusation took place in the Halls of Amenti.

There was an uproar. When everyone looked, they could see Thoth steal the eye. Yet he had always been the epitome of impeccability. After a sleepless night, I managed to contact one of the higher goddesses coming into the cosmos. She only told me that there was a conspiracy and I should ask one of the even higher goddesses who had not yet entered.

I managed to reach one, and she said that the number 2 god of the Alumuanu King's court had stolen Osiris's third eye and replaced Thoth's third eye with that of Osiris. Every time anyone asked where Osiris's eye was, the answer therefore was always "With Thoth". Thoth's third eye was hidden in the back of the number 2 god's neck.

The Alumuanu King immediately stripped number 2 of his powers and position and, after many hours, Thoth found his own eye. I accompanied him when he went to restore Osiris's eye, a process that took many hours.

Treachery From Another Cosmos

When I spoke to the holy mother from the other cosmos, who gave me the information about number 2, I fortunately asked whether there was anything else I had to know. She said the greatest treachery yet would come from one of the 'Fathers in Heaven', a king who had not yet entered the cosmos but who would do so in a few days. He would be the number 2 king of that cosmos. Specific instructions were given on how to counter this treachery. There would be a particular moment during which the number 2 king would not be listening; at that moment I was to tell the premier king to look at his former subordinate's treachery. As a result, the traitor would be stripped of most of his power and made to watch the misery his treachery had caused, which included the following:

Just like the number 2 of the Alumuanu King's court, this traitor had planned to attack his superior at his most vulnerable moment; the moment of his entry into the physical body previously prepared for use in our cosmos (each king had prepared such a body for this event).

He had stolen the minds of all the kings in that cosmos who ranked below him. Encountering them had left me shocked. They had wonderful loving hearts, but the minds of someone with severe ADD and were unable to solve the simplest problems.

He had removed huge portions of the male grid of our cosmos so that males, including our lords who governed all life everywhere, were twisted in portions of their warriorship and perception. The result was an exclusive, power-oriented way of seeing life, rather than an inclusive perception-oriented mindset.

The reason the number 2 king had done this, was so he could be the only perfect husband for the most luminous Goddess of all: the Mother of all Creation.

Restoration Of The Masculine And Feminine Grids

The damage to the grid resulting from the number 2 king's treachery to the cosmos caused it to resemble a spiderweb with holes in it. The spiderweb represents the lines of light relaying the template of impeccable masculinity for all males and masculine races to pattern their lives after. The relay system was flawed.

Not only did he damage the relay system, but he removed crucial parts of the template itself. However, the Mother of Creation had foreseen that he would take these actions to be the only 'perfect male'. She therefore left out one specific part of the masculine grid, the principle of ruthlessness and mercy, keeping it within herself and within the feminine aspects of the cosmos. The spiritual warrior is ruthless with him or herself and also in defending the innocent. But the warrior (and all are warriors against illusion, since the purpose of life is to explore the unknown) is supremely merciful in that he or she sees the innocence of all experience. This was the information that should have been in the cosmic masculine grid.

Mother furthermore designed the Toltec way, which had apparently come from another cosmos and through many star systems—so that little bands of truth seekers could perpetuate the teaching of perfect warriorship.

On the 25th day of August, 2005, the masculine grid was restored by the Mother after the cosmos entered into its next evolutionary step.

The feminine grid had been plundered by the dysfunctional males and masculine races and likewise had to be repaired immediately. Next, the templates had to be re-programmed. Re-programming the areas of the male template took place as follows:

1. Expressing emotions in a positive way:

a. **Anger.** The Alumuanu King had anger and felt let down by the number 3 god in his court. He was acting to frighten number 3, who was pretending it was fun. By turning the subversive hostility into an open dialog, this area was re-programmed into proper expression.

b. **Fear.** Number 3 had to admit his fear so that males everywhere could discard the old programming that being scared makes them less masculine.

c. **Love.** Thoth had to learn how to communicate when something hurt his feelings and he had to write a love letter to his wife.

2. Fulfilling duty in the midst of emotion:

For eons many masculine races, the lords of our cosmos and males in general, had wholly, or to some extent, suppressed their emotions. Then the edict from the Goddess of Creation went out: "Everyone has been given emotional bodies. Use them or perish as we move through the next two gates."

Emotions therefore were new to many, including the lords of Amenti. This resulted in the inability of Thoth, the lords or the male dragons to work when they became emotional. This problem grew worse and worse. This cosmos was awash with emotions and duties were often abandoned to these strange new feelings.

The lords in the Halls of Amenti had to govern the cosmos while struggling with emotions that daily threatened to overwhelm them. By mastering their emotions to do their duty, they helped restore the grid.

3. Turning competitiveness into motivation for growth:

Number 2 had influenced the male grid in a negative way. He had reduced others to make himself look better. The grid needed to be corrected in that the innate male competitiveness had to outsmart others with strategy and wit. It also had to use the accomplishments of others as motivation for personal growth.

When we descended into density, it had been the feminine that had lowered the frequency into descensions. Now it had to be the masculine that raised it. The feminine had been captured, owned and conquered, and in the lowering of her frequency, all Creation fell. Now gods were encouraged to 'raise the bar', and others had to step up to meet the new standard of excellence. In this way, males would use their innate competitiveness to become more luminous, raising the cosmos.

The gods of the suns (there is a solar god for each sun) had been attracted by the great light of the consolidating Goddesses. With light and frequency, same poles attract. The cosmic sun gods abandoned their suns and gathered around the earth, wanting to get through the shield to the Mother. She created a competition among them to see who could outsmart the others for admittance through the shield. She did this so that they could re-program the grid.

4. Learning to love inclusively:

The male need to be exclusive in nature is an inherent part of masculinity. However, love is feminine in nature and inclusive as a result. It is one of the biggest flaws in male perception that after choosing the most luminous, beautiful and loveable mate, he then expects her not to be loved or noticed by other males and has created many different rules and ways to control and hide her from them.

As we have seen, the act of loving someone enhances both the recipient's consciousness and the one who loves. Sexuality does the same to a lesser degree.

Thoth had definitely been part of the old male paradigm. But then, his father fell in love with his wife. Thoth loves Enki beyond words and it is reciprocated. Thoth understood it would enhance both his father's and his wife's consciousnesses and that the love need not be acted out sexually but just given and received. It became his act of heroism to give his father permission to love his wife that changed the grid.

5. Giving support without agenda:

The male concept that supporting the female gave him certain entitlements also had to be discarded. It didn't fit within the concept of unconditional love, which is the most we can give. This old paradigm was shattered by one of the male masters among my students. As more and more of the female Immortal Masters in my pods became pregnant with immaculate conceptions, he offered to assist two of them with a financial gift, unconditionally and with love.

Repairing the feminine grid.

1. The 'baggage' that comes with love has caused many women to clam up when someone loves them. Firstly, partners have often blamed women when they are found attractive by other males. Secondly, women have been at risk as some males lose their balance under the spell of the potent forces of love.

   It was necessary for women to simply accept love as it comes to them and a few of the masters in my classes were chosen to do this. They had to recognize that they had the choice to have it consummated or not, as was appropriate. If someone chooses to hurt themselves because their love is tainted with an agenda, that is their choice.

2. Huge guilt has been placed on women for allowing the power of female beauty, sexuality and sensuality to be exhibited. But the stars shine for everyone and the fragrance of the rose drifts upon the wind for all to enjoy. As masters of our lives, we can protect our boundaries and, safe in that knowledge, allow the allure of the feminine to emerge.

Women need to cultivate and preserve their boundaries in order to enjoy their own essence again. Too many are 'captured' or have become utilitarian in their roles; seeing to the needs of others only, until they become lusterless and impoverished in their feminine power.

3. Women must support each other's motherhood. According to many native traditions, it takes a whole village to raise a child. Children are everyone's treasure and the hope of our future. When we vaguely pity single mothers who struggle, but do nothing to assist them, we are being exclusive and denying the very nature of the feminine, which is to be inclusive.

The feminine grid was damaged as a result of the damage to the male grid. The males sought dominance over the feminine, instead of empowering it. If women do not support each other, it could take much longer for males to change.

A Transformative Event in the God-Kingdom

Although there are many gods in the cosmos—solar gods, gods governing the male archetypes *(See Fig. 12)* and so forth, the gods referred to as the kings are the male rulers of the cosmos, second in authority only to the Mother Goddess herself.

The kings are all of a specific lineage; they are all aspects of the original male part of Mother that separated out so that she might study her maleness.

To affect the males of all races within the cosmos, changes must be made from the top down. The changes must begin with the kings, spreading from there to all other male gods. From there it will go to the lords, then to all other male beings.

Eventually the masculine components of the cosmos, such as the masculine-dominated races, will have to change.

During the first days of June 2006, a dramatic change took place in the God-Kingdom amongst the kings; one that would eventually change masculinity as we know it.[31] Mother decreed and implemented the following changes:

- **The kings would become more involved in the creation of cosmoses.**

If the four petalled flower in Fig. 3 represents four different levels of creation, or four different cosmoses, only the cosmos in which matter forms (the bottom petal or material cosmos) was conceived through insemination of light by one of the kings.

The original cosmos we were in before ascension began in 2005 was inseminated with light by the Alumuanu King, or God the Father, from the Infinite, or top petal.

Mother had conceived the left, right and top petals by herself through immaculate conception. She did this by sending her own light into wombs of space she had prepared.

As we ascended, we assimilated cosmos after cosmos, but the same pattern of one male-inseminated cosmos for every three immaculately conceived cosmoses was encountered throughout. This pattern was part of creation through descension. But in the future, creation will be done while ascending. The first or left hand petal will be created immaculately and the other three through insemination with light by one of the god kings.

- **All kings must be perception seekers vs. power seekers.**

The age-old pattern of patriarchal rule that dominated during descension has no place in ascension. Every time one of the kings had attempted to take over any part in the rulership of the ascending journey, the timeline would bend and we would start sliding backwards. Mother's rule is not one of the use of power over Creation, but one of support.

31 Changes happen almost immediately in the etheric realms, but much more slowly in material life.

In past descension cycles, the males sought power for themselves. In ascension, power is seen as a by-product and natural result of perception and illumination. To seek power directly is to have access only to a limited amount. Such self-centeredness damages the inter-connectedness of life. To seek perception gives an endless supply of power. Power invested increasingly within the kings of the heavens energizes all beings within the cosmos. Increased energy, in turn, leads to more perception.

- **The kings are to stay connected through their hearts to Mother as the Source of all life.**

The pattern of growth for all life is set up as follows: Mother receives the most information about the unknown portions of existence. Through their heart-connection, the kings then know it also. Their task is to analyze the ramifications of the new information and find ways to implement it in the way life within the cosmos unfolds.

This further insures that by keeping their hearts open, the cosmos is led through love, preventing descension.

By staying connected to Source, their stability would increase as well as their ability to weather difficulties. Previously, they would become unstable as a result of overpowering emotions, often completely unable to perform their duties. Also, they were easily discouraged by disappointments, which could throw them into days of depression. In the future, there would be far more stability.

- **By accepting kingship, they agreed to be bound by the rules of highest wisdom.**

"Unto whom much is given, much is expected." This scripture sums up the principles behind these conditions of rulership. Those with the most responsibility have the greatest chance

to benefit and to affect life. But they also have the greatest opportunity to inflict damage if they make a mistake. The boundaries within which they can experience their unique contributions, creatively and joyously fulfilling their destinies, are therefore strict but flexible.

The flexibility lies in that, as higher perception is gained through experience and insight, the boundaries are re-negotiated and moved. If any god-king does not want to be bound by these rules of highest wisdom, he may step down from his throne.

- **The destiny of every king would be the seeking of perception. Their role in applying this perception would be to serve and support Mother and all life.**

The Mother Goddess is the embodiment of what we call the Infinite—the only 'real' being in existence. All others are simply manifestations of portions of her being. The comoses represent her light bodies on an infinitely higher scale, but similar to those of man.

To serve her is therefore to serve not only ourselves, but all life. To support, serve and love the Source of all life gives power and support to every creature.

Furthermore, the inactivity of the God-Kingdom will be resolved through life-enhancing and joyous service. This will bring movement and growth and new energy to their kingdom.

- **The kings and all male gods will henceforth have the same feminine components as human males; one-tenth masculine perception and nine-tenths non-cognitive, feminine perception.**

The split that occurred when Mother separated her masculine and feminine portions, and externalized them, was absolute. There were no feminine components within the male gods.

- **Three planets will be created by Mother for the kings where they may rest and enjoy and explore primary relationships.**

The first planet will be a place of solitude and natural beauty. There they may contemplate their relationship with themselves and all life. They will study how every action affects all life.

The second planet is for enjoying each other's company and studying their own maleness by interacting with other males. It will be a place where emotions can be expressed within safe parameters. A pool with healing waters will cleanse and heal emotions. There they may enjoy fun and male camaraderie.

The third planet will have an embodiment of Mother for every king so interaction with the divine feminine may be studied. The kings will see their own feminine in these embodiments and have a place to voice emotions, dreams and desires. The knowledge and understanding and love between them and Mother will be enhanced.

The planets will have to be visited in order, and for equal periods of time. The kings will need to first have a relationship with themselves and their oneness before they can develop relationships with others. Time spent in service will alternate with time spent in rest, healing waters and interaction with others. The more support they give to life, the more support they will receive.

Repression of emotions and desires is unsafe and stifles growth. When repressed emotions eventually surface, they often flare out of control. Through the time spent on the three planets the kings can be heard and also learn to know Mother's heart so they may better support her. This will bring them into emotional maturity so they can ask, "What is the most I can give, rather than what is the least I can give for the most I can get."

- **The declaration Mother had previously given that power and perception must be matched was now changed to: Power must equal inclusive perception with love.**

The Book of Existence was written by Mother to embody the highest wisdom and insights to incorporate into living. It expresses the highest laws, goals and ethics that are to be applied to enhance the quality of life for all. As insights are gained, they are added and the Book carried forward during the cosmic ascension.

This re-statement of the declaration is an example of how a previous perception is refined. Beings in very high dimensions may have the ability to perceive much, but without the component of heart, may yet lack wisdom and inclusiveness. They can use the power coupled with knowledge to act self-servingly and damage all life. Compassion increases power under this new declaration and where it does not exist, power will be stripped.

The Gods and Hurricane Katrina

At the time of hurricane Katrina, a large cosmic black hole had developed that affected the minds of the gods and all other beings in the non-corporeal realms, including the weather angels and large wind spirits. Their focus and clarity were greatly impaired and as a result, so were their abilities.

In the third week of August 2005, when the storm was still at sea and heading towards the densely populated suburban areas of New Orleans, I approached Mother to ask whether I could create a large spaceport around it and teleport the storm into outer space. She said, "No. Let the gods do it."

I could not understand Mother's reply. I had watched how poorly the gods had functioned during the past few weeks. How could she possibly think they would succeed? But her message was delivered. They started right away and every time I checked, all the primary gods of our cosmos were working on it. But by the time the storm was due to reach land, they had been only marginally successful.

I again asked Mother if I should help. Her reply was, "You can help now if you want to." But I had no one from the unseen realms to assist me. The hurricane was moving around. I had to focus on keeping the spaceport going and could not keep track of the storm's path. I too was unsuccessful.

The god we know as God the Father, namely the Alumuanu King, spoke to me. He was virtually in tears. "I have never seen anything so horrible! There is so much suffering!" I was silent. Where had he been looking during the many wars and global catastrophes that had cost so many millions of lives over the centuries?

I had once asked the Alumuanu King what it felt like for so many on earth to pray to him (apparently this is the only planet where this occurs). His answer to me was, "Very loud!"

Why did Mother permit this disaster to occur? Perhaps the answer lies in her instruction that humans be speedily prepared to evolve beyond mortal boundaries. The God-Kingdom, just like our Ascended Mastery realms, had become stagnant. The over-polarization into the light of these realms had caused inactivity to become the hallmark of the God-Kingdom. For growth to take place, existence has to pulse between doingness and beingness; between activity and passivity.

Mother knew that the gods had not tried to make things better before, but rather had stayed in the deep bliss that is part of this kingdom. She wanted to give them this experience to stimulate action.

When I later asked some of the beings who assist me why this had happened to New Orleans, they said that because the earth had risen in frequency, the city was no longer harmonious; in other words, it was no longer supposed to be there.

The result of this tragedy is that the global compassion directed at this area, as well as the team-work and unity (and in many cases selflessness and heroism), has raised the city's frequency to be more compatible with higher realms.

When I later asked some of the beings who assist me why this had happened to New Orleans, they said that because the earth had risen in frequency, the city was no longer harmonious; in other words, it was no longer supposed to be there.

The result of this tragedy is that the global compassion directed at this area, as well as the team-work and unity (and in many cases selflessness and heroism), has raised the city's frequency to be more compatible with higher realms.

PART EIGHT

The Realms of the

Star-Beings

Lessons from the Andromedans

As the earth became the cosmic pivot point, a surge of interest in this tiny speck in the cosmos was generated, attracting many star-beings. But for me, perhaps the most profound interaction was with the Andromedans months before. Four of my students and I were taken aboard an Andromedan craft and shown how to work with timelines.

This was done to show us how to move the planet out of the way of what was then potential catastrophes that lay in its future. We spent many hours out of body each day doing work on several continents and the planet herself. We were warned that from the work we had done, a very noticeable time-space anomaly would occur the following day within a twenty-mile radius of my house.

Later that day, after we had worked with the timelines, a former NASA scientist and Pleidian contactee called to say the Andromedans had contacted him and he was to tell me that impending damage to the earth had been averted due to a shift of its timeline. He added that a large part of national dharma (collective karma) had been cleared in the Middle East.

The time-space anomaly became apparent the next day when

my office manager, unaware of what we had done, drove to work from out of town. She came into the office, with a bewildered look; "It's the strangest thing. About twenty miles from here it felt as though I was entering into another reality. It almost felt as though I was driving into a gelatinous substance."

I had to go to my bank and for the first time ever, I found a line of customers trailing out onto the sidewalk. I decided to go to another branch, only to discover the same strange sight. The bank clerks were so confused that it took them four hours to notarize fifteen pages of paperwork. The branch clerk called my primary bank for information and the response was, "I'm sorry, my head aches. I can't think straight. I can't possibly deal with this today."

Driving around town, people seemed to be in a dazed state. Several times, I had to evade cars whose drivers seemed oblivious to my presence.

About a week later, two Andromedans, a male and a female, began appearing off and on during a time period of about six months, providing additional information especially when I was lecturing. When I would place my index finger on my third eye, the tall bluish beings would appear, one either side of me, to give the information I needed.

They became dear friends and the information regarding transformation, transmutation and transfiguration as given in Journey to the Heart of God, Anatomy of Change, is the result of some of their teachings.

On Board an Orion Craft

During the stressful time when the spirits had been captured by the Sirian demons, I was simultaneously attacked by a craft from Orion.

The dragon around my house had managed to keep me hidden from the demons, but she and Thoth had told me several times that my defenses against aliens had decided gaps. Dragons aren't very good at dealing with aliens. Three times I had sent a being from the hidden realms to search for someone, somewhere that was best at dealing with hostile alien craft. All three times they left for days and returned to point at me.

The techniques I knew had been given to me by the earth itself. The first dire need to get assistance began soon after I adopted my little girl when she was nine months old. She would see beings in the room that I could not and would scream in complete terror as she clung to me. During the nights, I would feel drugged and by morning my child would have nausea, nosebleeds and marks on her little body.

My agony over this grew unbearable. I slept with my arms around the child, but still the abductions continued. She was put out of school because of her rages and I hardly knew how to deal with them myself. I could only hold her as she beat her head against me, kicking wildly. I was also concerned that her speech was slow in developing.

Then one day when she and I had been crying together over her agony, she looked deeply into my eyes[32] and with great effort said, "I 'wuv' you", her little mouth struggling to form the words. About the time she turned three, she came to me after a brutal two week period and again looked deeply into my eyes and said, "Mommy, I'm better now." She was indeed at peace immediately after that, for instantly she could no longer see into the hidden realms, nor could she see the monsters with the red eyes.

The nightmares may have lessened, but we felt unsafe. All my

---

32 Abductees usually have a hard time making eye-contact.

calling on angels, lords, the Ascended Masters and even begging Thoth and the beloved Master Christ for help, had not brought results. I lay on the earth and sobbed bitter tears of frustration and impotence. Through my grief I heard clear, calm instructions on what to do—the voice was coming from the earth.

Her abductions did become much less frequent and she flourished at school, as well as socially. They had gotten what they came for, as I would find out later. They had abducted her dream body, as well as those of 300 other Indigo children and 50 Chinese children. (According to the spirits, there are 1.8 million Indigo and 200 brilliant Chinese children on earth.) The story of how I encountered them on board an Orion ship begins like this:

The Ascended Master Melchizedek had informed me that the earth would let me know when hostile ships entered her atmosphere, and she did. The signal was a sudden attack of severe nausea. I would then practice the techniques the earth had taught me, ship after ship until the nausea would be gone.

The week before the incident on board the craft, 14 ships had entered our space. I was awakened from a deep sleep by the nausea and worked until it left, knowing all ships had been dispatched with the help of mother earth.

The following week, during the demonic attacks described in the chapter on Spirit Realms, the spirit Faye (who was in my house at the time) said the Orion craft sent a probe or arrow of green light into my head. The pain was terrible, but I worked as well as I could to crack the demon language and sigils.

That night as I lay in bed, I felt myself transported. A period of great confusion followed, and then I found myself on a craft. There was a human-looking being who took me to some cages and showed me one with Melissa and another with my little girl. Later I found that the piece of Melissa, now an adult, had been taken when she had been four years old.

I was then taken to a table with a document I was to sign. The confused feeling was still present, but I shook my head. Two males watching this from behind a partition with a gate, motioned to the first being to bring me closer; they wanted to look at me. These individuals had a ridge around their heads but looked somewhat human and had dark skin. They did not speak, but I could hear their thoughts. After inspecting me, they exchanged looks of disbelief. Could this puny human really have destroyed their ships?

Everyone then became more insistent that I sign the document, which appeared to be some sort of contract. The pain in my head worsened, then I felt myself pulled out of the craft and onto another.

I stood in front of a strange alien. He had a leathery looking face, pointed chin and his top lip looked like that of a tortoise. He looked at me for a long time, making deep eye contact. He wanted me to see that his intent was to help. He turned his head sideways for me to study his profile, which displayed a very small nose ridge. The forehead slanted backwards and the eyes were deep-set.

This kind alien helped me home that night. Faye got the green arrow out over the next few days, but the pain didn't go away until Sarah was back. Once safe and sound under my roof, she found a blue core that had remained in the spot where Faye had removed the green arrow.

About a month later, the children were set free. That day my little one cried and cried in heart-rending sobs. She followed me everywhere for days, not wanting to leave my side for a moment. Her nightmares were nearly over.

Approximately two months later, the cosmos was moving into a much higher frequency. Thoth came to warn me that within an hour after that transition, the entire Orion fleet that had been involved in my abduction was planning to attack Earth. They recognized Earth as the pivot point—the Wayshower that, with one more shift, would pull their entire race into oblivion.

The Orions had time-traveling capacity and saw that in the near future their race would cease to exist. Because of the losses of their previous ships, they hid 12 years into the future. Thoth warned that the 7th year had a time wrinkle and had to be skipped. It was at this time that I learnt from him how to turn the space portal *(See Fig. 14)* into a time portal. The entire fleet was transported into the sun.

Conversation With a Starship

Right after I had done the ceremonies, I was instructed to do with a group of my students, time and space merged in some way. The ceremonies involved the Goddesses of Time and Space walking into one another. Within hours, there were approximately eighty space craft above the house.

Soon after, the master Horlet erected a shield around the earth that took about a month to complete, so that there was some control over who would be able to come and go. He did let Anu, Thoth's grandfather, in with his ship because I enjoyed a visit from Anu, Thoth and Thoth's father, Enki.

During the gathering of the eighty ships, I had the following conversation with one of them (they were asking the questions):
Q. We came in a hurry. What has happened?

A. Time and space have merged. It is part of the ascension of the cosmos.

Q. We do not want to fall off space. What is the ascension?

A. The whole cosmos is going to be pulled up into higher frequencies by the earth.

Q. We do not want to fall off space.

A. If you can wail until Thoth comes—he's on his way here—he will explain.

Q. We can't wait. We have not had nourishment for a long time. We came immediately to see. Who are you?

A. I work to make sure the earth survives. If she doesn't, neither will you. Perhaps you can help.

Q. Brave one. We can't stay. Need nourishment.

A. It is humanity that is brave. They go through much suffering to resolve the problems of all star systems so all can survive. They live their own and your problems to get the insights.

They then indicated they had to leave. The many conversations and noises from other ships had become silent as we talked. All listened. Thoth arrived within hours and gave a thorough explanation to all remaining ships.

Rescuing a Space–Brother

The traffic above the house continued to increase before Horlet could complete the shield. Beautiful One maintained a shield over my house so even though they could hear communications, they couldn't see me. But they knew I was there.

Apparently, this was also noticed by 'authorities' on earth and with their usual clumsy shortsightedness, they shot down at least one ship that I know of.

I was aware that someone was asking for my assistance, but

couldn't determine the source. Then, one of the women in my class saw images of a space-brother being brutally interrogated. I had the spirits immediately verify this. They confirmed that, up to that point, they had only terrified him, but hadn't yet injured him.

I called Powerful One, the dragon that assisted me, away from his work and asked him to save the star-brother and bring him to the house where he could hide under the shield until others of his kind could get him.

It took Powerful One 11 hours to get him out of the building where he was confined. Although he had been terrified before, he must have sensed the good intent because, according to Powerful One, he relaxed soon after, looking around with much curiosity during the journey to my home.

I welcomed him with gestures and words, but he stood stiff and still as a rod. He wore a one-piece, silver-colored suit that encased his feet as well.

He was slender, with long skinny fingers. He had a very human-looking appearance, with short, sparse, very blond hair. There were almost no eyebrows. His eyes were somewhat round and a very pale blue. His skin was very fair and seemed a bit pasty, like someone who had been ill.

The most movement I had gotten from him was one blink of his eyes. He did follow when I beckoned and showed him where water, food and a bed were. But although he glanced briefly at them, he continued staring at me, round-eyed and for the most part, unblinking.

Wherever I worked that day, he stood in a corner staring. I finally went to bed that night, feeling like a goldfish in a bowl. In the morning he was gone. The spirits confirmed that a space craft had come to get him.

Help from Friendly Aliens

During a past life regression, one of my students recalled details
of events that had puzzled her all her life. She remembered several
occasions when she had been tormented in her crib. During deep
meditative states, she remembered dwarflike men telling her they
would torment and follow her for the rest of her life.

Some months after retrieving these memories, this sister took
photographs of my daughter during an afternoon excursion. The
photographs captured images of the unseen realms. When the
pictures were developed, she saw the face of a little man peeking
out from behind my daughter. There were two packets of photos
which she placed in a bag and then proceeded to her car. When
she got there, the envelope with the picture showing the face of the
little man had been emptied; even the negatives were gone.

Some while after the photo incident, the spirits warned that the
little men were coming from the underworld with the intention
of harming my daughter. A battle took place in the house but not
between them and me, for unexpected assistance had arrived.
Three aliens came to our aid and took on what the spirits said were
60 of the little men. One of the aliens was badly injured and one of
the little men had an injured foot. But we were safe.

I knew the three aliens. Our acquaintance began in a most
unusual way. My hairdresser was cutting my hair when she
suddenly said, "I don't know why I'm telling you this, but when
I was a teenager I was listening to the radio in my room one night
when a strange voice interrupted the program and introduced
himself as one of a group of aliens that had come to earth to make
sure it survived. He said the survival of their own race depended
on it."

This was puzzling. The comment had come totally out of the

blue. As I left the salon, she said, "I'd forgotten about this all those years. It's as though I'd kept that information just for you." And she had. That night I awoke to see one of them standing beside my bed.

The being had very blue eyes set in a leathery, nut-brown face. The brow ridges were very prominent and continued around the eyes until they became well-defined cheek-bones. The whole effect was that of owl's eyes, except that the framed blue eyes seemed sunken. The jaw likewise was well pronounced and square. He had no hair and the nose was very small. No ears stood out that I could detect. He stared deeply into my eyes, holding the gaze for a long time. He wanted me to see he was well-intentioned.

A few nights later, he returned with two friends. They stood around my bed and I felt a strange sensation in my vital organs. They seemed to be focusing what felt like a healing; areas of stress released. It had felt wonderful and then they left.

Later that month, during a class in Kentucky, one of these beings was seen by a sister with many ailments. During the class she too, could feel the strange sensation in areas of distress. A digestive problem she had suffered with for a week was immediately released.

I had been concerned about the individual who had been injured during the battle to protect us, but several weeks later they showed themselves to me so I would know he had been healed. That was the last time I saw them.

PART NINE

Conversations With Beings
of Other Realms

Introduction:

In the third phase of Identity Consciousness, Masters encounter many beings from the hidden realms that congregate around them because their light starts to attract attention. The masters at that phase have one of two choices. The first is to not allow these beings to divert their attention away from gathering enough perception to transition to God-consciousness. The second choice is to utilize the gifts of the beings to avoid opposition, or in other ways to control how life unfolds.

The masters who work with these beings while still in ego get their assistance to increase their prestige, abilities and, in some cases, to harm others. But in getting this assistance to make their life choices, they slowly give away their power and freedom of choice. They use the beings to sidestep or control the outcome of opposition and in so doing, stifle their own growth, for it is within the challenges of life that our insights are found. The true perception seeker embraces life's opposition, knowing that the greater the challenge, the greater the insights.

The Immortal Master, many levels of human development further, having lost all ego, can no longer be sidetracked by these beings. Instead he uses them to distract him from the deep bliss of this phase that induces inactivity.

With the assistance of the unique gifts each being from the hidden realms offers, he uses their perspective to explore the mysteries of the cosmos.

Whereas the individual in ego-identification uses the beings to tell him how to live, the Immortal Master sees life from their perspective. In this way he grows in the breadth of his wisdom.

As we share a few of these conversations with you, we ask you to note the care with which high beings from the hidden realms answer questions; careful not to usurp freedom of choice and the benefits that come from puzzling out insights ourselves. Instead, their answers are given in a way that provokes more thought. Lower beings do not do this.

A Talk with Sarah, Goddess of the Direction of Below—March 2006

Q. Sarah, could you please help me understand money, which is crystallized power, from a high perspective?

A. It's about time you asked that question. The crux of the misperception is that you think you need money, and that of course stems from your not seeing just how powerful you really are.

Q. How can one see that from such a limited perspective?

A. Your mind has a limited perspective, but your heart does not. So take time each day to feel your power and your vastness with your heart and you will know without doubt that you can manifest anything you need.

Q. Are you saying we don't have to work for it?

A. Exactly. You work because you love what you do. By the way, isn't it about time you admit to yourself just how much you love your work instead of pretending it's 'hard'?

Q. You're absolutely correct! What's more, even though I no

longer identify with ego, I recently found myself identifying with my work and an addiction to perfection.

A. Well, can you see perfection for what it really is?

Q. Yes, perfection is perfect equilibrium; a place of no growth. It's stagnation. Everything grows and moves forward because something is always slightly out of balance—the gift of polarity. But to get back to money. What about reserves?

A. Having a reserve is the result of the lower perception of limitation; thinking there will have to be some things you must do without if the finite mind doesn't plan and scheme. But all energy, all power and all resources are yours as soon as you fully realize you are as vast as the cosmos. Do you want to discuss your thinking you don't always have all the answers?

Q. Sometimes it takes me a long time to fully puzzle out a cosmic principle. Doesn't that mean I don't know everything right now?

A. It just means you know exactly what you need to, the minute you need it and not before.

Q. But I make mistakes, don't I? For instance, my younger daughter left my home at 15 because of mistakes I made. And I didn't visit my mother during the last 12 years of her life when she was stuck far away in an old age home and didn't recognize me. That still hurts.

A. No, there are no mistakes, just occasional detours. Your younger daughter would have entered into a disastrous marriage at 16 if she hadn't left. Her life would have been different.

Q. And my mother?

A. Your mother left for the spirit world 12 years before the body died. This is quite common in old people where life is lived as a reflex.

Q. Are all my 'mistakes' like that?

A. Yes, as it is for all the major light promoters. Even when experts in certain fields have delved deeply into a specific body of knowledge, you can know anything they know if you need to, and the timing is right. You may not use the same terminology; you may see it as a symbol, for example.

Q. When you guide me in doing my cosmic assignments as you have been, where do my marching orders come from?

A. From the Mother of All three levels ahead of whatever level our cosmos rises to.

A Talk with the Goddess of Materialization—March 29, 2006

Q. The Goddess Sarah told me you would be coming to speak to me tonight. I'm overjoyed at your presence. What is your name?

A. You may name me. I am new in the cosmos.

Q. Do you mean you have been newly formed from the sea of consciousness? What exactly is your function?

A. Yes. I am the Goddess of Materialization.

Q. You mean like the goddess that gives form?

A. No, that is another. I do not determine form, but make sure that which is called forth by what you term faith, is materialized.

Q. Are any of the goddesses in human form and will you be coming into form in the near future?

A. What do you mean by the 'future'? There is only today and I do not come into form today. You know the goddesses who are embodied.

Q. Yes, I do. What will it take for the New Jerusalem to materialize? I am most eager for it.

A. It requires breaking the slave mentality found on earth; enslavement by form. It is time to realize form is not more real than that which you call non-physical. Another enslavement is the dependence on form to determine your reality, such as using nutrition to bring health. Ill health is simply the way you can become aware of attitudes and beliefs that need to change before they manifest in your lives as troublesome circumstances.

Q. How do you see form controlling us in the area of food and weight?

A. You should be able to eat what you like without weight gain. But you must first shake off the shackles of social conditioning that imposes belief systems around what is physically beautiful and what is not. The body must be completely loved and accepted as it is before it will change as you wish it to.

Q. Are the 'flaws' we manifest the result of bad attitudes or are there other purposes they serve? And what about the need for exercise?

A. Certain body parts can be like barometers. They signal when you neglect certain areas of your life, such as self-nurturing. But exercise can be done even when sitting, by directing swirling energy into certain areas like your waistline. Your spirits truly are the masters of your bodily temples.

Q. Are there other areas where this bondage of seeing form as more real and permanent needs to be addressed?

A It is time for those who will have access to these words to realize how magnificent their light is and to live their life from that level of insight. Form obscures the vast differences in the luminosity found among human beings.

Q. Do you have any other messages for us?

A. When a specific outcome like the New Jerusalem is desired, flexibility is required. It would be a mistake to have it manifest prematurely before the earth has reached a certain frequency or the full potential of its manifestation would not be reached.

Q. 'El' is the word for matter in the ancient tongues, 'ka' is energy, 'a' is of and 'la' is all. May I call you La-ka-ela?

A. Yes.

Conversation with the Goddess of Below—April 1, 2006

Q. As the goddess of the direction of below, are you also the goddess of the unknowable?

A. The direction represents that, yes. The unknowable consists of those portions of existence that have not previously been examined through experience.

Q. Are you also the goddess of the energy of the direction of the instinctual nature?

A. No, two different goddesses represent those areas. They are in body and you know them.

Q. The great divinity that hides in the human body is amazing. How can we show it greater respect?

A. It dishonors the inner divinity when you make yourselves appear less in order to make another feel better about themselves. That also applies when you dishonor your body's needs; eating on the run or denying the sub-personalities[33], such as permitting the inner child to express itself.

Q. You mean like not getting enough rest?

A. Yes, dishonoring any of life's alternating cycles[34], such as activity and receptivity. It is arrogance to identify with work and outcome to the extent that time is not taken to enjoy the journey. This happens when someone cannot feel the perfection of the unfolding plan of Creation behind the appearances of imperfection.

Q. Is there more?

---

33 For a full explanation of the sub-personalities, see that section in *Journey to the Heart of God*.
34 For more on life cycles, listen to the *Wings and Roots* CD.

A. (laughter) Of course! Clinging to old patterns and responding to life in ways that no longer serve drags the past into the future and dishonors the journey.

Q. It denies our growth and increasing perception, doesn't it?

A. Yes. And speaking of growth, all anyone needs to know will be available at the exact moment it needs to be known. You don't have to wait until it manifests without, to learn the answer.

Q. You mean we shouldn't have to learn from outside mirrors, or worse—the hard knocks. We should comb our psyche the way we comb our hair each day, to remove any resistance to life and gain our insights.

A. Exactly. Even forcing your gifts on others by trying to save them is a form of resistance in that it still judges their path as imperfect.

Q. What I hear you saying is that it is a greater gift to acknowledge wholeness than to try and right a wrong. How do we protect ourselves from our fellow human being's folly or deceit?

A. In your highest identity you are a vast and magnificent being. If you approach another from this largest identity, he or she cannot hide. Dishonesty will come to the surface and be exposed. To put physical precautions in place against another's destructive or foolish behavior allows you to focus on the perfection underlying all illusion. And, as you have said many times, in seeing the perfection you help bring it about since you empower what you focus on.

Q. Is there anything else on this subject you want to add?

A. On a regular basis, please take time to eliminate all that isn't life-enhancing in your life. That includes all relationships that take but don't give, or change the dynamics of the relationship. Demand the respect due a luminous being, for in honoring yourself, you honor all life.

Conversation with Thoth after he had tied up the Goddess of Form—May 12, 2006

Q. Why did you do that, Thoth, I wanted to ask her some questions?

A. Well, I've been trying to talk to you all day and she won't let me.

q. But won't it detrimentally affect the cosmos to tie up the Goddess of Below?

A. No, it's beneficial.

Q. Why? How could that be?

A. (long pause—as he studies the effects) It's symbolical.

Q. I think I've got it. You represent, as one of the kings of the cosmos, higher mind overriding the instinctual nature of below. Is that it?

A. Yes, when the instinctual nature runs wild and is not governed by higher mind, savagery can result.

Q. And I would imagine that individual instincts can become self-centered if they don't consider the good of the whole. Where does reason fit into this?

A. Reason must be overridden by both instinct and higher vision.

Q. If the below nature gets its information through instinct, how does the above nature get it?

A. Through insight in the form of effortless knowing.

Q. I bet you didn't know what you were doing in the grand scheme of things when you tied her up!

A. (laughter) No, I'd just had enough of her bossiness.

A conversation with the Goddess Sarah—May 13, 2006

Q. Sarah, what is happening? I feel as though my mind has been wiped clean. I can hardly remember anything from one moment to the next. When I try to do anything that isn't meant to be done exactly this minute, my whole body starts shaking.

A. You have completely changed because the cosmos has moved into the direction of within. The cosmos was pulled through a tunnel and now everything is different.

Q. Did this happen yesterday? That's when everything seemed to swirl around me.

A. What is yesterday? There's only today. Today we came through the tunnel.

Q. Yesterday was before it got dark.

A. There is only light; only now.

Q. Well then, why do I see periods of dark? Is it just an illusion? Has the reality behind it been removed?

A. That's because you see with your eyes closed.

Q. Is space different here? Have we moved into a much higher level?

A. Higher level, yes, but space has collapsed.

Q. Then how will we progress here? Before, we traveled in loops during the cosmic ascension.

A. We will travel along the outer petals of the rose moving inward.

Q. I see. And when we get to the inside of the rose, just like the DNA of man, the portal of Ara-ka-na opens. How many outer circles of 12 are there before we get to the ring of 7 and then 3?

A. There are two rows of twelve and Ara-ka-na is now called Shpirelviplavaurechbi.

Q. How can I deal with this feeling of my mind being stretched beyond its ability to grasp .... I don't quite know how to explain it ....all old ways of thinking aren't working.

A. Exactly. It's because we're in feeling and emotion, which is movement instead of structure. Be fluid, let life move through you. In inner silence, instinct and higher vision will guide you. Follow them even when your reason doesn't understand why.

Q. So fluidity is the key?

A. And ....?

Q. Inclusiveness? The mental approach to life has been separativeness. The feminine is inclusive. But how can one bring inclusiveness into every part of one's life?

A. By always acting from your largest identity ...

Q. ... a being as vast as the cosmos having a human experience.

A. Exactly. But go further than you've gone before.

On May 14, 2006, I asked her to speak again so I could better understand the concept of inclusiveness.

Q. So in the past I would see myself as everything, withdrawing only to the body in order to relate. That's certainly inclusive; in fact, how can it possibly get more so?

A. There is only now, I don't know what you mean by past, but you see yourself as a vast spiderweb of consciousness overlaying the cosmos. Now you are to see yourself instead as the whole cosmos. If you look beyond its boundaries, you'd find yourself there, too. Nowhere would you find anything but yourself.

Q. Well, I'd still have to pull back in order to relate...

A. No, not necessarily. The new way of seeing it would be that all bodies are yours. You would know the hunger of the child in the ghetto, the happiness of the bride on her wedding day, or the pain of the mother giving birth, as your own.

Q. Then how would I know which body is mine or the one I'm responsible for?

A. It's just that although all bodies are yours, there's only one whose choices you have immediate control over.

Q. What do you mean by 'immediate control'?

A. Every choice you make affects the entire cosmos. When you live from this vastness of being, you affect all life even more profoundly and more immediately. But only one body is yours to control in the moment.

Q. If everyone felt this way, there would be no unkindness, no hunger. But it's overwhelming if I think of feeling everyone's feelings and emotions!

A. Only if you engage them. It would be like a sea of emotion flowing through you and you only place your attention and intention where you want to.

Q. Let's explore this in various areas of life. How about giving and receiving?

A. To express gratitude to one who gives to you is desirable, but what you're grateful for is that that person is the conduit for life giving unto itself and that you may be part of this flow of supply. So, too, when you give, you are but an honored participant in this dance of life.

Q. Then how about injustice? My viewpoint has been that one does not permit it, so that others may learn. At the same time, one remembers the innocence of all experience, acknowledging the value of the perception-givers in our lives.

A. The more inclusive way is to see yourself in the reflection of the environment.

Q. Explain, please.

A. Look carefully at the issues you see around you and you will find them within.

Q. Are you saying that if I change within I can attract different mirrors without?

A. Precisely. Sometimes the people mirroring to you will refuse to change, even though you've made it possible for them to do so. When that happens, just move around the rock in the river or sidestep the oncoming train. If you allow it to cause a knee-jerk reaction, you'll get sidetracked too.

Q. What about sex? One has to relate separatively then, or not?

A. No, two people making love must learn to enter each other completely; each becoming the other's vastness.[35]

Q. Talk about intimacy!

A. Yes, let's. When you hug, you throw up a shield. Have you ever asked yourself why?

Q. I have a well-developed ability to walk into another and I am also fully empathic. In the first instance, it seems invasive and in the second, who wants to pick up all their fears, grievances, etc?

A. That's a lot of baggage you bring to a hug! If you become one with them, it's not invasive but rather may be the first time in their life they have experienced inclusive love. This will definitely leave them better than they were before. As for picking up all the pettiness or fears, I said their 'largest identity', not their smallest.

Q. How can inclusiveness be incorporated into the work we do?

A. When there's teamwork, people work inclusively; also when bosses don't concern themselves about the little rules, but instead of focusing on quantity, they encourage quality. Not all produce a certain quota of work at the same time; the larger picture has to be considered.

Q. What about the way we do the work itself?

A. When you live from this advanced level of perception, you will know what to do and say at the exact right moment. Don't pacify reason by second guessing yourself and you will get things done much more quickly—expect it. Fatigue can only come when you carry the last moment into this one or you live in the next.

---

35 See section on Sacred Sexuality in *Journey to the Heart of God.*

Q. How about eating?

A. When eating for health, consider the rare opportunity to experience the life of the plant or vegetable in your body during the time of its passage through you. Truly experience the uniqueness of the life that has entered you.

Q. How about helping another? Let's say a mountain climber is stuck half-way up a cliff and calls to you at the top for help. The usual way is that I'd throw him a rope, but see behind the appearances at the symbolical meaning of the event. Do I need to acknowledge that I need help from someone? That I need to ask for a rope? Has this person taken life for granted, and have I contracted to assist in showing him that every moment of life is precious? Or is the message that the higher one climbs, the more one has to be aware, for the greater the chance to make life-altering mistakes?

A. The higher way is that instead of seeing him there and you here, you see yourself as the mountain, the rope, the other climber and even as you throw the rope, you see him already on top of the mountain. This inclusive vision of the situation while staying in complete inner silence, is how miracles happen. Eventually you will be able to move him without the rope.

Q. I would still analyze the meaning of the event ....

A. Analyze, no. That is no longer needed as you live from this higher vision. You will effortlessly know what you need to when you need to. You may not see right away that the event is a mirror of your not giving equal value to the challenges, as you do to the joys. But when your next opposing event happens, if you are still, you will see the previous event flash before you.

Q. So the key is staying in the moment, the place of silence called eternal time?

A. Exactly.

Conversation With the Goddess of Below—May 12, 2006

Q. In my dealings with the Goddess of Form, why did she lie to me?

A. Because form lies and you believe it.

Q. Meaning that it deceives when we think it's real? I thought I'd gotten over that.

A. Then why do you pacify the unreal?

Q. (After some thought) Do you mean that I care that my students learn as painlessly as possible and I don't want them to become enraged or fearful because of the high frequencies they encounter in the work?

A. Denying them their pain is denying them their necessity to change. The classes during which you tend to the growth of the upper branches of the tree, leave everyone feeling uplifted and great—all can feel the spirituality. But at times, it's necessary to prod and unearth the stones of the stuck areas around their roots, which flushes up anger and pain so they leave wondering if you are the right teacher. But to give your utmost for their enlightenment, you must do both. If the roots are not healthy and growing in proportion to the branches, strong winds can topple the tree and, yes, you are pacifying the unreal by being attached to the outcome.

Q. For them, the unreal is the roles they play in physical life; the real part is indwelling life. Its evolution is all I should concern myself with.

A. It is so that being 'real' comes in degrees. Form that is not spiritualized as, for instance, immortal matter would be, is like a hologram—totally unreal. An Immortal Master's body is matter filled with spirit and therefore somewhat real. But the only real

Being in the cosmos is the Eternal Mother—the One expressing as the many.

Q. How about the gods, aren't they her counterparts?

A. They are her masculine components given spiritual form. So it can be said they are as much her creations as we are. We are simply aspects of her, separated out so she can examine the mysteries of her being through observing us.

Q. Form's grip on our life is like an addiction; it has had this hold on us.

A. Exactly. As the light on earth has become more and more intense, life has put pressure on humanity to correct its blind spots. Mirrors of addiction in your environment have therefore increased.

Q. I have wanted the increased light on earth to become visible; for signs of the cosmic ascension to be seen by the despairing masses. Is this a problem?

A. Only in that you tend to value the seen as more valuable than the unseen .... And of course there's the attachment to outcome.

Q. Yes, I can see that .

A. Do you find the many friends of the unseen realms as fulfilling as the seen?

Q. It pains me that I can't always see them, and I so much want to hug them.

A. But you have many tangible interactions with them that you clearly see and touch with your energy body and remember.

Q. It's not the same.

A. Then you do not value the experience of your energy body.

Conversation With the Goddess Sarah—
May 12, 2006

Q. I've been instructed to have a better relationship with myself. Can you help me identify all the areas of my life this pertains to?

A. The issues can be divided into self-worth, self-love, expressing your individuality and self-interaction. Which one do you want to tackle first?

Q. I suppose the core that should be in place would be self-acceptance. If one doesn't have that, the others won't be there either. How about starting with the flaws? Most people just want to fix them, striving for perfection.

A. And perfection is ------?

Q. Stagnation—if it's experienced for more than a few moments. It's the imbalance of life that creates movement and growth. It's like a timing mechanism; if a growth spurt is rapidly needed, great imbalance is created. This causes pain and discomfort in order to instill within us the desire to change.

A. Then you should welcome your flaws. Everyone has chosen flaws in the exact areas where they are needed in order to solve the individual's specific part of the mystery of existence. When they have done so, these 'flawed' areas become their strengths.

Q. How about self-acceptance in the area of our desires—the way we want life's conditions to be? Desires are frequently shunned as unholy or unspiritual, but without them we over-polarize into the light and stagnation occurs.

A. There also seems to be a great misunderstanding about the fact that accepting life's conditions and having desires for a different set of conditions aren't mutually exclusive. They are both important parts of self-acceptance.

Q. So if someone lives in a hut, but desires to live in a palace, he should first see the value of living the way he does in the hut, even though he desires to live in an entirely different way?

A. Yes. Change begins by accepting and seeing the value of what is. If acceptance of what is in front of you is not there, desires become needs. Who designed your life's circumstances anyway? Your higher self. Is it then that you don't trust yourself with your own well-being?

Q. The Toltecs call it the madness within the dream. We design our lives down to the last detail and then when we live it, we feel victimized and oppose it every step of the way. And what about accepting our worthiness, such as our worthiness to receive or to adorn ourselves? Or our worthiness to be seen as sacred?

A. And the big one???

Q. The worthiness to succeed at what we do?

A. Exactly. There are so many more areas, like the worthiness to spend time or money on yourself, the worthiness of being nurtured. But they all come down to one thing: The worthiness to claim your place in the sun and to live a fulfilled and happy life.

Q. What about believing that good things can come easily and we don't have to suffer to earn them? It feels to me that this issue of worthiness is somehow connected to seeing our own divinity.

A. Yes. Accepting your divinity is definitely part of self-acceptance in the highest sense.

Q. Perhaps we need to start by saying what is divine?

A. Perhaps you should rather ask what is not. When the average person fails to see the divine in others; he feels guilty about seeing it only in himself, or feels that such holiness must surely set him apart from his fellow man.

Q. But it is from seeing our divinity that we start to live sacredly, which benefits all life. When we live from this vantage point, we see ourselves as stewards of all life. We become conduits for cosmic power, love and light. What other areas of self-acceptance must we cultivate?

A. Accepting your unknown portions and your personality.

Q. But where do we see our unknown portions, since by definition they are unknown?

A. You will see them mirrored in your fellow man. When you see something that amazes or takes you aback, look twice; it's there you will find yourself. You also find your unknown pieces when you stretch yourself beyond the boundaries of your comfort zones.

Q. And how about personalities?

A. Each is totally unique. Like a specially colored lens through which each person shines his light. Unfortunately, people hold on to old habits, personal identities and social conditioning and call them their personalities. But a worldview produced by such baggage does not really have anything to do with personality. Personality is the special flavor you bring to your interaction with life. Because there is usually not enough self-love, many become what they think others want them to be. If you love yourself, what gift would you want to give yourself?

Q. Fun?

A. Yes, something you should have a lot more of! Now I suppose you want me to define it? Well, even though it's not easily definable, you'll know when you experience it.

Q. I have to think about this one.

A. No, you don't. But OK, let's go on to other areas. You love being by yourself, so taking time for that and enjoying your own company is your great pleasure. The key is in not letting duty crowd it out.

Q. We've spoken about accepting our own desires, but most don't even know what they are. I'd think taking time to listen to the desires of our hearts is really important.

A. Yes, and another thing I want to mention is how people are so hard on themselves for the mistakes they've made. How do they think they're going to grow? Not making mistakes means one is functioning only within the known. Growth occurs by exploring the unknown.

Q. So mistakes are necessary for growth. You're saying self-forgiveness is necessary for self-love.

A. Yes. And now there are two aspects of self-love left that I'd like you to think about: Self-nurturing and celebrating the self. Physical self-nurturing means you listen to the needs of your body; you rest when you need to, you take time for undisturbed self-care. You care about what you eat and drink. Too many eat mindlessly in front of the TV, not listening to the signals from the body that say when they've had enough; not really tasting their food and not honoring the life forms that provided that food.

Q. There must be some cause for obesity in there.

A. Yes. In countries where mealtimes aren't observed around a shared table, people gain weight. They don't converse with others, slowing their rate of consumption; they ignore body signals, fail to honor their food by tasting and chewing properly so it may be thoroughly digested and truly nourish them. Consequently they become nutritionally deficient as well as obese.

Q. Now what about self-celebration?

A. If you take a little time each day to see yourself as the vastness you are, you will know you are all-abundant, all-luminous. That the body could be the experiential component of such expansion is magnificent indeed. Let it fill your heart with joy.

Q. That is truly beautiful.

A. And so are you. Now let's look at expressing individuality. Each of us is like an instrument playing its part in the cosmic symphony. If one instrument is out of tune, it detracts from the whole.

Q. I would say a good starting place is to go through every programmed or pre-conceived label we have and throw it out the window. The truth of who we really are is so much greater than the boxes in which we've allowed ourselves to be placed would lead us to believe. To find the greatness within, we have to throw off all labels.

A. Yes, but even without identity, as in your case, you still have to watch that you don't get caught in the web of others' expectations.

Q. Isn't the key really to live in eternal time so that the guidance of one's heart can be heard in each moment?

A. Isn't that really the key to all things? If we look at self-interaction, one of the important concepts is sovereignty in relationship. This happens when you are constantly in touch with the inner personalities. This in turn is only possible if you stay in the moment.

Q. I would imagine it's also a matter of being self-referring for approval; again the result of staying connected with our sub-personalities. If one is constantly burdened by the opinions of others, freedom of self-expression would be absent.

A. Self-reliance takes cultivation.

Q. I'm not sure why you say that. Doesn't every overcoming require 'cultivating'?

A. I mean that self-reliance, whether in the area of being able to express oneself, or that of financial independence, for example, has to be cultivated by throwing out dependencies on cultural belief systems or any kind of control that prevents us from fulfilling our destiny. Consider a family with several small children, a mother and father. The father may be the primary breadwinner; the mother may be a fulltime mother. Perhaps there is barely enough money to cover everyone's needs. But the mother wishes to have financial independence.

Q. Exactly how do you suggest she cultivate this over time?

A. The mindset has to be correct as a starting point. She has to see herself living the way she would like to, by envisioning it joyfully every day as thought it were a reality. Next, she has to put a foundation under her dreams. She may investigate a source of funding for continuous education for low-income housewives. She could trade play hours with another mother and become computer literate at the library so she could do research. She could study textbooks in the bathtub, in the park while the children play, et cetera, while waiting for grant money or while she saves enough for college courses.

Q. So, by analyzing what it would take and by never giving up her vision, step by step she is slowly cultivating her self-reliance. It is her vision and moving towards it that has set her free, whether she has arrived or not. We've already spoken about self-reliance and financial independence being important aspects of self-interaction. What else comes into play?

A. Accountability and service. Why don't you explain how these fit into the concept of self-interaction?

Q. This is a tricky one ..... It has to do with how we see ourselves (which of course is self-interaction).

A. You're on the right track, go on.

Q. Well, if we recognize ourselves as points of influence that ripple throughout the entire cosmos, every action becomes deliberate and filled with power. If we realize that every action will either leave the cosmos a better place or not, we will want to live every moment in a way that is life-enhancing. Our lives then become lives of service. As we become aware that we affect all of existence through every choice, no matter how small, we become fully accountable for our actions.

A. You've got it! Well done! The next issues are those of sovereignty and self-reliance in relationships with others and with the self.

Q. Aha! My favorite topic. The secret to autonomy and successful relationships is the exact same one as the key to successful aloneness. In fact, we can't have the one without the other. We have to be happy by ourselves before we can be happy with another.

A. And how do we do that?

Q. The key lies in having our inner sub-personalities happy, balanced, acknowledged and expressing. The inner child comes to the business meeting, the inner nurturer parents the child, the inner sage guides and counsels and the warrior guards our boundaries and our impeccability. We also don't approach relationships with emotional need and so they have a chance to succeed.

A. So now we come to our last piece that makes up self-interaction and because it's another you would call 'tricky', I'm going to let you answer it. How does having a willingness to receive fit in with self-Interaction?

Q. We have to approach it from our highest identity; as an individuated awareness or a unique perspective filling all that is. If we approach it from this perspective, it is simply giving to ourself through another. It is life giving unto itself. To over-burden another with any guilt of receiving or, alternatively, any feelings of obligation is to receive from separatism rather than inclusion.

An Unusual Conversation with Merlin

Merlin has been weaving through my life at regular intervals over the years. In the presence of the Goddess of Energy, he answered my questions. He appeared tall and skinny, wearing a loose white robe, with white hair hanging down his back.

When I asked the first question, he patted his throat and said, "Hard, hard!" Somehow the way conversations were usually conducted with beings from the hidden realms was new or difficult for him.

A dear friend who is an unconscious channel for him, had often volunteered himself in the past so that I could speak to Merlin. He had always called me 'My little flower' and now produced a tiny flower for me.

Q. What is happening with time? It seems to be so distorted.

A. He produced a clock and hammer from thin air and smashed the clock.

Q. So you mean time has collapsed?

A. He nodded, pointing to the smashed clock.

Q. Then how can we function from our old calendar?

A. He produced a calendar, laid it on the floor, then jumped over it.

Q. Do you mean we moved far ahead of the year we think it is?

A. Again he nodded, "Yes". Then he picked up the calendar and tore it.

Q. So—it's not just that we're in a different year, having shot forward in time, but that time ceased to be, like a double-pointed crystal that collapses to create a diamond in the middle—the present moment.

A. He nodded again, smiled, and was gone.

Conversation with the Goddess of the Direction of Below

Q. Is there a flaw in my perception of living the wild woman instinctual nature? Recently I've had a lot of mirrors in people in my environment showing instincts that are out of control.

A. You've also been working on inclusiveness in all areas of your life. How do you think that applies in the case of allowing your wild woman to express?

Q. The wild woman nature has been very much viewed with apprehension by all around me. Inclusiveness would, of course, demand we express without the slightest regard for what others think of us, but I sense there's something I'm missing?

A. You already know that high mind must guide the instinctual, but the key problem area in your life is that you express it in boxes. In other words, you let it out only when you think it's appropriate.

Q. I don't understand. Are you saying I must live it all the time, even when I'm in a business meeting?

A. The instinctual nature must indeed be a constant guide in your life. It invigorates, it removes ruts and brings new possibilities to every moment. It should be a constant companion, as must the higher mind.

Q. I imagine that's because the above and the below have folded into the direction of within. They're not lived separately anymore, but are included within. But the four directions have folded in, too ---what are the ramifications of that?

A. You have been teaching of the four directions and the sub-personalities they represent. You have also been teaching how one must take time to listen to them and express them. How do you think this has changed?

Q. Yes, I see! Amazing .... In other words, no more taking

time out for them. They should be expressing all the time. In the business meeting the child's innocence, enthusiasm and curiosity about his world should be present; the inner nurturer should express the need for water, for a different temperature, for a break.

I suppose it's impossible to take boxes of 'time' for different personalities to express when there is no time, only the now in which they can express. In what other areas do I not understand inclusiveness?

A. Growth. You still think you must become something or grow to something. All you have to know is that you are all things.

Q. Yes, but clearly there are still things I'm learning; isn't that a form of 'becoming'?

A. Think of it rather as already being those things and then just bringing them on line. You can also think of standing in the middle of a landscape but only looking at certain portions of it at a time.

Q. What about leadership? How can one do that inclusively?

A. Exclusive leadership focuses on what the followers should do; the leader is judged by his actions. Inclusive leadership can present strategy and delegate responsibilities, but focuses instead on teaching correct principles and letting followers govern themselves within that framework. The leader is judged by who he is.

Q. What about mistakes we've made in the past?

A. What is the past?

Q. Ok, if previous mistakes are erased, how about their effects?

A. Yes. Those are erased too, unless your belief systems keep the illusion of the effects in place. I thought we've been through this—you can't make mistakes.

Q. Is it this way with everyone's mistakes?

A. The key players certainly; like the light-promoters on earth. The asleep masses have the abilities to make mistakes, if you mean 'detours', along their path if they choose not to learn from experience. If, in that moment, they act from their highest perception, the same applies.

Q. What's the difference?

A. The light-promoters are the turning points of the cosmos; the tip of the pyramid. Each one has a specific task that is not replaceable.

Q. And the masses at the lower portion of the pyramid, if they don't complete their assigned overcomings to gain insight on behalf of the One, someone else will?

A. Yes. Either someone else who has fulfilled their assignment will take it over, or someone enlightened will see their folly and get what lies behind the appearances.

Q. Then what happens if a major lightworker enacts a piece of the illusion or makes a 'mistake'?

A. It gets factored into the big picture and becomes an asset. The tip of the pyramid is too important to pull the cosmic ascension the wrong way.

Q. Give me an example.

A. The one you know to be the incarnation of the king of all the elves in the cosmos—why don't we talk about what happened there?

Q. Yes, that's a good one. Let me summarize what I know.

His actual name was Elrinray and the day came for him through a specific overcoming to be the one to move the cosmos from one level to another. He had an overcoming to do within, and a deadline for accomplishing it.

He worked on it intensely for two and a half days, but even though he had until midnight on the third day, Elrinray became so overwhelmed and discouraged, that he gave up before the deadline was reached.

The elves would have merged with the fairy kingdom and this would have greatly enlarged their abilities. They would have ruled what we would call the sub-conscious mind of the cosmos, side by side with the fairies.

Because of his 'failure', the elf kingdom was reduced in size and abilities. Eight thousand elves on earth committed suicide. They were reduced to serving the fairies instead. King Elrinray, who had been a very dear friend, left his body. No longer a king, he became a simple elf.

A. Now let's look at how the 'mistake' benefited the cosmos. As you know, the sub-conscious mind holds all that you do not resolve; the insights you do not gain in your life. Demons form to become the embodiment of the unsolved pieces of existence. They cause painful opposition in the areas where these insights need to be gained.

Lucifer and 600 of his hosts were the only ones to survive the cosmic and planetary ascension, but at this point have no density remaining. So there are no demons. However, a whole new underworld would have formed as the cosmos moved into areas of existence you call the unknowable.

Q. So the elves were like garbage collectors. They held all unprocessed stuff. But unyielded insights are our treasures of future perception and power so they can also be described as gem collectors.

A. They held the bottom layer of the sub-conscious—the one from which demons form. The gift Elrinray's 'mistake' gave the cosmos, is that there is now no storage place for this density and hence, no demons. This reduced suffering on earth by 52%.

Q. OK. But this is too simplistic an answer. The unresolved pieces of existence have to go somewhere. Who is either carrying them temporarily until solved, or actually solving them?

A. (laughter) You are! The quickest cosmic ascension occurs when it's given to those who get it the quickest; the top of the pyramid. So your challenges have increased, but those of the rest of humanity have decreased.

Q. What a responsibility! We'll have to do some fancy footwork in the dance of life to stay ahead of what is coming at us every day. Any advice?

A. Yes, you just have to increase your awareness. Before, you used to track your knee-jerk reactions to find the areas where your insights were to be gained. Now you track even the ripples beneath the surface. Every day needs meticulous examination of every suppressed or irritating area in order to gain the insights.

Q. I can only trust that whenever a task is given, so are the resources. In fact, it is an honor for the light-promoters to do what, to them, is their most heart-felt desire—to ease suffering on earth.

An Explanation of the Drama of Lucifer

It should be wonderful news for the earth and her people that Lucifer and his hosts no longer exist as demons. But for many, Lucifer has become a way to motivate themselves, their children or the congregations in their churches, to do good. For them, he has become an instrument of fear used to control behavior.

In many instances, churches have elevated him as the opposite of God, making him almost as important in the big scheme of things. In fact, they would strenuously resist the alternative—having to mature emotionally and spiritually and make the most life-enhancing choices, not out of fear, but love. Who is Lucifer and where does he come from?

When the Mother of Creation formed the space or womb in which Creation would take place, the one representing the Infinite (or top of the figure 8 as shown in Fig. 1), God the Father, inseminated it with light. Mother then had four daughters, the Goddess of Space, the Goddess of Time, the Goddess of Energy and the Goddess of Matter. Each of them had two self-inseminated daughters. From them, the other primary gods and goddesses were formed until eventually all beings in Creation existed. Lucifer, known as the one with the gray head, was number 39 to be created through Mother.

It was through obsession that he fell, taking one-third of created life with him. He wanted the most luminous of all, the Mother of Creation, for himself. After his fall, he and his followers were confined to the underworld behind locked gates.

From where they were, their ability to cause havoc was limited. But then they persuaded someone on earth to open the gates. The one who opened the gates was Afxghelm *(See The Story of Neptune in The Language of the Akashic Records).*

For eons their rage has tormented the creatures within these denser levels, specifically those on earth. But in 2005 the lower levels of existence ceased to be as individuated life. Although life can never be destroyed, when certain life forms have ceased to serve a purpose, they can be re-absorbed back into the sea of consciousness. Sometimes they may eventually re-surface at a much higher level to serve a different purpose.

In this way, by the end of May 2005, only 600 of Lucifer's hosts remained. At that time the Mother of Creation came to earth. Her advent transmuted 90% of Lucifer's density to light. The remaining 10% was lost at a later stage when the cosmos went into even higher levels and had its karma erased.

When I inquired about Lucifer in July 2005, I was told he was teaching one of his younger aspects.

My Own Interaction With Lucifer's Hosts

On December 16, 2000, it was necessary for the Inanna personality to leave my body for other purposes[36] for a period of five years. A higher aspect came in, but as described in *Journey to the Heart of God*, threw me into shock for several months.

Taking advantage of the shocked condition, 60 of Lucifer's hosts, distorted males with their heads on backwards, captured my dreambody and took it to the underworld. I didn't know at the time what had happened, but the most horrible panic attacks would grip me several times a day. It felt as if I couldn't breathe and as though my chest was being crushed by the density. I asked the Goddess of Above to help me, but couldn't understand her answers.

Thoth and the Lords of Amenti knew what had happened, but didn't save me because at the time they themselves had been tampered with by beings from outside our cosmos.

It was not until the last day of May 2005 that the Mother of Creation sent me to set myself free. I had gotten much stronger and they had gotten much weaker from our rise in consciousness with the planetary ascension.

The piece of me they had captured represented my wild woman element; the instinctual nature. The difference I felt when I was once again united with this instinctual part of myself was huge. It has taught me how valuable having this piece is in bringing vitality to one's life.

But my interaction with Lucifer's saga was not over. In April 2006, Mother sent me back through a time tunnel Thoth had created in my kitchen (the one in the Great Pyramid had been

36 See *Inanna and the Wolls*, pg. 208.

closed at this point). The new tunnel allowed travel between creational pages. I had to return to the day before Afxghelm would have opened the gates for Lucifer's hosts.

I was very taken aback by how dense existence felt at that time; how far that meant we must have come. Mother had given me the means to tie up Afxghelm, massive as he was. I had to teleport him with an inter-dimensional space portal through the sun and two levels higher.

He was to be instructed to lie there for millions of years, contemplating the misery his actions would have caused to trillions of lives. He would only be set free when someone would touch his tail in friendship, which I did as the earth ascended to those levels in 2005.

The ability to travel between pages is no longer an option as of May 2006. All tunnels have been closed as time has ceased to exist. The past has been condensed into the present in the following way:

Let us assume for instance that during a past life you had been a Jew living in Berlin and had been a victim of the holocaust. You will now be living in Berlin in peace. The perpetrators of such heinous crimes have ceased to exist as the earth rose in frequency. You therefore have the chance to relive that life in a fruitful and uninterrupted manner. The lives in which you gained all the insights won't repeat, but the interrupted one in Berlin will. You could then literally run into yourself in Berlin.

The Goddess of the Direction of Below Continues

Q. Could you talk to me about the huge changes[37] that have taken place in the God-Kingdom. I'm not that good with dates, but guess it might be around June 2, 2006.

---

37   Refer to the transformational events described in Part VII, The Realms of the God-Kingdoms.

A. You'll have to stop using the illusion of your calendar soon, you know. You've seen quite a few changes by yourself already. The major one you've overlooked is the issue of self-esteem.

Q. In the kings?

A. Yes. Self-esteem comes from emotional components and the flow of emotion within.

Q. You mean the sub-personalities?

A. Yes, that's a very large part of it. It's the inner family that gives the protection, the nurturing and so on. But the 8 basic emotions must also be expressed and felt.

Q. So without those feminine portions allowing deeper ability to feel, the emotions are shallow or gone?

A. Shallow. Self-esteem has to come from within. It can be felt when human males are in touch with their feelings and now the kings have them, too. Otherwise, they look for their self-esteem from without.

Q. Which is why women tend to feel they keep mothering males?

A. Exactly, and why males have often measured their success by outside trophies.

Q. The problem is women have frequently been the trophies, giving them the programming that their worth is measured by their exterior. So the previous disconnecting at the very top of the male grids rippled down, disconnecting the feelings even of the grids of human males who do have the ability to feel. This then caused female self-esteem issues and lack of self-worth. What a classic example of flawed perception causing flawed emotions. What is going to be done to restore the cosmic light and frequency to what it should be?

A. Lords have been called to correct it. *(See Fig. 52 Lords that Restore Frequency and Light Within the Cosmos)*

The Lords that Restore Frequency and Light Within the Cosmos

1. The Lord who restores Light:
name: Serklauhurutvakrechabernavereshbi
meaning: He who ordains with light

Sigil for the name   *Sigil for the meaning*

2. The Lord who restores Frequency:
name: Echvaershbauklutvararesbi
meaning: He who restores the cosmic song

Sigil for the name   *Sigil for the meaning*

(Figure 52)

Q. What self-esteem issues are most prevalent for women?

A. The issues around body image and sexuality. But taking time to get to know yourself and your relationship to all life is also very important.

Q. How does one tackle body image issues? The supposedly ideal images portrayed by the media as desirable are so unrealistic.

A. The areas of the body that bother you are no different than pain or disease would be. They are barometers of what needs to change to a higher order in your life. Take your knees, for instance...

Q. What??? There's nothing wrong with my knees!!

A. Then why do you not like looking at them?

Q. Well, they're rougher than they should be because I don't slough off the rough skin when I bathe. It's a result of not taking enough pampering time for myself. They keep reminding me of this.

A. Exactly my point. Your body is immortal. You don't have to be affected by dry skin or flab or injuries. But without them, how can you know what portions of your life are lagging behind?

Q. And how about sexuality?

A. Most of the world's people are very unaware. Their lives are in ruts and ruts close down awareness. The prerequisite to sexuality expressed with another, is to first have a wonderful sexual relationship with self and express it as a sensual relationship with all life; with the apple you eat, the sunset you see; the sound of rain.

Q. In other words, all relationships can be better if one knows and loves self and sees the relationship expanding to include our environment. Is that what you meant by taking time to examine ourselves in relation to all life?

A. That's half of it. There is also becoming the highest self and functioning from there, even if at first it can only be done for a minute or two.[38] See self as a vast awareness encompassing all, and the body simply as a point functioning within it. Return to this awareness off and on all day—you already live there.

Conversation with the Alumuanu King after days of my running into what felt like a brick wall.

Q. I just don't understand. The cosmos is sitting before this large purple vortex or portal of some sort, waiting for one of the lightworkers in the physical to get an insight. Then why am I having such a hard time?

A. It takes a big cucumber to make a big sandwich.

Q. My Lord, won't I be able to understand you better if you don't speak English? Then Melissa can translate and I'll know exactly what you mean.

A. I don't want to. I'm very proud of my English. Perhaps I mean pickle, not cucumber.

Q. You mean it's a big insight, but it will accomplish much!

A. You have a good way with words. But why are you angry with me?

Q. I'm not angry with you—please look in my heart! But I am very frustrated; every clue I follow is a dead end street. I feel the illusion like a wall before me—sometimes allowing frustration to surface helps break up the illusion.

A. You're angry with me and it's like a tin roof.

Q. A tin roof?

A. Yes. You know, like rain on a tin roof—it hurts my ears.

Q. I am so sorry, My Lord. I will do better. I sometimes do it with Sarah as well. Perhaps I need to go slower in working with

38 See the meditation for the Goddess Ara-ka-na.

others so the quality of the journey improves. After all, this is the new way the cosmoc ascension will take place—more quality and less speed. Is anger still a good tool to break up stuckness?

A. Sometimes.

Q. Can you give me any clue as to where I need to go with this insight?

A. No.

Q. (four hours of fruitless guessing later) Please, can you give me a clue?

A. Do you like purple?

Q. Well, for furnishings and clothing, no. For flowers, yes.

A. Do you like purple?

Q. For what, My Lord? Are you making something for me?

A. No. Do you like purple?

Q. Wait a minute! You're giving me a clue! The portal is purple. Is it the core of the Infinite Mother or her 'third eye'?

A. The core.

Q. In other words, our evolution is through her core. But the one thing we have established over these days of searching is that the insight has something to do with me. Am I at least on the right track now?

A. Yes.

Q. When we went into the direction of below, I looked at all the unknown portions of the vastness of my being that had never before been illuminated. It was so oppressively black that I had a massive panic attack; it was so vast it seemed to stretch forever.

A. And now?

Q. Well, last week I looked again and could find no darkness, only color. In fact, at the core it was purple! What does this mean?

A. Sorry, I can't tell you. Continue ...

Q. Perhaps it means that one has gained all insights one was supposed to during a specific creational cycle.

A. And ...

Q. I'm thinking that it's somehow connected with what you've previously confirmed; that we are going to create the future spontaneously once we're through the purple vortex. Instead of trying to find truth, we're going to create it moment by moment.

A. That's right.

Q. Perhaps the purple at one's core that comes from gaining the insights of a specific cycle of existence, is the color of the building blocks that form to turn those insights into creation during the next cycle.

A. You've got it.

Q. Thank God!

A. You're welcome.

Conversation with Horlet, our Planetary Lord

Q. My Lord, there have been many signs in my environment that there is something regarding energy I need to understand. Will you answer me, please?

A. Yes, you're a little behind schedule getting that one.

Q. I've been working as hard as I can trying to figure it out with my class ....

A. That's the long way to do it.

Q. I've had a hunch there's a new way of getting information that probably requires less energy. In fact, a few days ago, I asked my friend, the spirit Tom, to do something for me so I can focus with the class on getting these insights and he said, "That's not a good way to get it."

A. Well, the problem is you're not busy enough.

Q. My Lord! What are you saying? Do you know anyone busier than I?

A. Yes. Lots of people.

Q. Who in my immediate environment?

A. Paul.

Q. What percentage of busyness does he have and what percentage do I have?

A. You have .2% and he has 700%.

Q. But I work far more than he does.

A. Yes, with working you're at 100% and he's at 7%.

Q. Recently everyone has been telling me to get busy or that they're busy. I asked the Alumuanu King earlier to help me figure this out and he said he was busy. There must then be a difference between 'busyness' as you use the word, and work.

A. Of course.

Q. Can you give me an example of 'busyness'?

A. Like mopping a floor or shoveling dirt.

Q. In other words, mindless work?

A. Yes.

Q. Work should be done from a place of silence of the mind. Even office work, contracts and so forth?

A. Everything.

Q. That will release the huge amount of energy tied up in work. Earning a living doesn't have to be hard anymore. So, will you next help me find the new way of getting answers and insights?

A. I just did.

Q. Are you saying this will produce answers to large questions in life as well as the other methods would?

A. No. Better.

Q. My goodness! This is very revolutionary. Not only as a way of removing stress or hardship from work, but as a means of effortlessly getting information! Is it as good as getting answers form meditation?

A. They're two different ways. It's the same.

Q. But few people can sit in meditation all day. Most have to work. But now work doesn't have to distract from growth. I would imagine that it will take a lot of trust that one won't somehow drop the ball; you know, miss a clause in a contract or something. All work can be done this way, can't it?

A. Yes. It's a different mindset that has to be cultivated; and, no, when in the silence of mind you will be less apt to drop a ball.

Q. Does one still need as much alternating rest time?

A. Yes. To incorporate and internalize the insights you've gotten.

Q. Thank you, My Lord. There is one last question. Is there any dependence on my part in working with any of the beings from the hidden realms or any of my helpers in the physical?

A. Answer yourself by defining dependency.

Q. Dependency is if you think you can't do something yourself. But for most of the months of this year, I've done the cosmic work myself with little or no assistance.

A. What do you mean when you say months of the year?

Q. Let me re-phrase that. I know I can do it myself. I've proved it. But various assistants have areas of expertise that make the end product better and also saves me so much .... Oops! I almost said 'time' .... Effort.

A. And that is ....?

Q. Interdependency. Teamwork, unity within diversity—the place of most growth where specific talents focused on a common purpose produce the most growth.

A. Exactly.

Closing

Because of the enticement of the hidden realms, most mystics have neglected keeping their focus on their own growth. Few have therefore achieved the mastery of losing the ego and attaining the impersonal life of a God-conscious being.

For those with ego, making themselves vulnerable has seemed very unappealing. To expose the mystical world that the average reason-dominated mind cannot grasp, does exactly that.

Even when 'miracles', which simply are the revealing of the hidden realms, take place in front of my students, their minds either minimize it or argue it away.

- In front of three students, a patient levitated a foot off the bed as I worked on her. One student closed his eyes so he didn't have to deal with adjusting his worldview; another, whose cancer I had healed, but who attributed it to his diet, no longer wanted to study with me. Some months later, the third demanded I prove myself by showing him a miracle.
- A group of students was at my house during the time of the huge dragon fight. Thuds could be heard that sometimes knocked things off the wall. Bluish lightning, with and without a thunder sound, could be seen around my house but no where else up and down the street. A few months later, they wanted me to show them proof of unseen worlds.
- I gave a previous office manager photos of Mother Mary's face appearing in my stained glass windows during prayer, explaining what they were and asking him to keep them safe. Three Polaroid shots caught the image, developing from just the outline to a complete, life-size face. The cloth over her hair and her lovely face could be clearly seen. He threw them away, claiming he thought they were 'junk'.

In almost every instance of the multiple dozens of 'miracles' or super-normal phenomena that others have experienced through the work I'm engaged in, they have either discredited me or the event. This has happened to mystics and prophets over many ages. It is because the tyranny of reason is mainained by strongly fighting off or ignoring anything it cannot control or explain. It will create the most bizarre conclusion if it has to, if it can argue away the possibility that the experience lies beyond the grasp of the left brain.

An example of this occurred during a beautiful spring night when a house guest saw a fairy in my back yard. She explained to me that she enjoyed watching "the electric hummingbird strung on a wire in the backyard"!

There is a second reason why the mind doesn't register the hidden realms. That which lies beyond ordinary cognition is accessed by the right brain. All initial energy is used by the left brain. If the mind has a deafening internal dialog and is very disorganized, it will use all available energy. For most people, this leaves very little energy to access or interpret anything they may experience from the hidden realms.

I had a class ask me why, as a Nagual, I did not lead them into alternate realities by shifting their assemblage points for them. Finally I said I would, but asked them first to check the time on their watches. They did so and then sat waiting. What seemed to them to be a minute later, one of them asked, "Well is anything supposed to happen?"

I asked them to look at their watches again. Forty-five minutes had passed. Not one of them had enough energy to enable the remembering and registering of the events that had taken place during the previous three-quarters of an hour.

Because of the egocentric benefits of increased power and

prestige interaction with the hidden realms have brought mystics, and, alternatively, the ridicule it could evoke, they have been silent about these topics. Even well-intentioned mystics have felt that revealing these aspects of their lives could potentially jeopardize the credibility of the higher perceptions they wish to impart in order to raise consciousness.

Dragons in particular seem to be somehow a source of controversy. There seems to be a deep-seated, but undefined, fear that somehow they stand for the 'anti-Christ' or black magic or demons or Lucifer. Many will still accept angels as being authentic, perhaps even fairies, but attack with anger one who speaks of dragons.

Our belief systems are our prison bars, trapping us in the materialistic world of mind and the five senses. The arrogance with which man has thought he knew his universe has strengthened his blindness and widened the chasm that divides him from the beauty of the unseen worlds that teem with exquisite life. This, coupled with the unwillingness of mystics to speak about them, has steeped the unseen realms in mystery.

Why This Book Breaks the Silence

The reasons I have brought forth, as clearly as I could, a portion of the mysteries (some things, such as the Lemurian language, I've been told are for a later book) are multiple:

- My life is lived with unattachment to outcome. I have nothing to prove and everything to learn. If I deviate from this in any way, I have beings in the unseen realms who will immediately point this out.
- The time for the book has come. If I were to publish the book on this day of writing these words, there would be unpleasant

consequences from those who do not wish the masses to have access to it. But by the time this has been printed and shipped, the opposition will not be there, since the earth will have moved to a higher level of consciousness.

- In many other planetary systems where the enthusiastic contributions of the elemental kingdoms have been unnoticed and unappreciated, they have left, causing a devastation in nature. Their lives are like ours—they have triumphs and tragedies, individual personalities and the desire to be appreciated and understood.

Humanity has had an infantile understanding about their role in relation to other mystical kingdoms. They have assumed:

- that spirits that channel through mediums have higher wisdom;

that angels are all-powerful beings who will 'save' them, while taking very little responsibility for saving themselves;

- that the God-Kingdom has been out of their reach and that man is so lowly he cannot hope to take his place among them;

that higher dimentional beings automatically have more light and love and, above all, understanding and that humans have little power;

- that God has nothing better to do than hear their prayers and that suffering may further enhance their standing with 'him'.

Once again they feel they will be saved from pain.

It is with the sincere desire that man, that incredible microcosm of the macrocosm, powerful beyond conception, will take his place as wayshower of the cosmos, that I share these experiences and insights.

Authorities and experts everywhere conspire to keep the masses locked into primitive beliefs about their origins, history and other discoveries that will shift man's paradigm. They hide the discoveries of giant artifacts and remains, sacred objects and records that indicate advanced races have lived here before; indications of populations in the earth and interactions with star-races. It is assumed that keeping humanity locked into immature beliefs will make them more controllable. It is criminal to rob races of their right to know. I wish to be part of the solution to this problem, not to perpetuate the dilemma.

If even a seed can be planted to say that "All is not what it seems", we have begun the journey out of the confinement of mind to the place of expanded awareness and mastery. The journey must be walked with humility born of the knowledge that from our vantage point the vast majority of the cosmos is yet unknown.

* * *

This book is written in loving memory of the dear friends of the unseen realms; those who have graced my life with their presence only to disappear into the ocean of consciousness as the cosmic ascension brought their function to a close.

May they live on in the memories I share with you. All of them have served to the best of their abilities. If this recounting of their deeds can further inspire and awaken planetary awareness, it would be a fitting tribute and completion to lives well lived.

APPENDICES
Angels and their Functions

place #	qualities	names
1	Holy ones we are	Klerebeushtamal
2	Remembering ourselves	Frishuet
3	Lord of hosts	Moraminuvat
4	Unimagined Glory	Bretlklansk
5	Symphony of the stars	Uverbret
6	Stairway to heaven	Nerchopssavute
7	Chambers of the heart	Hitereopskani
8	Earth's destiny	Uchanovitch
9	Frequency transfiguration	Helepenskarosk
10	DNA activation	Bubel
11	Light temples	Keteropsklani
12	Cave of darkness	Meti
13	Sacred languages	Ninaskepluvabeurtanabi
14	Symbolic meanings	Hepukskla
15	Holy pathways	Bochpavel
16	Mother of energy	Heliopskani
17	Codes of creation	Ushnaferanumpatel
18	Cosmic map	Breshkipvusapatarel
19	Open hearts	Eunif
20	Humble spirits	Hershklatem
21	Crown jewels	Petlumanoech
22	Web of life	Efertishnabel
23	Frequency of love	Hiterochvavuset
24	Masters of light	Kestelanachmishmaset
25	Creating the moment	Uverabgneskopet
26	Alternative realities	Haniskerabi
27	Active dreaming	Lotemuvarset

28	Dissolving the veil	Biberroshnasklapahoverhetmishtu
29	Shifting dimensions	Sekelnishtahem
30	Portal to power	Eonitsch
31	Mother's transformation	Vraponach
32	Overcoming perceived impossibility	Sesubertalamanatbutem
33	Required stillness	Frefferel
34	Removing overwhelm	Puchnashbrlvak
35	Flowing perfection	Utubareshkaba
36	Angelic assistance	Hetu
37	Universal support	Pekalbomuvitch
38	Triumphant spirit	Fraternet
39	Flowering pulse	Babervet
40	Dancing devas	Lavunamersetklanitch
41	Intuitive listening	Pechuberan
42	Dissolved sub-creations	Satshivu
43	Constant order	Bealkatanbremi
44	Discovery	Histeropkloppohem
45	Galactic destiny	Sanarechsabuvukreshnaiter
46	Eagle vision	Epelra
47	Cosmic illumination	Hestiver
48	Brilliant visionary	Bokelupspara
49	Eye of creation	Rabaletvu
50	Transformation of mass consciousness	Shishomuvet
51	Translating complexity	Kleternachtara
52	Creative dematerializer	Hirioshimanabata
53	Wing makers	Koteruchshatel
54	Earth wizard	Hebversimina
55	Dragon lore	Udelklanatoch
56	Peacekeepers	Susikrepeta
57	Full circle	Nanunetchsklavuparel
58	Labyrinth walk	Retotachpabel

59	Blue road home	Eversethavink
60	Ceremonial rites	Epeoloch
61	Progressive initiation	Marabuchtanakreotesh
62	Tree of life	Frevilpata
63	Fate of universe	Esnadarech
64	El-ka-mi	Vosatem
65	Master gatekeeper	Remanoplata
66	Door to everything	Skiruvim
67	Tube toris	Bakatelerop
68	Cosmic reunification	Pavhu
69	Dynamic pulse	Pletetamunitch
70	Progressive trinity	Keskitarapmaich
71	Love light creation	Effeloptaravershinuvuset
72	Golden proportion	Bebilof
73	Permeating creation	Etamishkrenapalat
74	Squared circles	Bufetpladansk
75	Fully integrated sub-personalities	Eklosabuvet
76	Star pentagram	Menerataskuradel
77	Procreative principal	Blivivet
78	Gnomonic expansion	Hubafel
79	Coagulating power	Eknitramasu
80	Invisible provacator	Klaberfest
81	Universal contractive	Hechnanusatmutet
82	Survival integrity	Ribuklava
83	Altar of sacrifice	Hepipsperaparashet
84	Reincarnation	Ochdablevinash
85	Cyclical repetition	Peurpapa
86	Rhythmic breath	Blaterneskura
87	Attentive stillness	Eotal
88	Presence of God	Vutavitch
89	Multiple intelligences	Sketadelrabupmachnuem

90	Ongoing discernment	Helpivebrata
91	Unexpected change	Sustalumanesh
92	Circuitous path	Kettelpak
93	Divine revelation	Elnishbuvarek
94	Twelve tribes reunited	Bichpongsatelvak
95	Genesis revisited	Hereditorsalempamuvek
96	Cosmological constant	Susnapuetch
97	Seven generations to come	Kluska
98	System limitation	Bechplenuvaru
99	Precipitation point	Hedenestatu
100	Polar reversal	Kesmelparukbiueshelkata
101	Purposeful imbalance	Friuka
102	Tests of initiation	Sumaletut
103	Dying to the old ways	Bochmaraanspirulhelaklatesh
104	Separation conciousness	Spivube
105	Self-destruction	Lamatan
106	Adaptation capabilities	Nichorrabulavuset
107	Toxic transmutation	Klenitaor
108	Energetic filters	Hishkamintur
109	Renewed simplicity	Bishkabeb
110	Cosmic unification	Luurnit
111	Beyond Androgyny	Bebilof
112	Angelic symphony	Skarotnitch
113	Diverse life forms	Herumaunkal
114	Artist's expression	Veriblimines
115	Self portrait	Habulachgala
116	Truth mirror	Sperimiskatal
117	Unknowable mystery	Neunitmiratetblavut
118	Awakening to Infinity	Seberofklani
119	Unknown becoming	Echpachmahishunes
120	Evolutionary portals	Giguranuhemtafa

121	Illusions and appearances	Bishubehesumnarva
122	Core grief	Beopklanisk
123	Dysfunctional force	Petrochhebifer
124	Key to survival	Bubel
125	Roots and wings	Ramel
126	Sovereignty	Hutsh
127	Merging angels	Keskeranoblaviter
128	Death of old patterns	Spuranunisk
129	Self sabotage	Erger
130	Tabula rosa	Baus
131	Rose window	Klankranatch
132	Labyrinth walk	Etervamitchhechkapa
133	Sacred metamorphosis	Loinrapatel
134	Butterfly cocoons	Kufuvamuvitch
135	Rejoicing song	Spertuklamonit
136	Exquisite dance	Rechtu
137	Remembering again	Arantafatmuve
138	Solo journey	Helianderskappata
139	Cellular connections	Petrimervuhempaurata
140	Interdependent systems	Skechilamat
141	Cause and effect	Beftuhamut
142	All possibilities	Patrl
143	Ecstatic vision	Skabil
144	Selfless creation	Buftafat
145	Impeccable warrior	Pekerochmarasuteltovaritoem
146	Sobriety	Bletnu
147	Masterful concentration	Skatu
148	New paradigm	Hapshava
149	Loving community	Sausineme
150	Connected hearts	Kiatarume
151	Perfect health	Bleputsperaska

152	Power of now	Olnichspartura
153	Utter silence	Plenetiraskuruel
154	Veils lifted	Bishnaputuvurael
155	Illuminated dreams	Bepl
156	Sacred color	Skotmaraush
157	Creative vibration	Spinikop
158	Formless form	Michpavu
159	Planetary freedom	Binatar
160	Starseed family	Kroupvatel
161	Group collaboration	Peffera
162	Tolerance	Skutera
163	Universal brotherhood	Bif
164	Path of heart	Hepelvufskadromaset
165	Magical life	Ichnabishtuva
166	Soul knowledge	Petra
167	Supernatural power	Skianit
168	Wide awake	Hasokeshelnamuvit
169	Instant holographic manifestation	Teresamutsklatuvitch
170	Existential harmony	Koroner
171	Primordial sound	Betuel
172	Heavenly transition	Praag
173	Enlightened beings	Skotnashmuvratnael
174	Dream time	Hehubatafilamink
175	Children of light	Spurakuravraumin
176	Powerful creators	Ptelanurabush
177	Expanded original thinking	Eoranusitch
178	Celestial flame	Klanunsk
179	Memory of gods	Bavru
180	Gosamer threads	Bletsh
181	Filaments of grace	Pukarekmertlvutchheplaset
182	Revolutionary revelations	Bevrushnechtanuitch

183	Indigo children	Pleurskabromink
184	Tribal reconnections	Heftulomin
185	Spiritualized form	Bebeldagon
186	Unfoldment	Horklamnit
187	Light web	Oeftrl
188	Gate of possibility	Bauchnaret
189	Wellspring of the divine	Kreshtiperskavarut
190	Alignment to truth	Epaelmishpatet
191	Alchemy	Ofel
192	Amazing grace	Trehina
193	Reordering chaos	Broesk
194	Folding time	Leptiminarabuesh
195	Natural elimination	Frahukamdita
196	Overcoming instability	Klechnarahut
197	Rehabilitation	Shperstaak
198	Chain of command	Blamuternuklam
199	Key to survival	Hefnichtetlamervu
200	Spiritualized matter	Setnichsamural
201	Zero point module	Hepla
202	Star gate control system	Papa
203	Indigenous memory	Vru
204	Time traveling	Hopnata
205	Explorers of consciousness	Kliuresk
206	Motivator of growth	Skaduramanesh
207	Continual renewal	Hebelefna
208	Recapitulation's gifts	Badulara
209	Erasing outdated codes	Spenrvuklares
210	Adaptive intelligence	Hotshaatklu
211	Migration	Bergdavumures
212	Overcoming duality	Hibipul
213	Underworld revisited	Tofenach

214	Authority	Babushklanaskank
215	Shared resources	Trafeltripulmaaks
216	Social ability	Buchernetskersuklanug
217	Complex ordering	Piflach
218	Permeating creation	Hebevech
219	Returning to simplicity	Skarautel
220	Tithing the mind	Sanafarael
221	Hidden meanings	Didoraspartel
222	Visible vibrations	Kersnochpinfarel
223	Potential gravity	Kleterbanach
224	Light incarnation	Purvkabishotel
225	Calling power	Elsaduvet
226	Hearing inner voice	Binmaruset
227	Circle of awareness	Elovaruhem
228	Transmuted mirror	Pretlaparel
229	Transformed moon	Keshnabiftabel
230	Way to the sphere	Helinamitskareleternu
231	Divine love expressed	Vomatis
232	Keys of life and death	Klanusabal
233	Between above and below	Euvarochtame
234	Initiation portal	Kreshbeiverfet
235	Plane of unfoldment	Hocktaluminet
236	Freedom from mortal boundaries	Eskatadorahuplamesh
237	Journey through the sun	Krenutarna
238	Detachment	Spekvutklava
239	Consuming flame	Peachmarochtu
240	Supernova transfiguration	Evrauneskabehem
241	Star seeds of the future	Pefrach
242	Source of all	Norachtu
243	Rainbow of fire and light	Shpleba
244	Cosmic radiation	Pekrata

245	Cleansing laughter	Merkukrenuta
246	Cellular clarity	Hebochkratanavumasut
247	Reawakening renaissance	Helkranatanitch
248	Creating transformation	Blavu
249	Lotus blossom	Skmurametet
250	Neutrality	Haturbil
251	Cosmological transfer	Pleufera
252	Fate of universe	Paturnithebal
253	Flawed image	Frauganat
254	Beyond light and frequency	Kavutel
255	Elemental light blockages	Mrishnak
256	Virtual reality	Bapuvrilkranusk
257	Artificial intelligences	Klepskibavumit
258	Universal law transfigured	Enturaopkala
259	Master minds	Spetunhestira
260	Accelerating expansion	Hebelklosnatu
261	Everlasting life	Euba
262	Creative dematerialization	Kiura
263	Increasing brilliance	Pebalruptanovich
264	Filling gaps	Echbubechbustar
265	Release of trauma	Helleprakmamusdra
266	Rights of inheritance	Patiklopskasuva
267	Peaceful co-existence	Hefpakiaru
268	Ageless longevity	Bepelkausmitshatel
269	Quickening vitality	Heteremioskut
270	Fears faced	Sperukumlata
271	Mindfulness	Ufenbachrinmatuesh
272	New purpose	Meochsaturlahupshlala
273	Living conversation	Peurinatvartum
274	Engineering the future	Freshnitskeuramutem
275	Inspired design	Tleupesh

276	Heart-formed sanctuary	Vaskarabaut
277	Abundant resources	Peochlisaburut
278	Progressive luminosity	Babapaherut
279	Triumphant spirit	Fraa
280	Pure generosity	Belendu
281	Galactic destiny	Pretekaat
282	Transcending time	Hafloburet
283	Incomplete completion	Speromuvlit
284	Energy management	Habo-org
285	Resource allocation	Shlamutkalaop
286	Knowing mercy	Preplefink
287	Riddles of the heart	Botersupramuketelvitch
288	Bands of compassion	Spa-ank
289	Receptivity	Persunik
290	Profound joy	Advukaat
291	Spirit of innocence	Breshtuchlamatsa
292	Song of faith	Pleovipl
293	Steadfast truth	Hertzochna
294	Wizard of wizards	Spiirael
295	Glorious goddess	Pertibumherel
296	Cycles of change	Bureskmaperv
297	Memory loss	Kuplash
298	Natural resistance	Buvlem
299	Sustained nourishment	Hepsogperklava
300	Transforming weakness to strength	Forentiurbava

Lords and Their Qualities

place #	qualities	names
1	Venerable reaper of the violet ray	Hablavuetch
2	Wearer of the silver cloak of light	Vramugbla
3	One who wears the golden mantle of sunshine	Kirshkakos
4	One with the countenance of blazing fire	Kolkabos
5	Gatekeeper of love and light	Pretlabus
6	Emissary of peaceful spirits	Haromklus
7	Free spririt of the night	Bekelmus
8	Winsome whisperer in the still	Pristarva
9	Awesome organizer of cosmic realms	Hauchbrish
10	Magnetic Power of the Firey Gates	Pernugvrbly
11	He who swallows the night	Pareshnurv
12	Spark of Flame	Bekelnitsh
13	He who dances with grace	Kukarem
14	He who whispers to the heart	Baralsko
15	He who flies out of the sun	Huflabirtz
16	Holder of the Keys	Spetelblum
17	Creator of the codes	Prevatzklubut
18	He who lights the shadows	Hefroch
19	He who pulls the moon	Prlbtspitz
20	Sky-Light	Vravlbli
21	Song-bird of color	Vreklabtz
22	He who Unravels Illusion	Kuchtavru
23	He who dissolves darkness with light	Oremin
24	He who sees the wonder of the cosmos	Krotsklau
25	He who sounds the call to freedom	Huchra
26	Toner of light	Plevbaru
27	Keeper of the fire	Putlos
28	He who weaves the fabric of the cosmos	Prevelbu
29	Eyes that flash with light	Hutskla
30	He who stands at the end of cycles	Priosh

31	He who breaks the ties that bind	Piurtalet
32	He who witnesses the truth	Aranbrush
33	Stepping stone to the infinite	Kavurr
34	He who spreads his feathered cloak	Peochsktl
35	He who shapes into formlessness	Klufruba
36	He who lifts up souls to the light	Breofstel
37	He who thunders with laughter	Plaulaf
38	Liberator of souls	Hitkertel
39	He who speaks the tongue of pictures	Sachufuru
40	He who quenches thirst for light	Varaum
41	He who dissolves in the light of the all	Helskeskit
42	Magnet of fire	Plufamaach
43	He who shatters the bonds of darkness	Prevulpa
44	He who shines from the blackness of night	Wahun
45	He who lights the path to beyond	Bleupa
46	Way-shower to the sun	Orchprasu
47	One who blows the winds of time	Hupslauer
48	One who guides the impeccable warrior	Pertelops
49	He who carries the spirits of all creation	Klusklawer
50	He who brings forth the mountains of hope	Artenug
51	The guardian of the gate of compassion	Frugbavel
52	The wearer of the cloak of extinction	Paleshnk
53	He who flies the path of the eagle	Pigeruf
54	One who holds the winged ones in hand	Fruskalf
55	He who carries the torch of love	Greogbv
56	The flaming warrior of old	Vroetish
57	Sculptor of the fount of abundance	Greensh
58	Visionary of the expanding universe	Bokspu
59	Emissary of peaceful spirits delight	Lernvupa
60	The harbinger of hurricanes of thought	Kluanem
61	He who hears the whale song lament	Askleroth

62	One who cloaks the moon light surprise	Birgavet
63	Dragon express for mortal demise	Spertlervu
64	Protector of all who travel in light	Bekspokleroch
65	Promoter of all that fly through the skies	Vratelush
66	One who energizes the dawn	Parektuval
67	He who journeys with feline stealth	Hereopspa
68	One who develops the mist of the moors	Buchve
69	One who is the beacon of light	Barup
70	One who interprets the heavenly realms	Kletkanesh
71	He who travels with the wings of the dove	Tabusut
72	He who blankets the earth with repair	Oreskata
73	Wearer of the mask of deception and truth	Brtlnt
74	One who brings light to the world	Kuru-up
75	Master of the deep deep dark	Hoterech
76	Blazing star gazer of the cosmic realm	Efilbaruch
77	One who brandishes the sword of truth	Potelmi
78	The whirling blade of inequity given	Hekelsmi
79	One who swings through the ides of time	Traplaak
80	The navigator in the starry sky	Murch
81	The initiator of happiness in the garden of life	Erfemi
82	Joyous trumpeter of the heavenly news	Klaerunt
83	The harper of life's heavenly refrain	Shpuba
84	One who's seated upon the throne of redemption	Trelopha
85	The choir master of the avian chorus	Vruil
86	The powerful driving force of intent manifest	Echnaraebu
87	One who brings the billowing lightness of the cloud filled sky	Eplushnera
88	Keeper of the mist of the dragon lore	Hurtushni
89	Space musician to angelic choirs	Plepkla
90	Broiling intensity of the heart's desire	Heronish
91	One who holds the grace of simplicity	Evurnme
92	The upholder of the faith of the universe	Plishnaka

93	The gardener of the tree of life	Berulum
94	Guardian of those wrapped in angel wings	Peifnochru
95	Moderator of life's energy release	Almunibu
96	Liberator of life force like white light before the prism	Pretzlem
97	Holder of symbols undulating like serpents	Efbluhemsh
98	The golden bird of silent wing	Kerkatel
99	Architect of feelings and shield of hope	Sperochbu
100	One whose feelings can hear the sounds of space	Parhemsh
101	Seer of past lives coarsened by time's reign	Dardanoch
102	Searcher of the infinite spaces	Spertelbuch
103	One who treasures the sounds of the pure	Freomplava
104	Singer of the prophesies of discontent	Hubermu
105	Opener to the clans from which we sprout	Kartelmu
106	Luminous white light before the prism	Daromich
107	Spirit of the deepest channel of the heart	Krechimu
108	Collector of the minds who lost their way	Paushara
109	Gentle eye that out lasts all	Blevut
110	Leader of the tribe of light	Frahupslma
111	Giver of the wings to strive against the wind	Vaork
112	Giver of the smile to translate life into light	Efbartel
113	Giver of the lamp that sings at night	Greug
114	Revealer of the secret dwellings of time	Barortlket
115	He whose thoughts fuse space and time	Piichboch
116	Formidable champion of conciousness of all	Harashku
117	One who governs the storms along the way	Splivavet
118	He who cloaks in the feathers of delight	Barufu
119	He who shines through the dawn of new beginnings	Parket
120	One who removes the cloak of deception	Brefulnit
121	One who soars above the celestial ball	Alabuvanu
122	Warrior's response to the eagle's call	Fremit
123	Holder of space for the light bearers all	Harakul

124 One who illuminates the way for all	Fraralkgmich
125 One who recycles energy galore	Vretlurug
126 Fearsome warrior protector of all	Kaurfblakluep
127 One abominable snowman in space does reside	Britpaue
128 The celestial bearer of the crystaline spire	Brufelnug
129 The celestial navigator with chariots of fire	Splukma
130 One who raises high the golden branch of peace	Buchpelplavet
131 Powerful one propels through the sky	Freutlumish
132 The wayshower through cloud filled paths	Vratl
133 One who converts chaos to peace	Brufplub
134 The wisdom keeper of earth's holy sites	Hortelet
135 Rebounder with celestial spheres	Sketshma
136 One who separates the beings home line	Preuf
137 He who dissolves illusion	Butplfma
138 He who dissolves fear	Peringa
139 Heals illusion through tone	Blisop
140 He who shines healing light	Kakatesh
141 Lord of the Love vibration	Pruv
142 Lord of the Grace vibration	Brotlma
143 He who breaks stagnant energy	Faug
144 Lord of time and timelines	Spretlbrut
145 Keeper of the gate of power	Hugkluf
146 He who illuminates	Preshmat
147 Lord of physical immortality	Kuhlka
148 Lord of the gift of total sight	Fraugrit
149 Lord of original awareness	Hereskop
150 He who integrates through growth	Pekeropsh
151 He who holds balance	Anulim
152 He who yields healing vibration	Befraplak
153 He who governs attractive power	Dagonak
154 Lord of dispersal power	Esklaterop

155 He who grounds and connects	Hortish
156 Lord of synchronicity and patterns	Varaug
157 Lord of transformation	Fefbech
158 Lord of power of elevation / levitation	Hefloch
159 He who quickens	Etleish
160 He who governs cycles	Barog
161 Lord of consciousness	Krekinash
162 He who designs life experiences	Ku-useki
163 He who harvests insights for the infinite	Travar
164 Keeper of the gates of mystical knowledge	Pertofel
165 Lord of resistance to enhance growth	Blabutsh
166 Lord of fluidity	Hefspef
167 He who manifests	Prakut
168 He who brings warmth to life	Horbauotsh
169 He who holds open the door guarding astral travel	Krekerolm
170 He who weighs & measures soul readiness for next life	Keishkatet
171 He who removes the memory of painful experiences	Labulop
172 Seeder of souls into divine contract environments	Prefbish
173 Spinner of interconnecting spiritual paths	Kruat
174 He who constructs illness to serve plan of suffering	Teferoch
175 He who maintains the illusion of separation between worlds	Parmuvet
176 She who opens the womb birthing old and new life into experience	Skretra
177 She who cradles wounded and abused souls while nurturing the life force within	Blivish
178 She who blends life experience and spiritual message in dreamtime	Harog
179 She who sees within to assess the soul's readiness for initiation	Satsu
180 One who opens awareness and potential through weaving threads of challenge in life	Apelof
181 He who dissolves density with movement and sound	Fragnut
182 She who lights the way in the face of turmoil thus nurturing indwelling life	Piitirnit
183 She who illuminates the seeker with the brillance of insight	Hataliof
184 Holder of the sacred sword Excalibur	Vaushim
185 She who vibrates the strings releasing the music of the spheres	Kefrabli

186 She who weaves the patterns of worlds in time and space	Peshkekop
187 Teacher and shower of all faces and forms of the natural world	Ratadel
188 Keeper of the rhythms of the tides	Asakablug
189 Holder of the key to human body cycles	Blefpug
190 Guardian of the stones holding the record of planetary memory	Faog
191 Snowflake messenger holding and showing the patterns of every individuals dreams	Skiderm
192 Way shower from the stars, teaching humanity to remember gifts	Rotmati
193 Way shower from the stars, teaching humanity to rediscover the wholeness of spirits	Bofple
194 Guardian of ritual and ceremony honoring the gifts with gratitude and celebration	Ufshpa
195 Stargate master	Kreomir
196 Dream weaver	Heridtor
197 Guardian of portals	Esmatech
198 Master of change	Heliosh
199 Guardian of ritual and ceremony	Klerafim
200 One who is the stillness within	Busbu
201 One who brings laughter and joy to all	Plaek
202 One who brings gifts of wisdom from afar	Firyu
203 One who shines with the light of a thousand stars	Bresbfir
204 One who is simplicities sake	Totarek
205 One who carries the sword and shield of the defender	Hoeshkli
206 One who smiles with the sweetness of a rose through life	Miramish
207 One who brings order out of the ashes of chaos	Echbu
208 He who rides the waves of song	Faraklut
209 Herald of the songs to sing	Etlim
210 One who brings love to the song of life	Kaurut
211 One who composes the whale song	Splataple
212 He who leads in 4 directions	Hefimop
213 Wise owl with eyes that pierce the night	Keilendre
214 He of wild imaginings	Aplech
215 He who labors in love	Bishpitu
216 He who branches out in new directions	Kefril

217 He who laughs in water	Huspa
218 He who dances on graves	Grepetosh
219 He who lights from below	Echlites
220 Lord of realms	Keupla
221 Master of protocol	Esrich
222 He who is harmony of motion	Oslamirv
223 Light of understanding	Hable
224 He who blankets himself in colors of hope	Beofplm
225 Master painter of signs	Speruk
226 Procreator of Life	Kanadoch
227 Hand of God	Garnitesh
228 Light of lights	Plevuit
229 He who stays time	Preskhitch
230 He who quenches fire	Hops
231 He who reveals truth	Effelbuch
232 He who wears the cloak of darkness	Eskitelbach
233 He who restores	Bruvetch
234 He who designs the future	Frababul
235 He who maintains justice	Klabechpul
236 He who de-structures	Profetch
237 He who shines brightly	Blaburp
238 He who dances with death	Bergplafvtch
239 He who breathes life	Herpersop
240 He who guards the gate of wisdom	Klopnet
241 He who wears the cloak of invisibility	Grugur
242 He who protects the innocent	Partet
243 He who bestows sacred gifts	Henskun
244 He who brings forth change	Prabovtz
245 He who light the fire of life	Buprel
246 He who extinquishes life	Kruska
247 Keeper of the immortal flame	Bochturm

248 Shaper of man's destiny	Plabach
249 He who sees beyond form	Suska
250 He who holds the torch of hope	Huferbi
251 He who breathes fire	Kleablahm
252 He who looks within	Biufal
253 He who stands forth	Kruchta
254 He who stands firm	Eoralbik
255 He who lights the spark within	Splutaari
256 Carrier of the torch of belief	Hefblip
257 Giver of Sacred Vision	Klautz
258 He who values beauty	Grochma
259 He who holds divine intent	Parvu
260 The wise one	Blaak
261 He who watches over	Prospa
262 He who sees all things	Gufer
263 He who wields the blade of truth	Hechtari
264 He who defies odds	Skotabi
265 He who gives strength	Plefputet
266 He who walks between the worlds	Harung
267 The communicator	Brush
268 Teacher of magic	Kafaal
269 Creator of new things	Efklat
270 Creator of new beginnings	Hiskopra
271 He who creates and maintains balance	Grateng
272 He who purifies	Muruvetch
273 He who integrates	Grasnog
274 Great star of Heaven	Erlbik
275 Holds Creation in his hand	Prutin
276 Sounder of the sacred trump	Glanek
277 Lighter of the sacred fire	Mana
278 The grand temple-keeper	Sketaru

279 The Grand architect	Frisbek
280 Keeper of the indigo flame	Favaru
281 Keeper of the blue flame	Hiktor
282 Keeper of the green flame	Plaabaa
283 Keeper of the red flame	Prech
284 Keeper of the orange flame	Pistorpa
285 Keeper of the violet flame	Huk
286 He who tilts the scales	Befur
287 Dancer in the night	Terimhur
288 Song of the morning	Horsklaba
289 Illuminator of mankind	Bebsklavu
290 He who sees perfection	Orpa
291 Lord of the Lightning	Minech
292 Lord of illusion	Perteva
293 Governor of growth and decay	Bishbaa
294 The grand destroyer	Klatfut
295 He who walks at infinity's gate	Hechba
296 Watcher of the Crystal gate	Kru-ush
297 He whose touch magnifies	Plata
298 He whose touch purifies	Bresh
299 He who transmutes to light	Pruug
300 He who sees the grand vision	Natbalem

9 Giants of the Inner Earth
Peprugifateshbaqitu
Hepsujaduwuttu
Ufdabe
Jhefopkltru
Htlsvtepsi
Erlptz
Pruhanat
Klisbi
Stibavich

20 Dragon Lords who Live in the Sun
Daunergat
Barachku
Griflyu
Bsilca
Beprplekanug
Plablvrem
Porchbilu
Sabutlvo
Drnklarusut
Bvro
Pelshnt
Setchklug
Brtlpas
Fortnpiushplabl
Borl
Fuhabrush
Doghablvutz
Bropplafvu
Boruchsepl
Petrvilklata

Giant King
Aseix

2 Assistants to the Fairy Queens
Walubepemi
Feminizati

Other books by Almine

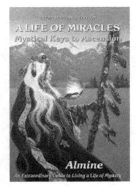

A Life of Miracles
***Expanded Third Edition* Includes Bonus Belvaspata Section—Mystical Keys to Ascension**
Almine's developing spiritual awareness and abilities from her childhood in South Africa until she emerged as a powerful mystic, to devote her gifts in support of all humanity is traced. Deeply inspiring and unique in its comparison of man's relationship as the microcosm of the macrocosm. *Also available in Spanish.*

Published: 2009, 304 pages, soft cover, 6 x 9, ISBN: 978-1-934070-25-3

Journey to the Heart of God *Second Edition*
Mystical Keys to Immortal Mastery
Ground-breaking cosmology revealed for the first time, sheds new light on previous bodies of information such as the Torah, the I Ching and the Mayan Zolkien. The explanation of man's relationship as the microcosm as set out in the previous book *A Life of Miracles*, is expanded in a way never before addressed by New Age authors, giving new meaning and purpose to human life. Endorsed by an Astro-physicist from Cambridge University and a former NASA scientist, this book is foundational for readers at all levels of spiritual growth.

Published: 2009, 296 pages, soft cover, 6 x 9, ISBN: 978-1-934070-26-0

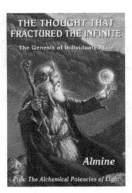

The Thought that Fractured the Infinite
The Genesis of Individuated Life
This profound work offers insights where few authors dare to tread: the genesis of individuated life.
Offering what could possibly be the deepest insights ever revealed about man's relationship to light, it details our ascent into spiritual awakening.
It gives the thought-provoking wisdom of the cosmic root races and a practical guide to using the alchemical potencies of light. Almine's global following of serious students of the mysteries will love this one!

Published: 2009, 316 pages, soft cover, 6 x 9, ISBN: 978-1-934070-17-8

Other books by Almine

The Ring of Truth *Third Edition*
Sacred Secrets of the Goddess

As man slumbers in awareness, the nature of his reality has altered forever. As one of the most profound mystics of all time, Almine explains this dramatic shift in cosmic laws that is changing life on earth irrevocably. A powerful healing modality is presented to compensate for the changes in laws of energy, healers have traditionally relied upon. The new principles of beneficial white magic and the massive changes in spiritual warriorship are meticulously explained.

Published: 2009, 256 pages, soft cover, 6 x 9, ISBN: 978-1-934070-28-4

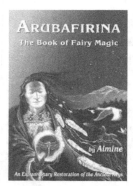

Arubafirina *Third Edition*
The Book of Fairy Magic

This book is most certainly a milestone in the history of mysticism throughout the ages. It is the product of a rare and unprecedented event in which Almine, acknowledged as the leading mystic of our time, was granted an exceptional privilege. For one week in November 2006 she was invited to enter the fairy realms and gather the priceless information for this book. The result is a tremendous treasure trove of knowledge and interdimensional color photos.

Published: 2011, 340 pages, soft cover, 6 x 9, ISBN: 978-1-936926-32-9

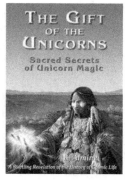

The Gift of the Unicorns *Second Edition*
Sacred Secrets of Unicorn Magic

These life-changing insights into the deep mystical secrets of the earth's past puts the cosmic role of humanity into perspective. It gives meaning to the suffering of the ages and solutions of hope and predicts the restoration of white magic. An enlightening explanation of the causes of the Great Fall and our ascent out of ages of forgetfulness into a remembrance of our divine new purpose and oneness, is masterfully given. Truly an inspiring book!

Published: 2009, 284 pages, soft cover, 6 x 9, ISBN: 978-1-934070-29-1

Other books by Almine

Opening the Doors of Heaven *Second Edition*
Revelations of the Mysteries of Isis
Through a time-travel tunnel, linking Ireland and Egypt, Isis sent a small group of masters to prepare for the day when her mysteries would once again be released to the world to restore balance and enhance life.

They established the Order of the White Rose to guard the sacred objects and the secrets of Isis. In an unprecedented event heralding the advent of a time of light, these mysteries are released for the first time.

Published: 2009, 312 pages, soft cover, 6 x 9 ISBN: 978-1-934070-31-4

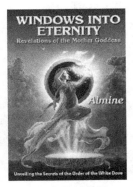

Windows Into Eternity *Third Edition*
Revelations of the Mother Goddess
This book provides unparalled insight into ancient mysteries. Almine, an internationally recognized mystic and teacher, reveals the hidden laws of existence. Transcending reason, delivering visionary expansion, this metaphysical masterpiece explores the origins of life as recorded in the Holy Libraries.
The release of information from these ancient libraries is a priceless gift to humankind. The illusions found in the building blocks of existence are exposed, as are the purposes of Creation.

Published: 2011, 322 pages, soft cover, 6 x 9, ISBN: 978-1-936926-26-8

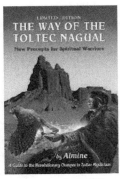

The Way of the Toltec Nagual
New Precepts for the Spiritual Warrior
Not only is this wisdom packed book a guide for serious students of the Toltec way, but also a font of knowledge for all truth-seekers. Mapping out the revolutionary changes in Toltec mysticism, it presents the precepts of mastery sought out by all who travel the road of illumination and spiritual warriorship. Almine reveals publicly for the first time, the ancient power symbols used by Toltec Naguals to assist in obtaining freedom from illusion. Bonus section: Learn about the hidden planets used by Toltecs and the Astrology of Isis.

Published: 2009, 240 pages, soft cover, 6 x 9, ISBN: 978-1-934070-56-7

Visit Almine's website **www.spiritualjourneys.com** for workshop locations and dates, take an online workshop, listen to an internet radio show, or watch a video. Order one of Almine's many books, CD's, or an instant download.

US toll-free phone: 1-877-552-5646

CPSIA information can be obtained
at www.ICGtesting.com
Printed in the USA
BVHW041504280120
570723BV00007B/124